MONEY LAUNDERING COMPLIANCE FOR SOLICITORS

MATTHEW MOORE AND DIANE PRICE

Published by Professional Compliance Publishing Ltd

Copyright © 2015 Professional Compliance Publishing

The moral rights of the authors have been asserted.

Professional Compliance Publishing
2 Crown Lane
Sutton Coldfield
B74 4SU

ISBN 978-0-9933833-1-1

First reprint: March 2016

British Library Cataloguing in Publication Data.
A catalogue record for this book is available from the British Library.

Typeset in Calibri by Troubador Publishing Ltd

Printed and bound in the UK by TJ International, Padstow, Cornwall

FOREWORD

This book builds on our earlier collaboration on this topic and is intended to be an in-depth analysis of the law and practice on the linked topics of law firm money laundering and terrorist financing compliance. The title combines our respective experiences as a consultant trainer on the issues covered within the text on the one hand and as a compliance director in a major top 100 legal practice on the other. We have covered not just what is known about the current compliance regime but also the numerous areas of uncertainty in relation to both the main statutory offences and the regulatory obligations.

The book is arranged in five parts, starting with the main legislation and the offences contained within it, and then the regulatory obligations to be found mostly in the Money Laundering Regulations 2007. Part C deals with certain of the related areas of financial crime which will be of concern to most firms – the avoidance of the linked issue of mortgage, or property, fraud most obviously. Part D examines the legal and regulatory concerns from the perspective of the main specialisations to be found in most law firms and part E sets out a template anti-money laundering policy. The policy is taken from the Solicitors Office Procedures Manual and is available to Infolegal subscribers for download as part of that publication – see www.infolegal.co.uk.

The Fourth EU Directive on Money Laundering was finally brought into European law on the 5th June 2015, requiring all member states to implement its provisions into domestic law by the 26th June 2017. We are unlikely to see new draft Money Laundering Regulations until 2016 but we have explained the requirements of the Directive and have suggested how they are likely to be addressed within the UK. For the time being, however, there are challenges aplenty in addressing the regime that already prevails: there is common acceptance that part 7 of the Proceeds of Crime Act 2002 is in need of an overhaul and David Anderson QC, the UK Government's independent reviewer of terrorist legislation, has made similar comments in relation to those related provisions. Unfortunately there is little prospect of the root and branch review, which it is accepted that both areas require, for the foreseeable future.

Our thanks are due to Soo Darcy, also Jennifer Parker and her colleagues at Troubador Publishing. Whether you are a reporting officer or have general responsibility for compliance we hope that the book will assist you in your understanding of the topics we cover and will enable you to better judge the suitability of your compliance policy and procedures for your legal practice.

Matthew Moore   Diane Price

ABOUT THE AUTHORS

Matthew Moore LL.B, MCIPD, C.DipAF, Solicitor

Matt is a director of Infolegal Ltd, which provides a range of support and advisory services to the legal profession, and is also a consultant solicitor with the regulatory specialists Jayne Willetts & Co., where he is also the firm's reporting officer. He was the authorised trainer for the Law Society in its Lexcel scheme from 1999 to 2007, writing during this time four editions of the widely used "Lexcel Office Procedures Manual" (his last version having appeared in 2007). His very first publication was "The Law and Procedure of Meetings" (Sweet & Maxwell: 1979) and he has been responsible for numerous other titles since. Other than this title his other current publication is "The Solicitors Office Procedures Manual" (2015: second edition) – with Vicky Ling – also published by Professional Compliance Publishing and also appearing in a separate Sole Practice version.

After a first career teaching law at a number of colleges in Essex and Devon he was admitted as a solicitor in 1984 and worked for a while in high street practice in Coventry. He was subsequently appointed Co-ordinator, and then Marketing Director, of the then M5 Group (later NRM5) – an association of a number of leading commercial firms. He now has over 25 years' experience of law firm management and compliance consultancy and training for a range of firms from sole practitioners to the largest international commercial practices. He is actively involved as a trainer and adviser on money laundering compliance and mortgage fraud avoidance issues on public courses and at in-house events.

mattmoore@infolegal.co.uk

Diane Price LLM, Assoc CIPD, Solicitor

Diane was formerly Director of Compliance at SGH Martineau (now Shakespeare Martineau) where she set up the compliance function following the introduction of the

SRA Handbook and also had responsibility for the firm's anti-money laundering programme. This included resolving all internal CDD queries and also liaising on behalf of the firm with the National Crime Agency in relation to suspicious activity reports. Her responsibilities also extended to the operation of the firm's quality systems under ISO9001, risk management and business continuity planning.

Diane studied law at University College, London and Clare College, Cambridge. After attending the College of Law at Guildford she undertook her training contract at Ryland Martineau, specialising in corporate and commercial work on admission. Subsequently she specialised in intellectual property and competition law at the University of Birmingham, before re-joining Martineau Johnson (as it had then become) in 1991 to establish a human resources and training department. She was Director of Human Resources and Compliance until 2012 when her role became exclusively compliance and risk management.

Infolegal
The various template materials contained in chapter 18 are available for download from the linked business of Infolegal Ltd, a specialist law firm compliance and risk management consultancy and training company. In addition to being able to download The Solicitors Office Procedures Manual Infolegal subscribers receive a monthly e-newsletter on recent developments of note and are also able to access an extensive range of guidance notes and single topic factsheets. A number of computer-based compliance training modules can be accessed by subscriber firms, not just explaining some of the more complex regulatory issues facing legal practices but also enabling users to satisfy various of the training requirements in the Lexcel standard and, in the case of money laundering awareness, the law of the land.

For more details please see www.infolegal.co.uk, or contact co-author of this title and Infolegal director Matthew Moore, at mattmoore@infolegal.co.uk.

CONTENTS

REFERENCE TABLES

1 Proceeds of Crime Act 2002

Section number(s)	Page
266(3)	61
327	27
328	27,30,31,33,47,59, 84,168,197,199,202, 210,211,217,224
329	29,31,202,204,205, 221
329(3)(c)	32
327-329 (collectively)	18,26,46,53, 197,198,200,203,205, 208,224
330	10,19,21,24,25,45, 49,51,52,97,103,176, 200,201,203,204,205, 208,209,216,224
330(4)	25,53
330(5)	25,53
330(6)	22,168,201,209,216
330(7)	23,25,76
330(14)	45
331	5,12,24,27,52
332	5,12,24,27,52
333	28,33,34,36,48,54,60, 64,179,217,235
333A(3)	35,54
333B	36,48
333C	36, 49,202
333D	35,36,48,49,223
336	34,52
336(3)	56
336(7)	56
337	51,54,58,59
338	32,51,54
338(2)(A)	53,54
338(3)	31,53
338(5)	54
339(1)(A)	54
340	197
340(2)	18
340(3)	6,18,224
340(11)	6,18,209
341	63
342	33,35,36,49, 64, 235

2 Terrorism Act 2000

15	31
16	32
17	32
18	31,84
19	10,25,46,210
19(3)	25,46
21	10,25,45,51,53,97, 203,209,210
21D(2)	34

4 Other Statutes, Orders and Provisions

5 SRA Handbook References

6 Table of Cases

PART A

The Main Legislation

CHAPTER 1

Understanding the regime

The anti-money laundering regime came of age for the legal profession with the implementation of the Proceeds of Crime Act (POCA) in 2002, replacing some earlier and more limited provisions. The Act was introduced in response to the requirements of the Second EU Directive on money laundering, with the main aim of the legislation having been to establish the prospect of recovery proceedings in suitable cases through the new Assets Recovery Agency which now forms part of the National Crime Agency (NCA). The Act is, for the most part, the general law of the land and applies to the public at large, but part 7 of the Act ('Money Laundering') does contain certain provisions that are limited to the 'regulated sector', i.e. those organisations that are subject to the Money Laundering Regulations 2007 (MLR 2007).

Money laundering is the process of converting illegal funds into apparently legitimate property. It is very much in the interests of criminals to launder their funds so as to escape recovery proceedings if they are apprehended; to do so they will almost certainly need the involvement of banks and, more often than not, lawyers and/or other professionals. An extensive compliance regime has therefore developed whereby the cooperation of the professional sector is required in adopting anti-money laundering (AML) policies. Combating money laundering, and the linked topic of terrorist fundraising, has thus become a major strand of law firm management over the last decade, particularly for those with direct responsibility for compliance issues.

Although the Terrorism Act 2000 (TA) predates POCA it is usually dealt with as an adjunct to it. There are good grounds for doing so in that the TA makes much the same requirements for disclosures as the AML regime but establishes no statutory arrangements for so doing. The Third EU Directive required that a "Financial Intelligence Unit" should be established for the prevention of terrorist financing and the Serious Organised Crime Agency (now the NCA, which replaced it on 7th October 2013) was nominated for this purpose.

In most other respects POCA and TA have many more similarities than differences, and it is therefore common to deal with AML policies in conjunction with the issue of countering terrorist financing (CTF). Much the same duties to avoid involvement in prohibited acts and to make disclosures in certain circumstances can be found in both regimes. The separate offences relating to tipping off did not originally form part of the TA but have since been written into the Act through the Terrorism Act 2000 and Proceeds of Crime Act 2002 (Amendment) Regulations 2007. Since a reporting officer might not know whether he or she is dealing with terrorist fundraising or other criminal behaviour we have chosen to combine our treatment of the AML and CTF regimes in the more detailed chapters that follow.

In addition to the various statutory provisions that law firms, and those working within them, are subject to there are also extensive regulatory obligations. Quite apart from the 'catch-all' nature of Principle 1 of the SRA Handbook to the effect that there is a fundamental duty to uphold justice and the rule of law, there is a specific requirement at O(7.5) of the SRA Code of Conduct ('the Code') to "comply with legislation applicable to your business, including anti-money laundering and data protection legislation". Legislation is not, of course, optional and so this provision might seem to be superfluous, but the likely intent was to stress that all such issues are also therefore capable of being dealt with instead of or as well as disciplinary issues. Outcome 7.5 highlights the need to comply with money laundering and data protection requirements, but in its first draft referred instead to money laundering and terrorist financing obligations.

So far as the SRA is concerned the primary obligation to ensure compliance with the firm's AML and CTF obligations will rest with the Compliance Officer for Legal Practice (COLP) since his or her first duty is stated to be to ensure compliance with all of the obligations – statutory or regulatory – that the firm is subject to, other than the SRA Accounts Rules. In most practices, however, it is more likely to be the Money Laundering Reporting Officer (MLRO) who will be regarded as being responsible for this area of compliance management. The job of the MLRO is actually confined in the MLR 2007 to making the necessary disclosures to the appropriate authorities – now the NCA – but most MLROs will assume a wider responsibility in relation to compliance with the AML and CTF regimes. The issue of how the COLP and MLRO share these responsibilities between them is therefore one of the many issues that will need to be addressed in the firm's practice manual and/or compliance plan.[1]

Estimates of the value of money laundering activity are little more than inspired guesswork since money laundering is, of its nature, a hidden and secretive process, but the SRA suggested in November 2014 that the actual amount could be as much as £57bn per year[2]. On a wider scale it was reported in early 2014 that the value of corruption throughout the EU was reckoned to amount to a "breath-taking" £100bn per year and the international Financial Action Task Force (FATF) has suggested a global money laundering trade of just under 3% of all financial activity. Also in early 2014 the Serious Fraud Office expressed its concerns that an increasing share of the total illegal international finance was being processed through the London market, the reasons given being the vast nature of its banking and investment activities and the City's increasingly cosmopolitan profile. As we will see, this has led to increased calls for lawyers always to investigate the source of any funds they are handling.

With over a decade of managing money laundering compliance programmes in the legal profession it might have been hoped that by now the requirements made of law firms would be clear and there would be widespread appreciation of what constitutes 'best practice' for the sector. Few would argue that this is the case, however, and there is growing evidence that the operation of the regime is far from ideal. In a thematic review of conveyancing work conducted by the SRA in March 2013 one third of the respondents admitted that they did not know when to make disclosures to the then Serious Organised Crime Agency ("SOCA"), with a further 15% admitting to doing so on "gut instinct". It seems fair to suppose that the proportion of firms admitting to being uncertain as to the extent of this critical obligation might have been higher still had it not been for the fact that it was the regulator that was conducting the research.

There seems to be a general consensus that part 7 of POCA, dealing with money laundering offences, is unfit for purpose and in need of a radical overhaul. By way of illustration, when the Government consulted on the operation of the disclosure and consent regime in 2008 it wrongly described the arrangements on which it was consulting.[3] It is regrettable, AML being a compliance concern of such potentially serious implications for law firms and their personnel, not to mention the significant administrative burden it places on firms, that there should be such continuing confusion on an issue that is accompanied by such considerable risks if problems arise.

One of the most obvious causes of confusion within the anti-money laundering regime is differentiating between the requirements of POCA and TA and the regulatory obligations as contained in the MLR 2007. The obligation to appoint an MLRO, for example, is to be found at r.20(2)(d)(i) MLR, but the potential liability of that individual is spelt out in POCA at ss.331-332 and in part 3 TA. Liability for the offences within the Acts will attach to those individuals concerned, but liability for non-compliance with the regulations lies with the "relevant person" – in effect, the management of the firm, whether the MLRO or other. It should also be stressed that non-compliance with the MLR continues to be a criminal offence under r.45 despite widely publicised promises that this would cease to be the case some time ago. In practice, however, non-compliance will almost certainly be dealt with as a disciplinary issue through the powers provided to the Law Society (but exercised by the SRA) at Schedule 3 of the MLR 2007.

In other places the law has been poorly conceived and rushed through. A good example is the changes to the operation of the tipping off offence, in particular through the Terrorism Act 2000 and Proceeds of Crime Act 2002 (Amendment) Regulations 2007[4], with its short title referring to the "Prevention and Supression" (sic) of illegal activities hardly inspiring confidence in the user. More generally, there are wider concerns about the operation of the key provisions of POCA and the Act has been described as "legislation of which Dracon the Athenian legislator would have been proud",[5] whilst the authors of Blackstone's Guide to the Act have commented that part 2 "seems to occupy some parallel legal universe which has no apparent relationship with the normal rules of criminal process".[6] The distinctive features that they had in mind in making this comment were the placing of evidential burdens on the accused, the use of civil standards of proof in criminal proceedings and the availability of penalties even where criminal conduct has not been proven. Notwithstanding the widespread concerns as to the operation of the law, and the disclosure regime in particular, there seems to be little prospect of any significant change to the legal provisions and the operation of the regime for the foreseeable future.

Money laundering

Most lawyers will be concerned primarily with part 7 POCA, which deals with money laundering. The offence of money laundering is defined by s.340(11) as being anything which amounts to an offence under the principal offences under the Act or an attempt, conspiracy or incitement to commit any of them, or aiding, abetting, procuring or counselling any such offence. The definition of "criminal conduct" is anything which is a crime if committed in the UK or which would be a crime if it were to occur here. This initial definition in the Act was modified by s.102 of the Serious Organised Crime and Police Act 2005 (SOCPA) so that activity will not generally be prohibited if committed abroad and legitimate where conducted, but illegal here. This amendment addressed the often-quoted 'Spanish bullfighter' example, under which a bullfighter who had earned their money lawfully in Spain would risk being dealt with as a launderer here since their earnings would have amounted to criminal property, bullfighting being illegal in the UK.

Where criminal conduct as above results in "criminal property", money laundering will become a concern. Property is defined as criminal property if it:

> "constitutes a person's benefit from criminal conduct or it represents such a benefit (in whole or part and whether directly or indirectly), and the alleged offender knows or suspects that it constitutes or represents such a benefit." (s.340(3))

It should be stressed that it does not matter who carried out the criminal activity or who will benefit from it, with the result that the offences apply to the laundering of an offender's own proceeds of crime as well as somebody else's. Most of the problems for practitioners have stemmed from the fact that the UK Government chose to extend the provisions of POCA to "all crimes", whereas the Second EU Directive which inspired the provisions merely required prohibitions in relation to "serious crime". This is what has been referred to as 'gold-plating' by the Law Society and others in their objections to the provisions.

Another unfortunate aspect of the definition is that there is no *de minimis* level, this lack of proportionality being seemingly quite deliberate. Whereas SOCPA introduced a threshold level of £250 for banks and other "deposit taking bodies" (s.103), this concept was quite intentionally not extended to professional advisers for fear that they would break down higher value transactions into multiple agreements below the threshold amount. So far as solicitors' firms are concerned the law therefore remains as stated in *P v P* 2003:[7] that "an illegally obtained sum of £10 is no less susceptible to the definition of 'criminal property' than a sum of £1m."

For what it's worth, an insight to a more sensible and workable regime can be found quite close to home in Jersey. The Proceeds of Crime (Jersey) Law 1999 defines criminal conduct as "any offence in Jersey for which a person is liable on conviction to imprisonment for a term of one or more years". As we will see, the filtering out of the numerous minor regulatory offences from the AML regime that would have been achieved had this sort of definition been adopted in the UK would make the reporting officer's job much easier, especially in their dealings with corporate teams. The effect of the UK definitions has been that even minor regulatory offences, such as non-registration with the Information Commissioner under the Data Protection Act 1998, will be covered, posing the challenge for reporting officers as to whether to observe the letter of the law and make multiple reports of trivial irregularities or adopt a more pragmatic, even if technically illegal, approach to their responsibilities.

The stages of the process

Placing

The money laundering process is generally reckoned to have three stages. First, where the criminal activity results in cash, 'placing' involves introducing the cash into the banking system. With the various controls that are now in place this represents quite a challenge for the would-be launderer, with the most common strategies involving:

- Supplying large amounts of cash to established cash retailers (and sometimes purchasing such concerns as a front for cash banking) and the issuing of false invoices for subsequent payment;

- Making bulk cash purchases of travellers cheques in foreign jurisdictions where controls are more lax and banking them on return to the UK, with the NCA having expressed particular concerns in this regard to the availability of €500 notes which can be imported to the UK (though not obtained from UK banks);[8]
- Cash payments to unregistered employees using dirty money to generate a profit; and
- 'Smurfing', in which large amounts of cash are broken down into multiple smaller units for payment into separate bank accounts and subsequent repayment to the criminals.

There are growing concerns about the opportunities provided for laundering by the gaming industry. It was reported in a trade magazine in November 2013 that the Gambling Commission had fined one large betting concern £90,000 for its profits in allowing a drug dealer to pay around £1m through its high street stores.[9] The use of fixed odds betting terminals (so-called 'FoBTs') has also been highlighted of late. These mechanised devices are capable of processing £300 cash per minute whilst offering a guaranteed rate of winnings to the gambler, and were described in one newspaper report by one young drug dealer as "what turns dirty money clean". By all accounts the criminal will regard the slice of funds taken by the operator as the fee charged for the written receipt which can then be presented to the bank as evidence of the source of funds.

Since law firms will not generally deal with substantial amounts of cash (in contrast to the common practice of many firms in years gone by) they could be seen to be largely exempt from the risk of becoming involved in the laundering process at the placing stage, but it does sometimes occur that clients or others will seek to deposit substantial amounts of cash directly into client account at a branch of the firm's bank. Arguably this is the responsibility of the bank first and the law firm second, but the accounts department should nonetheless take care to monitor the sources of receipts into the firm's client account.

Layering

Having banked the funds there will then be attempts to disguise their origins through 'layering', where the funds are re-invested in one or more transactions to disguise the original source of the funds. If placing is more a concern for the banking sector, layering is where professional advisers such as accountants and lawyers come much more into the frame. Since this is just as much money laundering as the initial placing of funds, the view often encountered (stubbornly so by many lawyers) that "it can't be m... laundering if the money comes from a UK bank account" is clearly mistaken. The most comprehensive analysis of the ways in which lawyers assist money launderers, wittingly or otherwise, can be found in the June 2013 report of FATF – the body established by the G8 nations to combat the problem. The main risks listed in 'Money laundering and terrorist financing vulnerabilities of legal professionals' were:

- Misuse of client account – As through large payments (in cash or bank transfer) for matters which then abort resulting in a request for repayment. The launderer can be confident that a receipt from a law firm will not be questioned by their bank or could be explained as an award of damages if so;
- Property purchases – Always the most obvious investment on which to instruct a solicitor, but the creation of trusts and companies are also mentioned as other common methods of recycling suspect funds;
- The appointment of a lawyer to a company board, or an appointment as a trustee, on a professional basis with the aim of their lending credibility to a scheme set up to launder funds (or to defraud others); and
- Bogus litigation – Using an imaginary dispute as a front to move large sums of money between collaborators.

Ongoing training in money laundering awareness is required under r.21 MLR 2007 and the contents of any such programme should include risk awareness in relation to the likely patterns of attempted laundering activity in the delegates' areas of specialisation.

Integration
Finally, 'integration' is the completion of the process whereby apparently legitimate income is achieved – as where rental income is received from tenants in an apparently lawfully purchased property. Although this money might appear to be completely lawful it will still be capable of being the subject of recovery proceedings if the prosecution can show the necessary link between it and the alleged criminal activity.

The Terrorism Act 2000
As we have seen, the regime in place for countering terrorist financing is applied in conjunction with that dealing with money laundering concerns. There are, however, a number of critical differences between the two compliance areas and these should be noted at the outset. First, whereas the offences under POCA – and part 7 on money laundering in particular – require criminal conduct and proceeds to be involved through

some "predicate" offence, this is not the case under the TA.[10] Although many of the funds that might trigger alarm in a law firm on grounds of suspected terrorist activity may well be criminal in their origin, this is not a requirement in relation to terrorist financing. In relation to the terrorist offences it is the intended use of the funds, rather than their provenance, that prompts liability.

Second, whereas liability will only arise for the principal offences under POCA where normal subjective criminal intent or *mens rea* can be shown to have existed, their equivalent provisions in part 3 of the TA place a reverse burden on anyone accused of such an offence to show that they "did not know and had no reasonable cause to suspect that the arrangement related to terrorist property". This could be seen to represent a departure from the normal principle that a person is innocent until proven guilty, and also to place a duty of disclosure on members of the general public, as evidenced by the conviction of the wife of one of the so-called '21/7' bombers in 2008.[11] The former Independent Reviewer of Terrorism Legislation, Lord Carlile, commented on a number of occasions on the "considerable responsibilities" that these provisions placed on members of the public.

The most significant difference between the two regimes, however, is that the "duty to disclose" offence – found in s.330 POCA – is not limited in the TA to the regulated sector. The duty to disclose offence can be found at s.21A of the TA in relation to the regulated sector, but s.19 also extends this obligation to suspicions that arise in the course of a "trade, profession, business or employment" so would include, for example, teachers developing concerns about the activities of a pupil's family or building contractors becoming suspicious on-site.

It is important to maintain a sense of perspective in relation to the risks that any given law firm is subject to for possible liability under the TA. In his annual report on the operation of the legislation David Anderson QC – the UK Government's Independent Reviewer of Terrorism Legislation – reported that only one person had been charged under ss.15 to 18 of the TA as a principal offence in each of the years from April 2008 to 2012, whereas there had been five annually in the preceding seven years from 2001. The legislation is subject to much the same level of criticism as POCA with the report also stating that the Reviewer would welcome:

> "a root-and-branch review of the entire edifice of anti-terrorism law, based on a clear-headed assessment of why and to what extent it is operationally necessary to supplement established criminal laws and procedures." (para 4.5)[12]

This was a theme to which the Reviewer returned more recently in his 2014 report,[13] arguing this time for changes to some of the base definitions in the TA and to the whole review process. As he acknowledges in his most recent report, however, and in common with the AML regime, there is little prospect of any major change to the CTF provisions in the foreseeable future.

The Money Laundering Regulations 2007

The EU-inspired Money Laundering Regulations were first extended to the legal profession in March 2004 when the Money Laundering Regulations 2003 took effect. The later 2007 version (MLR) replaced the earlier and simpler 2003 regulations on the 15th December 2007. The main changes were a move to a risk-based approach with less identity checking being required in some cases but more in others. Greater checking of controlling or beneficial interests would also become necessary as would the ongoing monitoring of existing clients. The checking would also need to be above a mechanistic approach to the collection of identity evidence with advisers needing to understand the "purpose and intended nature of the business relationship".[14]

More specifically, the new provisions adopted a wider approach as to who was covered by the regulations and included clearer references in the definitions to certain professional groups. Specific changes included a wider definition of "trust or company service provider" at r.3(10) and the introduction of certain exemptions for financial activity on an occasional or very limited basis. The full applicability of the regulations can be found in the Proceeds of Crime Act 2002 (Business in the Regulated Sector and Supervisory Authorities) Order 2007, which took effect at the coming into force of the revised regulations so as to amend Schedule 9 of POCA. Under the TA the definition of the regulated sector has been amended in like form because of the Amendment Regulations by the Terrorism Act 2000 (Business in the Regulated Sector and Supervisory Authorities) Order 2007.

Where the Regulations apply there will be a need to:

- Appoint a "nominated officer";
- Establish formal reporting procedures for occasions when disclosures are needed;
- Conduct "customer due diligence" checks on clients and others;
- Train "relevant personnel"; and
- Maintain certain records of identity checks and transactions.

Although the appointment of a nominated officer (usually referred to as a reporting officer or MLRO) is only a legal requirement if a firm is covered by the MLR 2007, the Law Society has suggested in its anti-money laundering practice note ('LSPN') at para 3.3.1 that other firms should still consider making such an appointment in case disclosures to the authorities become necessary. The Law Society's guidance also suggests a voluntary appointment would be useful, perhaps as evidence of running the firm in accordance with "proper governance and sound financial and risk management principles" as required by Principle 8 or the general supervisory requirements of chapter 7 of the SRA Code of Conduct ('the Code'). Much the same requirement would appear to apply to firms that are outside the scope of the MLR 2007 under Lexcel v6 at para 5.13, though subsequent guidance has suggested otherwise.

Where there is a voluntary appointment of an MLRO that person would appear to open themselves to potential criminal liability. This is because s.332 POCA imposes much the same obligations to pass on disclosures as can be found for their counterparts within the regulated sector. Whether the MLRO within a firm that is part regulated and part not is subject to potential liability under both ss.331 and 332 is one of the many points that remain unclear and is not addressed in the LSPN.

Where the MLR do apply, the most significant requirements are those relating to customer due diligence (CDD), which is stated by r.5 to mean three things:

- Identifying and verifying the client on the basis of "documents, data or information obtained from a reliable source";
- Identifying if there is a beneficial owner other than the client and taking "adequate measures, on a risk sensitive basis, to verify his identity" including measures to understand the ownership and control structure of any "legal person, trust or similar legal arrangement"; and
- Obtaining information on the purpose and intended nature of the business relationship.

The whole regime is stated to be "risk-based" in relation to the need to establish and monitor the issue of what is commonly referred to as the "know your client" identity checking obligations. There is accordingly a duty under r.7(3) for all firms to undertake their own risk assessment of their potential exposure and to be able to justify their approach, if questioned, to the SRA. In some circumstances "simplified due diligence" is permitted, in which case no formal checking is needed, but in others – such as where the client is not physically present or where the client is a "politically exposed person" – more checking than the norm is required by way of "enhanced due diligence". The risk-based approach has its merits – there is little point in having to establish the identity of a major plc or local authority client – but it has introduced more confusion as to the precise requirements. Conducting the necessary risk assessment is yet another responsibility for those in compliance roles; the lawyers then need to understand and support the firm's risk assessment and resulting procedures.

The regulations also introduced obligations to undertake greater checking on the beneficial ownership of most corporations, trusts and other such organisations, along with their management controls. There is a need to apply CDD to beneficial owners, generally defined as anyone having a 25% plus interest in any relevant entity, though the level of checking required here does not usually have to be to the same degree as clients.

Finally, there is a need to ask the client about control and management structures. These requirements might be simple enough in domestic family owned companies, but can be much more impenetrable if dealing with an international client base operating through, often deliberately, the most complex of corporate and holding structures. Nor can the practice relax its guard completely once the client has an established relationship with the firm since there is an obligation to continue to monitor the relevant data. The Law Society advice suggests renewing the full CDD process if, for example, there is a three year gap between retainers,[15] but it may well be that more limited checking of address details, at least, is needed if the gap between instructions is less.

Strained relations

Although the current regime should by now be well embedded the various relationships that exist within the AML regime are often tense and there are occasional outbreaks of recriminations. The law enforcement agencies – including the SRA for these purposes – have often accused the profession of being too lax in its AML controls and too accommodating in relation to suspicious clients. The Law Society, along with many compliance officers within firms, will point to the substantial compliance costs incurred by firms in addressing the regime and question whether the regime can be seen to be cost-effective in relation to the results achieved. Lawyers also respond that their obligation is preventive first and foremost, monitoring instructions so as not to become involved in illegal activity, rather than policing their clients. The publication of the FATF report on the legal profession in June 2013 was rather typical of this dialogue: the report criticised the levels of due diligence levels in many European firms and claimed that different interpretations of legal professional privilege acted as a disincentive to prosecution. In response Evangelos Tsouroulis, President of the Council of Bars and Law Societies of Europe, criticised the report as being based on "hypotheses", also "lacking interest" and with "no pedagogical purpose".[16]

Closer to home Steve Wilmott, Director of Intelligence and Investigations at the SRA, berated the profession at the 10th annual Ark Conference on Money Laundering in February 2014 for making an inadequate number of suspicious activity reports (SARs) to the authorities and for the quality of reports being made, the latter criticism being based on how often the authorities request supplemental information. In response various other speakers and delegates pointed out that:

- The available figures do not show how often lawyers meet their obligations by turning suspect work away – prevention rather than detection being the main aim of the regime for law firms; and
- The operation of privilege would mean that solicitors would be acting in breach of the relevant provisions in the SRA Handbook – and also the law of the land – if they were to disclose all of the suspicions they form when acting, or to disclose confidential information in breach of their duty in order to do so.

Similar tensions have arisen in many of the dealings reported by firms in relation to police investigations. Prosecutions – let alone convictions – may be rare, but the experience of an interview under caution is much more commonplace and often no less daunting. Many such investigations have been conducted in a hostile and intimidating manner by officers with little understanding or sympathy for the restrictions that arise under legal professional privilege, causing understandable distress and anxiety for those concerned.

The reported cases from both the courts and the Solicitors Disciplinary Tribunal might show that it is those who have knowingly involved themselves in illegal activity that will be most prone to legal or disciplinary process, but there have been findings against those who have simply missed the warning signs. Currently the UK subjects its lawyers and other professionals to a level of risk of prosecution that is unmatched in the rest of Europe, notwithstanding that the relevant AML and CTF provisions are EU inspired. In its response to the 2008 Home Office consultation on the reporting regime the Law Society protested about the continuing use of serious criminal offences to achieve a reporting obligation – the principal offences attracting up to 14 years' imprisonment and a fine. The Society also highlighted that the criminalisation of non-reporting by professionals and non-compliance with the regulations are both uniquely British concepts.

It is also worth pointing out that the current level of 4,000 SARs by lawyers is substantially more than in any other European nation, and does not take account of how often lawyers turn away potentially lucrative work on their understanding of their legal and professional obligations to do so. Nonetheless, in September 2014 the SRA announced that it would be "stepping up its efforts to ensure solicitors firms do not become embroiled in money laundering activity and are compliant with the various regulations and legislation associated with anti money laundering compliance".[17] A "specific piece of focus work" would run from the date of the press release (8th September 2014) to May 2015, "working with firms to ensure robust systems are in place to guard against solicitors becoming involved in money laundering." This announcement followed on from the July 2014 SRA Risk Outlook update, which placed money laundering as one of the issues that were "widespread, current and posing a significant risk to the public interest."

The outcome of this initiative was less critical than had been anticipated, but such criticism that is still made would be more palatable if the requirements of the disclosure regime and, to a lesser extent, the CDD processes under the MLR 2007, were more clearly stated in law and practice. There is instead widespread continuing confusion as to what precisely the compliance and disclosure provisions require of firms and their compliance personnel. The current state of affairs within most firms may be judged to be just about workable most of the time, but with continuing criticism of the profession by both its regulator and the NCA the position is far from satisfactory. In the meantime lawyers and reporting officers remain open to arbitrary action from the authorities which might end their careers and cause untold damage to the reputation of their firms. Little wonder, therefore, that so many reporting officers see their AML and CTF responsibilities as an unwelcome, if mandatory, burden.

The Fourth EU Directive

The Fourth EU Money Laundering Directive finally received formal approval on the 5th June 2015 and will need to be implemented by all EU national governments by 26th June 2017. The provision was first proposed by the European Commission in response to the FATF report of February 2012 and also followed a review by the Commission of the operation of the Third Directive. Delays in the consultation process have postponed the likely development of the next version of the MLR until late 2016 at the earliest with implementation now unlikely before 2017.

The key changes effected by the Directive are:

- Risk assessments being required at national level also. The concept has always been that the measures adopted should be commensurate to the risks that present themselves and so it will be at the national level also. This might suggest that more stringent measures are called for in the UK given the level of concerns as to London becoming an ever more popular destination for international money launderers.
- Enhanced due diligence requirements in relation to politically exposed persons. Currently the provisions relating to such people have excluded domestically based

high ranking individuals but this will cease to be the case. In addition, PEPs who have ceased to hold office within the last 18 months will also be covered by the provisions.

- There are no longer prescribed categories for simplified due diligence where full identity checking is not required. Instead, where a member state or an "obliged entity" (regulated firm) considers there to be lower risk member states may permit this lesser level of checking.

- An obligation for companies, trusts and other entities to maintain their own details of their beneficial owners, making the task of checking such details when conducting CDD that much more straightforward. Companies will also be required to hold this information on a public register, such as the Companies Registry, and make it available to competent authorities, "obliged entities" (including law firms in the regulated sector), Financial Investigation Units ("FIUs"), and anyone else with a legitimate interest. Information in relation to beneficial ownership of trusts must be maintained in a closed centralised register available to competent authorities and FIUs, whilst member states will be able to decide whether to allow access to obliged entities.

Other changes will include amended record keeping obligations in the light of data protection requirements and the imposition of minimum sanctions for breaches, though still defined in disciplinary rather than criminal terms. All in all the changes are not likely to be great given the current level of requirements on firms under the UK arrangements, nor, sadly, can any relaxation of the additional responsibilities placed on banks and other regulated concerns within the UK be expected in the short term, notwithstanding a recent announcement by Sajid Javid, Business Secretary, that he intends to review the current regime.[18]

As we have seen, the SRA has announced initiatives to address what it sees as poor levels of compliance in law firms in relation to money laundering activity by clients. More generally, there are concerns in Government about an imminent inspection of the UK by FATF which could well result in a more active approach to law enforcement for all concerned, law firms included. All in all, a review of this area of law firm risk management should be a priority for all firms since the risks of non-compliance are quite clearly on the increase.

Notes
1   See guidance note (iii) to s.8 of the SRA Authorisation Rules.
2   "Cleaning up: Law firms and the risk of money laundering" SRA: November 2014
3   A comment made by the Law Society in its response to the Home Office consultation – see 'Obligations to report money laundering: The consent regime', The Law Society, March 2008

at para 4.6.

4   SI 2007/3398.

5   *UMBS Online Ltd v SOCA* [2007] EWCA Civ 406.

6   Rees QC, E., Fisher, R, and Bogan, P. *Blackstone's Guide to the Proceeds of Crime Act 2002*. Oxford: Oxford University Press, 2011, para 3.03.

7   *P v P* [2003] EWHC Fam 2260 para 56.

8   See *The Guardian*: 12th February 2016 "EU Finance Ministers call for restrictions on 500 Euro notes over crime fears".

9   Reported in www.casino.org 16th November 2013

10 On the need for the prosecution to prove criminality see *Regina v A* [2007] EWCA Crim 2862 in which mere suspicion of fraud was ruled insufficient to support a conviction under s.327 POCA.

11 Yeshiemebet Girma and others were convicted of failing to provide information about acts of terrorism, contrary to s.38B(1)(b) of the Terrorism Act 2000.

12 David Anderson QC, 'The Terrorism Acts in 2012: Report of the Independent Reviewer on the operation of the Terrorism Act 2000 and part 1 of the Terrorism Act 2006', July 2013.

13 David Anderson QC, 'The Terrorism Acts in 2013: Report of the Independent Reviewer on the operation of the Terrorism Act 2000 and part 1 of the Terrorism Act 2006', July 2014. See 10.26 onwards.

14 MLR 2007 r.5(c)

15 Law Society practice note: Anti-money laundering, 13th October 2013, para 4.4.

16 Law Society Gazette 8th July 2013

17 'SRA steps up anti money laundering work', SRA, 8th September 2014.

18 'Ineffective money-laundering rules under scrutiny in Javid's bonfire of red tape' (*Daily Telegraph*, 28th August 2015).

CHAPTER 2

The main offences under the Proceeds of Crime Act 2002 and the Terrorism Act 2000

The risks of liability under POCA and TA have become major concerns for most law firms in recent years. The wide definitions of "criminal property" and "criminal conduct" within POCA have made money laundering a more regular issue than terrorist fundraising, but both sets of provisions carry the prospect of criminal liability and the drastic consequences that this would bring for any individual and the firm concerned. It follows that every sensible precaution should be taken to safeguard against involvement in the various offences in the Acts. This needs to include an awareness of the risks of the offences and how to avoid them in each adviser's practice area.

The money laundering offences are to be found for the most part in part 7 of POCA, with direct equivalents in relation to terrorist financing in part III of the TA, dealing with "terrorist property". Whereas liability for the money laundering offences will require proof of some illegality in relation to the funds or property in question, the like offences in the TA can be based on funds that are in all other respects legitimate. In the counter-terrorism offences it is the intended use of the property that is relevant for issues of liability, rather than its source.

As we have seen, "money laundering" is defined by s.340(11) POCA in somewhat circular fashion by reference to the "principal offences" at ss.327-329, i.e. money laundering is anything that constitutes an offence of concealing (s.327), arrangement (s.328) or acquisition, use and possession (s.329), an attempt, conspiracy or incitement to commit one of these offences, or aiding, abetting, counselling or procuring the commission of one of these offences.

Whether any particular conduct could be seen to constitute any such offence then depends upon the definitions of "criminal conduct" and "criminal property" under s.340(2) and (3). The fact that no proportionality exists in relation to the extent of the criminal conduct or improper gains remains a problem for professional advisers. In practice, the more trivial the criminal activity or the gain involved, the lower the risk of prosecution for the adviser. Many will nonetheless be understandably concerned to avoid even the most theoretical of risks.

The main defence to liability under this part of POCA is to make a disclosure of the knowledge or suspicion of money laundering that has arisen, or in some instances, should have arisen. Key to understanding this disclosure regime is to understand that there are two distinct reasons to make a disclosure: because of the legal obligation or *duty* to do so; and for fear of committing one of the principal offences, most probably that of "entering an arrangement" under s.328, and thus the *need* to do so to gain a defence to one of these offences. Since the definition of money laundering depends on an appreciation of the principal offences, and since these carry the most severe sentences on conviction, these form the most common starting point in any examination of the POCA offences. Professional advisers are likely to find it more helpful, however, to examine the possible offences in the same sequence as managing a client matter, and so starting with the process of taking instructions. There are then additional considerations in relation to "tipping off" if a disclosure to the authorities is needed, or if a disclosure has been made outside the practice.

This approach identifies three categories of offences as follows:

- Category 1: Non-disclosure offences: taking instructions
- Category 2: Principal offences: putting instructions into effect
- Category 3: Tipping off: discussing disclosures

Category 1: The non-disclosure offences
Failure to disclose: s.330 POCA
The first reason why an adviser might need to make a disclosure is that they are under a specific legal duty to do so. POCA builds on various earlier provisions, such as those contained in the Drug Trafficking Offences Act 1986 and the Criminal Justice Act 1993, by placing a legal obligation on those in the regulated sector (i.e. those conducting "relevant business" under the MLR 2007) to disclose their knowledge or suspicions of money laundering activity as defined by the Act. The obligations are to be found in the "failure to disclose" offence at s.330.

As originally enacted this provides that an offence is committed where a person:

- Acquires a knowledge or suspicion of money laundering, or should reasonably have done so; where
- That knowledge or suspicion comes to them in the course of business in the regulated sector; and

- They do not make the "required disclosure" as soon as practicable after the information comes to them.

Section 330 has since been amended in the light of the Serious Organised Crime and Police Act 2005 ("SOCPA") so that a disclosure is only needed where the person who is known or suspected to have committed a crime can be identified, or it would be reasonable to suppose that the information that could be disclosed would be helpful. This amendment was introduced mainly to deal with the sort of situations frequently confronted by accountants who would realise, for example, that shoplifting had had an effect on retailer accounts. There would be little to be gained by making a disclosure to this effect to the authorities since the information would be of no practical use, but until this change they were technically required to do so.

It is important to note that the knowledge or suspicion of money laundering must be acquired "in the course of a business in the regulated sector". The intention of this provision was to exclude the general public from the duty to make disclosures, but its precise application remains uncertain. It is not clear, for example, if a partner or staff member would be obliged to report a social conversation concerning a client. Likewise, if an accountant has some building work done for them at home by a client who then suggests payment in cash "to avoid VAT" have they acquired a knowledge or suspicion of likely tax evasion in the course of their work in the regulated sector, or merely as a private citizen? There has never been any definitive guidance on such situations.

Another point of concern in relation to the drafting of this offence is that the duty to disclose is not technically discharged when information is in the public domain. If an adviser reads in a newspaper that a client organisation is being investigated for criminal offences they would seem nonetheless to be required to disclose this fact to the NCA.[1] As ever, the risks of prosecution for not doing so might be theoretical, but it is a matter of concern that the boundaries of criminal liability should be so poorly defined.

It is important to stress that the duty to disclose is not limited to clients of the firm; the offence talks about learning about money laundering by "another person", so will quite commonly be the other party in a matter rather than the adviser's own client. It is thus the policy of various major practices, when acting for a purchaser or lender, to disclose as a matter of course all prohibited actions such as taxation irregularities revealed in the disclosure letter. Whether this is what was truly intended by this provision seems unlikely.

The greatest concern with this offence, however, is the application of the "reasonable grounds" test to the level of criminal conduct needed for liability. An adviser is obliged to make a disclosure not only when they know or have suspicions about criminal activity by their client or another, but also where it is felt that they should have known or suspected that something was untoward, meaning that the test is both subjective and objective. The application of criminal sanctions to what is potentially an offence of negligence can produce worryingly harsh results. As to the required mental state, it was suggested by the Court of Appeal in *R v Da Silva* 2006 that a person could only be said to "suspect" criminal activity if they thought there was a possibility which was more than "fanciful" that the other person was or had been involved in criminal activity. They also suggested that a "vague feeling of unease" would not suffice.[2] In relation to the objective "reasonable grounds", the Law Society suggests that this will depend upon whether an "honest and reasonable person engaged in a business in the regulated sector would have inferred knowledge or formed the suspicion that another was engaged in money laundering".[3]

The first solicitor to be convicted of this offence was the Northern Ireland lawyer David McCartan.[4] During the course of a conveyancing transaction an accomplice of the client came into the office with over £70,000 of cash and cheques with the suggestion that the funds should be used in the transaction. McCartan refused to take the monies but assisted this individual by completing a client account paying-in slip to take to the bank, having satisfied himself that the money came from the earnings of a related car dealership. He pleaded guilty at trial but at the appeal on sentence it was stated that "all the evidence that has been put before us has led us to the unmistakable conclusion that the applicant was gullible rather than malign." The report of his appeal on sentence shows that the remainder of his six months' prison term for this offence was suspended.

The concept of what amounted to a "reasonable" suspicion was more of an issue in the later case of the Shrewsbury solicitor Philip Griffiths.[5] After a trial lasting some two weeks Pattison, an estate agent and financial adviser who was known to Griffiths, was convicted of the more serious offence of entering an arrangement contrary to s.328 POCA. The owner of a house in Birmingham had approached Pattison asking him to buy the house for £43,000. The true value of the property was nearer £150,000 and the aim of the transaction was to defeat confiscation proceedings following a conviction for drug trafficking. There was some dispute as to what Pattison had said to Griffiths about the transaction, but it was claimed that he had explained the under-value as being the amount of the outstanding mortgage in a transaction within the owner's family. Although Griffiths was acquitted of the more serious arrangement offence he was convicted nonetheless of failure to disclose under s.330. There was evidence of the solicitor's innocence in relation to the main charge in that he charged his normal fee for the matter. In relation to the failure to disclose offence. However, it was held that there were reasonable grounds for him to have suspected that Pattison was involved in money laundering and he should therefore have made a disclosure to the authorities. For his failure to do so he was initially sentenced to 15 months imprisonment, reduced on appeal to six months. He was also subsequently struck off the roll of solicitors, thereby losing his livelihood.

Various concerns have been expressed about the application of the twofold subjective and objective suspicion test in cases involving professional advisers. First, there is a tendency for the prosecuting authorities to treat lawyers as if they have expertise in all areas of the law – complex fraud cases included. A career in conveyancing does not make an adviser expert in VAT carousel frauds, for example, but in all probability the average juror will suppose that experience of any one area of law equates with expertise elsewhere, which could operate unfairly against any professional charged with an offence. Secondly, an objective test generally works unfairly when applied with the wisdom of hindsight: things tend to seem more obvious when considered at a later stage than they might have done at the time. During the course of an investigation it is likely to be extremely difficult to work on the basis of what was not known at the time. There are bound to be concerns as to the extent to which a jury can truly assess what should have been obvious to a professional adviser at a previous stage of a process that, in any event, they are unlikely to understand.

The main defence to liability under s.330 is for a partner or member of staff to report their concerns to the firm's MLRO and then to follow that person's instructions. In the circumstances where the disclosure to the reporting officer is as a result of a legal obligation to do so it is referred to as a "required" disclosure. Most firms take the view that it is better that all suspicions and concerns are reported to the MLRO in order for them to address what is and is not a required disclosure for these purposes, rather than expect members of the firm to take a view on such issues. One modification is to use Heads of Department or other specialists as a filter, but unfortunately the MLR 2007 do not recognise the concept of deputy reporting officers. Either way, once a disclosure is made responsibility then passes to the reporting officer and he or she will have to decide whether to report on to the NCA. In making this decision they will have to take into account the other defences for this offence, which include reasonable excuse (s.330(6)(a)) and, more importantly, legal professional privilege (s.330(6)(b)). More than ten years since the law first took effect there is still no judicial guidance on what amounts to "reasonable excuse", with the Law Society having suggested in the past that any such instances will be "narrow".[6] One possible application might prove to be the circumstances where an adviser was subject to serious threats or intimidation.

In practical terms it will seldom be necessary to report on to the NCA at this stage as a result of the operation of privilege, as examined in Chapter 3. Privilege is the client's right to have their confidential information withheld from disclosure outside their relationship with the adviser or the firm and is enshrined in anti-money laundering provisions by the Third Directive. A breach of common law privilege is potentially a professional offence under the Principles of the SRA Handbook and could also give the client contractual rights against the firm for the misuse of their information. In relation to this offence, however, it is the statutory format of the "privileged circumstances" defence that applies. This is explained in the LSPN at para 6.5 as excusing non-disclosure by a professional legal adviser where the information concerned is communicated by:

- The client or their representative in connection with the adviser giving legal advice;
- The client or their representative in connection with their seeking legal advice; or
- Any person for the purpose of or in connection with contemplated legal proceedings.

The scope of this defence is likely to cover the taking of instructions in the great majority of cases with the only major likely exception being where there is an attempt to perpetrate a fraud through the adviser, as in sham litigation. Privilege will also break down where the information that causes suspicions is extraneous to the work in question, but a broad view should be taken of the issues that might be covered in the course of consultations between client and adviser. In the LSPN on this point the Law Society quotes the following extract from the case of *Three Rivers District Council and others v the Bank of England* 2004, para. 111:

> "All communications between a lawyer and his client relating to a transaction in which the lawyer has been instructed for the purpose of obtaining legal advice are covered by advice privilege, not withstanding that they do not contain advice on matters of law and construction, provided that they are directly related to the performance by the solicitor of his professional duty as legal adviser of his client."[7]

It should also be stressed that where common law privilege exists it is not merely the case that the lawyer has a defence to non-disclosure of the money laundering – they have no right to reveal the privileged information unless they have a waiver from the client to do so. Privilege, it should be remembered, is the client's entitlement to have their confidential information kept secret and is more onerous in this regard than the adviser's duty of confidentiality.

The less common defences that might apply are where there is a "reasonable excuse" for not reporting (s.330(6)) and the specific defence for s.330 only at subsection 7 that the adviser does not know or suspect money laundering and has not been provided with "such training as is specified by the Secretary of State by order for the purposes of this section" – a defence that does not have a parallel in the TA. In such circumstances the authorities would no doubt turn their attention to the firm that had not provided the required training and it might be expected that a prosecution under the MLR or, more likely, disciplinary measures under O(7.5) of the SRA Code of Conduct might follow. The specified training, if of interest, is subject to The Proceeds of Crime Act 2002 (Failure to Disclose Money Laundering: Specified Training) Order 2003 *(SI 2003/171)*.

Failure to disclose (Reporting Officers)

The MLRO of a regulated firm is subject to a separate "failure to disclose" offence under s.331. Completing the set of non-disclosure offences is s.332, which applies in very similar terms to s.331 but in relation to reporting officers outside the regulated sector. The appointment of a reporting officer will only be mandatory for concerns within the regulated sector, but it can be good practice to make such an appointment for others. So far as law firms are concerned this might apply to firms providing services in areas such as crime or personal injury law, which are generally regarded as being outside the ambit of the regulations. The LSPN at para 3.3.1 suggests that such an appointment will be advisable in order that fee-earners have a process to disclose concerns that might otherwise lead to possible liability, especially for the principal offences, or for in-house legal departments that are outside the scope of being "independent" legal professionals under r.2 of the MLR. The point has already been made that in such instances the firm's reporting officer would appear to volunteer for potential liability under s.332 in that there is in law no need for such an appointment but, if one is made, the office holder assumes potential liability under s.332.

What is unclear, from either the statutory wording or the LSPN, is whether the reporting officer in a mixed firm that is part regulated only will find him or herself subject to both s.331 in relation to the regulated work and s.332 for the other parts of the practice. Either way, these offences are the reporting officers' version of s.330 "failure to disclose" liability, but with one material variation: whereas privilege is a specific statutory defence to non-disclosure under s.330 it is not to be found in either of ss.331 or 332. This has led to considerable uncertainty as to the operation of a disclosure regime within a firm. Initially it was suggested that privilege would be lost as soon as an internal report was made to the reporting officer, an approach doubted by the Law Society on grounds that the MLRO would have a "reasonable excuse" not to report on to the NCA in such circumstances.[8]

There was a more specific resolution of sorts on this issue in s.106 SOCPA, which provides that privilege will not be lost if a "professional legal adviser" is to make a disclosure to their reporting officer for the purpose of obtaining advice about making a disclosure under s.330, and does not intend that communication to be a disclosure under the firm's procedures. On the basis of this amendment the LSPN now advises at para 6.4.4 that it is not a breach of legal professional privilege to discuss a matter with a nominated officer for the purposes of receiving advice on whether to make a disclosure. This amendment is far from ideal, however. Advisers would seem only to acquire the "required disclosure" defence under s.330(4) when they make the disclosure to the nominated officer and this, along with the definition of "disclosure" at s.330(5), seems to suggest that it must be a formal disclosure in accordance with the firm's procedures. If this is the case the adviser is placed in a difficult position if they consult the reporting officer informally only to be told that no report is needed, and would be within their rights to insist on serving a formal notice of their concerns to gain a defence to any possible charge. See also s.330(9A) on this process.

Failure to disclose (Terrorism Act)
The TA contains a similar failure to disclose offence at s.21A for the regulated sector and s.19 more generally. Whereas s.330 POCA is limited to those in the regulated sector, s.19 TA talks instead of a duty to make a disclosure when a person believes or suspects that another person has committed one of the main terrorist financing offences in ss.15-18, and this is based on information that has come to them "in the course of a trade, profession or business, or in the course of his employment". The obligation is then to disclose "to a constable" (but in practice the NCA) their belief or suspicion and the information on which this is based, and should be through any process established by the employer for the purpose. Section 19 TA could apply to solicitors' firms to the extent that they are outside the regulated sector, and the defence of privilege can therefore be found at s.19(5), along with "reasonable excuse" at s.19(3).

In relation to s.21A and the regulated sector, and therefore most transactional legal advisers in particular, "reasonable excuse" applies as a defence, as does the statutory format of the "privileged circumstances" defence for professional legal advisers, provided the communication is not intended to further a criminal purpose (s.21A(8)-(9)). Liability under s.19 outside the regulated sector is on a subjective basis only and does not arise where the accused should have developed suspicions but did not do so. The reasonable grounds standard can be found, however, at s.21A(2) for those in the regulated sector as well as the subjective test. Finally, there is no equivalent under either offence in the TA of the defence found at s.330(7) POCA of personnel not having received training in AML and CTF issues.

Category 2: The principal offences

The second and more common reason for a firm to make a disclosure to the NCA is that it needs to do so to gain a defence to one or more of the principal money laundering or terrorist offences. A disclosure to gain a defence to any of the principal offences is referred to as an "authorised" disclosure and is subject to extensive statutory provisions. As the title suggests, these are the most serious offences under the regime, attracting up to 14 years' imprisonment and/or a fine. Unlike the non-disclosure offences these crimes can be committed by anyone, and so apply just as much to private citizens as to those working in the regulated sector or who are designated as reporting officers. It follows that many businesses that are outside the regulated sector would be well advised to establish a reporting regime in order to provide their employees with a defence to a charge under the principal offences.

Sections 327-329 POCA could be seen to penalise those who benefit from any acquisitive crime or those who assist them to do so, those who use any such criminal property and finally those who come into possession of it. This is achieved by the three complementary offences of:

- 327: Concealing
- 328: Entering into an arrangement
- 329: Acquisition, use and possession

There will often be considerable overlap between these offences and the authorities might therefore be in a position to choose which they wish to pursue. An accomplice who agrees to take criminal funds into their bank account and then pay them back to the criminal or to a third party at their instruction could be said to "conceal" the source of the funds, have "entered into an arrangement" with the criminal, and also be in "possession" of the funds while they are under their control, as when they are in their bank account.

It is important to note that the normal criminal *mens rea* applies to these offences. This would mean that if, naively, a solicitor were to get involved in accepting and processing a payment as above, without appreciating that what they were doing was wrong, none of the principal offences would be committed. The test in relation to any suspicions that they might have had is therefore subjective only, not objective, and would probably be judged as suggested in *R v Da Silva*. It would therefore be for the prosecution to prove that the relevant act was done with the knowledge or suspicion that the property derived from criminal conduct. If it were established that the adviser was not in fact suspicious the proper verdict would be "not guilty", though convincing a court that a skilled legal adviser was blameless in such circumstances might prove to be quite a challenge for the defence.

Concealing: Section 327 POCA
Section 327 provides that a person commits an offence if (s)he

"(a) conceals criminal property

(b) disguises criminal property

(c) converts criminal property

(d) transfers criminal property

(e) removes criminal property from England and Wales or from Scotland or from Northern Ireland."

Concealment or disguising is explained to be concealing or disguising the nature, source, location, disposition, movement or ownership of any rights with respect to it. As with so many of the provisions in this Act, the wording of s.327(1)(e) does have some strange connotations. It is made an offence to remove assets from one of England and Wales, Scotland or Northern Ireland, meaning that it is therefore an offence to take property from Edinburgh to Belfast or London, but not – under this provision at least – from London to Cardiff or Manchester.

Concerns were expressed when POCA was first passed that "concealing" could embrace omissions to act in addition to positive steps taken to hide the criminal property – a risk that was dealt with in the Law Society's earliest guidance on the topic. The concern was that not revealing or disclosing concerns could be taken to be "concealing" the property. Had this interpretation been adopted the offence could have been used as a more general "non-disclosure" offence that would not have been limited to the regulated sector, as are the non-disclosure offences at ss.330-331. This would have been out of line with the earlier offences that appeared in provisions such as the Drug Trafficking Act 1994 and the Criminal Justice Act 1988, however, and recognising this the Crown Prosecution Service guidelines still talk of the need for an "act" of concealment. Fortunately there appears to be no evidence of these fears having been justified.

Arrangement: Section 328 POCA
In cases where professional advisers are involved the "arrangement" offence seems to be the preferred charge. It is committed where the person:

"... enters into or becomes concerned in an arrangement which he knows or suspects facilitates (by whatever means) the acquisition, retention, use or control of criminal property by or on behalf of another person." (s.328(1))

There is a good deal of clarification on the arrangement offence in the LSPN and, in particular, the point at which an arrangement can be said to come into existence (para 5.4.3). It is important to be clear on this, as it is at this point that the adviser enters into that arrangement, usually with the client. There will be a "predicate" offence, i.e. some pre-existing criminal conduct by the client or another person which could trigger a subsequent scheme that could amount to an arrangement. In these circumstances the adviser needs to toe a careful line between providing advice to the client on their potential liability and becoming complicit in that offence or some scheme that arises in its furtherance.

Most of the early cases in relation to this offence involve banks and the difficulties they face when concerns arise as to the operation of accounts that become suspect or are subject to an order under the Act. In *K Ltd v NatWest Bank* 2006[9] it was held that a banker who knows or suspects that money in a customer's account is criminal property, and who processes the funds without making the necessary disclosure to the NCA, facilitates the use or control of those funds and cannot use his/her contractual duties to the customer as an excuse for doing so. Furthermore, the banker could not explain to a customer why their accounts would be frozen in such circumstances for fear of liability for tipping off under s.333 POCA if they knew or suspected that this might prejudice an investigation.

Other cases have since elaborated on the point at which a person can be said to have entered an arrangement. In *R v Geary* 2010[10] there had been a complex bank fraud and the accused was approached to "hide" some of the money. He was told that this was to safeguard funds in relation to a pending divorce and he had no knowledge of the fraud. Although he initially agreed to do so he then developed second thoughts and returned most of the money. It was held that although he might have risked liability for perverting the course of justice he could not be liable for the arrangement offence as he had no knowledge of the nature of the funds handled, and so did not have the necessary *mens rea* for the offence. The view of the court was that the natural and ordinary meaning of the offence was that the arrangement to which it referred must be one that related to property which was criminal property at the time when the arrangement began. To say that it extended to property which was originally legitimate but became criminal only as a result of carrying out the arrangement was to stretch the language of the section beyond its proper limits.

The case of *R v Amir and Another* 2011[11] is helpful in relation to attempted fraud and also the possible liability of the borrower in mortgage fraud cases. Money laundering offences could only be committed where the property in question was "criminal property" at the time of the relevant arrangement. In this case Amir, who sold mortgage leads to brokers for a fee, encouraged clients to falsify their applications. It was held that he was not guilty of the arrangement offence on grounds that when he entered into the relevant arrangements with the mortgage brokers the property in question was not criminal in the hands of the mortgage company. Furthermore the borrowers were not liable under s.329 for the "possession" offence since they had provided adequate consideration for the loan.

The first major decision that examined the disclosure regime for lawyers was *P v P* 2003.[12] The case involved a substantial divorce matter involving some £19m of joint assets. The wife's advisers had developed suspicions in relation to the husband's activities and had disclosed these suspicions – then to the National Crime Intelligence Service ("NCIS") – for fear of becoming concerned in an arrangement relating to a financial settlement involving their client. It had been assumed before the *P v P* case that it would be necessary to make a disclosure for the adviser to protect him or herself from liability under the principal offences and that decision was made accordingly, but this approach was then reviewed by the Court of Appeal in *Bowman v Fels* 2005.[13] The main element of this Court of Appeal decision was to question whether it could truly be said that a lawyer becomes concerned in an arrangement with their client where, for example, they learn of tax evasion or some other irregularity that emerges in the course of representing them. Litigation, it was observed, is a state sponsored process and viewed as such it would be a "nonsense" to suppose that a lawyer somehow enters into a criminal scheme with their client by acting for them in such circumstances.

Bowman v Fels was greeted as a much needed dose of judicial commonsense at the time and removed the need for disclosures in most litigation cases – and ancillary proceedings in family law in particular – which at that stage had become commonplace. If the lawyer does not become concerned in an arrangement with their client they do not need to make a disclosure to protect themselves from liability. It was, however, stated to be very much a case that was limited to litigation and so did not remove the need for a disclosure in transactions where there are concerns as to the legitimacy of funds or assets that are being transferred by the firm if not acting in litigation. This has created, in effect, two sets of rules on the issue and the reporting officer will need to be clear as to which track they are on in any given report that is made to them.

One of the more complex issues in relation to possible liability for the principal offences is the point at which an arrangement can be said to have come into existence from the point of the lawyer's involvement. This was a point first examined in *P v P*, with a ruling by Dame Elizabeth Butler-Sloss that:

"In my view, the duties under section 328 of a barrister or solicitor engaged in family litigation are straight-forward. There is nothing in that section to prevent a solicitor or barrister from taking instructions from a client." (para 49)

The issue was reviewed more fully in *Bowman v Fels* and the current LSPN on this point is based on that judgment, and para 67 that:

"To enter into an arrangement involves a single act at a single point in time; so, too, on the face of it, does to 'become concerned' in an arrangement, even though the point at which someone may be said to have 'become' concerned may be open to argument."

The Law Society therefore advised in the LSPN at para 5.4.3 that it considers that *Bowman v Fels* supports a "restricted" understanding of how and when an adviser enters into or becomes involved in an arrangement, and that an offence is only committed once the arrangement is actually made. This means that "preparatory or intermediate steps in transactional work which does not itself involve the acquisition, retention, use or control of property will not constitute the making of an arrangement under section 328". This, in turn, has generally been interpreted to mean that steps taken in pursuit of instructions will fall short of an arrangement until funds or property are actually transferred. The LSPN does not go quite this far, however, and advisers are cautioned instead to consider at all times "whether an arrangement exists and, if so, whether you have entered into or become concerned in it or may do so in the future" or, if no arrangement yet exists, "whether one may come into existence in the future which you may become concerned in" (LSPN para 5.4.3).

By way of a cautionary note, there would now have to be greater care in relation to the lawyer's freedom to undertake "preparatory acts" short of actually entering an arrangement, especially where criminal clients of the firm are concerned. In *Fitzpatrick v Metropolitan Commissioner of Police* 2012[14] a client of the firm (X) had been convicted of conspiracy to supply drugs and had been imprisoned. A restraint order had also been made in relation to his assets. The police believed that X owed another client of the firm (Y) money and hoped to transfer it via a power of attorney in contravention of the restraint order. An adviser in the firm – Fitzpatrick – visited X in prison to secure his signature to a power of attorney and was duly arrested on suspicion of money laundering offences – a search warrant was also granted for an inspection of the firm's offices. Fitzpatrick and a partner of the firm were questioned and bailed for almost two years, at which stage charges were dropped. This claim for compensation for assault, wrongful arrest and false imprisonment was rejected on grounds that the police had acted reasonably.

The Law Society's most recent advice on *Bowman v Fels* is dated the 2nd December 2014 and is headed "Matrimonial property challenges". This report might be seen to be a slight rolling back of the earlier advice that family work was unlikely to prompt the need for disclosures to the authorities as a result of the Court of Appeal's decision in this case. Difficult issues of tax evasion have been highlighted in particular and the suggestion is made that the payment of any outstanding tax should be factored into any order or settlement in order to address all parties' obligations. More than anything, however, this note re-asserts that the matrimonial lawyer (and perhaps, therefore, litigators more generally) should not usually have to make disclosures to the NCA to protect themselves from the arrangement charge at s.328 as a result of the main element of *Bowman v Fels* to the effect that a litigator does not join in an arrangement with their client by acting for them.

Acquisition, use and possession: Section 329

The third of the principal offences is found at s.329, which provides that it is an offence to acquire, use or have possession of criminal property. One of the implications of this offence is that money does not need to be moving for an offence under this provision to become a possibility, since possession is likely to be a passive state of affairs as opposed to actively "acquiring" the same property. If a firm has funds in its client account and suspicions then arise as to its provenance, liability could arise if the adviser does nothing. In such cases the disclosure should be made "as soon as practicable" under s.338(3)(c).

Terrorism offences

The TA contains a number of offences in relation to financing at ss.15 to 18 that are again very similar to POCA provisions, in particular the "money laundering" offence at s.18:

"A person commits an offence if he enters into or becomes concerned in an arrangement which facilitates the retention or control by or on behalf of another person of terrorist property–

(a) by concealment,

(b) by removal from the jurisdiction,

(c) by transfer to nominees, or

(d) in any other way."

The other main terrorist offences (to which disclosure is again the main defence) include:

- Fundraising (s.15): Committed by inviting others to make a contribution, receiving contributions or making contributions (including gifts and loans);

- Use or possession (s.16): Liability can also arise where a person should reasonably have suspected that money or other property could be used for terrorist offences;
- Funding arrangements (s.17): Where a person knows or has reasonable cause to suspect that an arrangement that makes money available to others could be used for terrorist offences.

It is a defence for a person charged with any of these offences to prove that they did not know and had no cause to suspect that the arrangement related to terrorist property. It should be noted that whereas the principal offences in POCA require normal criminal *mens rea*, liability for their equivalents in the TA can be based on a failure to act on reasonable suspicions.

Defences to the principal offences
The main defence is that the person makes an "authorised disclosure" under s.338 POCA and obtains consent to the act, which we examine in Chapter 4. There is also the more general defence of "reasonable excuse" which is still, as yet, unexplained in case law. Finally, in relation to s.329 POCA only there is a defence that the property was acquired for "adequate consideration". This is intended primarily for those who are paid from criminal funds in relation to the provision of their ordinary goods or services – the window cleaner need not question the source of their payment, for example. There is an important restriction to this defence at s.329(3)(c) to the effect that the goods or services supplied must not be to help "carry out criminal conduct". The Law Society takes the view that there should be no risk of liability under this offence through a firm being paid its fees and disbursements as long as the fees are reasonable and proportionate.[15] Without this defence a criminal firm representing a client who was convicted of an offence under the Act would risk liability itself for having received questionable funds into its office account.

Category 3: Tipping off and disclosing an investigation
Tipping off is probably the most readily intelligible offence in the anti-money laundering regime. Revealing information that could hinder enquiries by the proper authorities could compromise the criminal process and might itself lead to criminal liability. An offence that seeks to restrict what advisers may tell their clients causes obvious tensions for professionals whose primary duties include the need to disclose all relevant information to their clients. Managing the conflict between the statutory duty not to reveal disclosures on the one hand, and complying with the duty of disclosure to the client at O(4.2) on the other, requires a detailed understanding of how this group of

offences works. This tension is recognised in the Code of Conduct, with Indicative Behaviour 4.4.c acknowledging that there are situations where the provisions in the money laundering or terrorist financing legislation will prohibit the lawyer from passing information to others.

In relation to disclosing dealings with the authorities there were initially two POCA offences to consider – "tipping off" (s.333) and "prejudicing an investigation" (s.342). These offences were originally general in their application and were thus not limited to the regulated sector. Although always an important element of the money laundering legislation they did not appear in the TA. The offences were subject to extensive changes in the Terrorism Act 2000 and Proceeds of Crime Act 2002 (Amendment) Regulations 2007 ('the Amendment Regulations'), which took effect at the end of 2007. The main purpose of these regulations was to make the necessary amendments to UK law to accommodate the Third EU Directive.

The main offence of tipping off is now specifically written into the TA, but in relation to both proceeds of crime and terrorism is limited to those in the regulated sector. A new offence of "disclosing an investigation" was also introduced for the regulated sector, but the general offence of "prejudicing an investigation" in POCA at s.342, with an equivalent offence of "disclosure of information" at s.39 TA, now carries an immunity for those in the regulated sector. These offences are still relevant to partners and staff in firms or departments whose work falls outside the scope of the MLR 2007, such as those that deal with crime or personal injury work or, presumably, those in the regulated sector acting in a personal capacity.

The defence of statutory privilege that formed part of the original offence of tipping off at s.333, and which was the main issue examined in the case of *P v P*, was replaced by some specific defences for most professional groups. To further complicate matters – as if this were needed – the defence of statutory privilege remains for any adviser outside the regulated sector who is charged under the "prejudicing an investigation" offence at s.342.

As elsewhere in the regime, uncertainty remains in the operation of this offence. Suppose that the 'nightmare scenario' arises for a conveyancer. They have made a disclosure to the NCA in relation to their concerns about completion monies, but they are within the seven working days period within which consent may not be deemed to have been granted. They have still not received the consent they sought to continue with the transaction at the start of business on completion day – a situation that has been encountered, though seemingly rarely. If they complete without having obtained the necessary consent they risk liability under s.328 for having facilitated an arrangement at a time when they did not have consent to do so, or the firm's reporting officer risks liability under s.336 if he or she gives approval to the completion in advance of being granted formal consent by the NCA. If they do not complete, however, could it be argued that they have, in effect, tipped off the client about the disclosure since this might be seen as the only logical explanation for delaying completion? A further and rather obvious practical problem is what to tell the client in such circumstances when they ask what they should tell the removal company that is now waiting to load up the van for a move which appears not to be happening. There is unfortunately no advice on these potential problems in the LSPN.

The offences

There are two separate offences that can be committed by those within the regulated sector in relation to both s.333 POCA and s.21 TA.

First, it is an offence under s.333(A) POCA to disclose to any third party – the client or another – that a disclosure has been made by "any person" – not just the firm in question – "to the police, HM Revenue and Customs, SOCA [now NCA] or a nominated officer". The same applies now to terrorist situations under s.21(D) TA.

It is important to note that the point at which this offence becomes a possibility is when an internal report is made to the reporting officer and should thus be taken as the trigger for the point at which tipping off could arise as an offence (sections 333A(2) POCA and 21D(2) TA). An issue for internal reporting procedures is therefore to recognise that the point at which a disclosure is made, and tipping off liability therefore becomes a possibility, is the point at which a formal report is made internally to the reporting officer. Some firms have in consequence restricted the availability of the internal reporting forms to the MLRO in order that there is some form of prior discussion before a formal report is made.

It also follows, therefore, that until this point an adviser may, and under his or her professional duties probably should, be explicit about the risks of the disclosure regime in their advice to clients. Many advisers seem still to fear that explaining the risks of the regime – for example, in selling a company without dealing with taxation irregularities – will amount to tipping off. This will not be the case since, at that stage, no disclosure will have been made. Far from providing as little information as possible about such processes, Principle 4 of the SRA Handbook – to act in the best interests of the client – suggests that detailed advice should be given on the risk to the client of a disclosure needing to be made unless they modify their instructions. The Law Society therefore provides that:

> "There is nothing in POCA which prevents you making normal enquiries about your client's instructions, and the proposed retainer, in order to remove, if possible, any

concerns and enable the firm to decide whether to take on or continue the retainer." (LSPN para 5.8.3)

This might also be helpful in relation to the common situation where an opponent makes an allegation of illegality to the adviser about their client. The above provision would appear to encourage the adviser to investigate the situation rather than disclose on the basis that they have now formed a suspicion based on a third party communication which could prove to be unfounded or malicious.

The second tipping off offence is to be found at s.333A(3) POCA and s.21D(3) TA and consists of "disclosing an investigation". This offence is probably best seen as the equivalent of "prejudicing an investigation" (sections 342 POCA and 39 TA) for the regulated sector, but as yet we have no judicial guidance on it. Unlike the main offence above, this offence can be committed even where the adviser does not realise that a disclosure has been made.

The specific nature of this new offence has perhaps inspired the Law Society to withdraw its earlier advice that if a client is aware that his bank has been in contact with the police, he is entitled to seek advice on his legal position and his legal adviser is entitled to advise him that he may be the subject of a money laundering investigation, even if as a result such advice might prejudice the investigation.[16] The adviser in this situation would now have to be more careful as providing an explanation on the disclosure process might well prejudice any investigation. The safer view would be to be very cautious about the firm's ability to provide advice in such circumstances.

Liability for both offences can only arise where "the disclosure is likely to prejudice any investigation that might be conducted following the disclosure". The LSPN seems to suggest that this will apply in subjective terms: at para 5.8.1 it suggests that the offence is only committed "if you knew or suspected that the disclosure would, or would be likely to prejudice any investigation." This is based on s.333D(3) POCA and s.21(G)(4) TA, which do seem to be worded in subjective terms.

Defences

It should first be noted that one of the ingredients of the tipping off offences is that disclosure is "likely to prejudice any investigation that might be conducted following the disclosure", so a report to a senior level compliance professional in a client bank, for example, might at first appear to be prohibited but is unlikely to constitute the offence. At first, legal professional privilege was a specific statutory defence to the offence of tipping off but the Amendment Regulations 2007 replaced this with a list of specific defences that allow disclosures:

- Within a group or undertaking (i.e. internally within the firm) (s.333B);
- Between institutions, including "by a professional legal adviser to another professional legal adviser" or by "a relevant professional adviser of a particular kind to another professional adviser of the same kind" but only in relation to a shared client or service or a transaction involving them both, and where the disclosure is "for the purpose only of preventing an offence under this Part of this Act" (s.333C);
- To the appropriate regulatory body under the MLR 2007 (the SRA) (s.333D); or
- To the client "for the purpose of dissuading the client from engaging in conduct amounting to an offence" (s.333D(2)).

The final defence in this list seems to envisage that the lawyer should be able to talk freely to their client to dissuade them from criminal conduct, even if a disclosure has been made. If there is any hesitation to engage in such conversations it is important to remember again Principle 4 from the SRA Handbook and the obligation to act in the best interests of the client. This objective will usually be met by being as open as possible about the client's behaviour within these new provisions in order to dissuade them from illegal activities and to be sure of the facts before a disclosure is considered.

Prejudicing an investigation

The offence of prejudicing an investigation remains at s.342 POCA and has a broad equivalent at s.39 TA. Neither offence applies any longer to those in the regulated sector through r.8 of the POCA Amendment Regulations 2007. In all other respects the offence remains the same and could be committed, for example, by a litigator whose firm or department was outside the scope of the MLR 2007. Such an individual would still have the defence of privileged circumstances that formerly applied to the main tipping off offence at s.333.

Serious Crime Act 2015

Section 45 of the Serious Crime Act 2015 should now be added to the list of the main offences that fee earners need to be wary of. This makes it an offence to participate in the "criminal activities of an organised crime group", which is so defined to consist of three or more persons who act together to further the purpose of carrying on criminal activities. The offence has been planned to target those who head up criminal organisations or who do not directly participate in such activities, and would seem to be an alternative to a more general conspiracy charge. Fears have been expressed that solicitors might unwittingly become liable under this section as liability is stated to apply to those who know or who should "reasonably suspect" that criminal activities are afoot. This suggests that, rather like the "failure to disclose" offence at s.330 POCA, liability might be based on an objective test of what the adviser should reasonably have been aware of, rather than their actual suspicions at the time.

Notes

1   See on this point Mark Humphries and Suzie Ogilvie, 'End this money laundering madness', *Legal Week*, 17th April 2008.
2   *R v Da Silva* [2006] EWCA Crim 1654.
3   LSPN 5.3.3.
4   *R v McCartan* [2004] NICA 43.
5   *R. v Griffiths and Pattison* [2006] EWCA Crim 2155.
6   See, for example, para 5.5.1 in the September 2007 LSPN.
7   *Three Rivers District Council and others v Governor and Company of the Bank of England* [2004] UKHL 48.
8   LSPN para 5.7.1.
9   *K Ltd v NatWest Bank* [2006] EWCA Civ 1039.
10 *R v Geary* [2010] EWCA Crim 1925.
11 *R v Amir and Another* [2011] EWCA Crim 146.
12 *P v P* [2003] EWHC Fam 2260.
13 *Bowman v Fels* [2005] EWCA Civ 226.
14 *Fitzpatrick and Others v The Commissioner of Police of the Metropolis* [2012] EWHC 12 (QB).
15 LSPN para 5.5.2.
16 See, for example, 4.71 in the Law Society pilot guidance of January 2004.

CHAPTER 3

Legal professional privilege

Legal professional privilege provides a defence to various non-disclosure offences and, as such, is an essential element of both the AML and the CTF regimes. Unfortunately the application of privilege to the need for disclosures is widely regarded as being one of the most problematic elements of the subject; knowing when a disclosure needs to be made can be quite complex enough, but working out when and how legal professional privilege should then apply can tax even the sharpest of legal minds. The complexities are made that much the worse as there are different forms of privilege in both common law and statute which apply in different circumstances, with multiple formats of privilege sometimes applying to the same situation. The vagaries of which form of privilege applies when, and the practical implications that therefore follow, have inevitably made this one of the most troublesome issues for the reporting officer to contend with.

The nature of legal privilege was examined in detail in the case of *R v Special Commissioner and Another, ex parte Morgan Grenfell & Co Ltd* 2002[1] where it was described as:

> "...a fundamental human right long established in the common law. It is a necessary corollary of the right of any person to obtain skilled advice about the law. Such advice cannot be effectively obtained unless the client is able to put all the facts before the adviser without fear that they may afterwards be disclosed and used to his prejudice."[2]

More than just an element of the laws of evidence, legal professional privilege has been described by Colin Passmore in his authoritative work on the topic as now being "a substantive common law and human right that confers an enhanced form of protection over the confidentiality of certain types of communication made between a professional legal adviser and his client".[3] Where privilege exists there will be no need for a disclosure to the authorities and the adviser will have a defence to any charge that is brought against them in this regard. It follows that for the reporting officer much depends on getting the issue of privilege right. The stakes on this issue are high and those responsible are confronted with an invidious choice. Solicitors are under a duty to act in the best interests of each client under the SRA Handbook (Principle 4) and must also protect confidential information (Outcome 4.1), so any confidential (and damaging) information provided to the NCA will require a clear and justifiable basis. Failing to disclose to the authorities when it is necessary to do so brings with it the risk of criminal liability under both POCA and TA, but disclosing without good reason could just as easily amount to a serious dereliction of professional duties. Many reporting officers have come to the conclusion of "better the risk of the SRA than going to jail", but reporting officers who adopt the approach of referring to the NCA anything that might be suspicious, without regard to possible issues of privilege, are at risk of disciplinary action by the regulator and civil liability to the client.

The normal application of privilege is to protect documentary evidence from the need for disclosure to opponents or the court, but within the AML and CTF regimes it operates in relation to the personal knowledge or suspicions of the adviser. Only in exceptional circumstances is privilege set aside so as to require the disclosure of oral information elsewhere, such as in a limited number of statutory taxation provisions. This distortion of the operation of privilege accounts for most of the problems in trying to get to grips with the topic, and also makes the extensive case law on privilege of limited value to the extent that it focuses on which documents attract privilege rather than what information the adviser is obliged to disclose.

The *Morgan Grenfell* case quoted above provides a good example of the way in which privilege arises as an issue in relation to documentary evidence only in the normal operation of the litigation process. The case involved the Revenue questioning the company's treatment of a lease premium as an allowable expense. The company was served with a notice in pursuance of s.20(1) of the Taxes Management Act 1970 to produce their instructions to and advice from their lawyers on this point. The company's objections on grounds of privilege were upheld, at which point a further application was made by the Revenue to the effect that although the documents in question might have been privileged there was nothing to prevent the lawyers being ordered to answer interrogatories on the position. This further application was rejected, with the result that the information known by the lawyers through acting for their client remained secret. The critical point to understanding the operation of privilege in the AML and CTF regimes is that the adviser risks liability not simply for refusing to disclose the documentation that they possess but also for refusing to share the professional knowledge which they have acquired unless, in both cases, it can be shown to be privileged.

Confidentiality and privilege

The first step in getting to grips with privilege in the disclosure regime is to distinguish privilege from confidentiality. The easiest way to explain this distinction is that all privileged information is confidential, but that not all confidential information is privileged. Whereas everything that a solicitor does for and with a client is to be treated as confidential, only some of it will be privileged. It therefore follows that if information loses its confidentiality, it will also lose its privileged status.[4] Both concepts require elaboration.

Confidentiality is one of the basic aspects of any professional/client relationship and the nature of the obligation is to be found in chapter 4 of the Code of Conduct:

> "...you keep the affairs of clients confidential unless disclosure is required by law or the client consents" (Outcome 4.1).

The more detailed guidance that accompanied the like provisions of the 2007 Code of Conduct listed a number of situations where the duty might not apply, and the equivalent section can now be found at IB(4.4). It would have been helpful if the former guidance note[5] to the effect that the reporting obligations in relation to money laundering "override the duty of confidentiality" and "often require difficult judgements to be made" had been retained as an indicative behaviour in the revised SRA Code of Conduct 2011. The starting point is in any event to keep all client information confidential and only disclose to the NCA when specifically obliged to do so.

Confidentiality is therefore best seen as the adviser's obligation to safeguard information provided to or acquired by them within the professional relationship. Breach of this obligation could be dealt with as a disciplinary offence and might also give rise to civil rights for the client for compensation under the "fiduciary" or implied contractual duties owed by the solicitor to their client. The nature of these duties was examined in *Hilton v Barker Booth & Eastwood* 2005[6] where they were described as being essentially common law, but then as varied between the parties by contract through the retainer process (paras 28-31).

Privilege, by contrast, is probably best seen as the client's right not to have their confidential information shared outside the practice and is a professional obligation under the Principles of the SRA Handbook, most notably the duties to "uphold the rule of law and the proper administration of justice" (P1) and to "act in the best interests of each client" (P4). Whereas confidentiality is a duty that arises under most professional relationships, privilege is therefore best seen as the client's entitlement to safeguard the secrecy of their information. Failure to respect privilege could also amount to a contempt of court, this latter point having been made in the judgment in the leading case on money laundering disclosures – *Bowman v Fels* 2005[7] at para 88.

How privilege operates

Within the AML and CTF regimes there are two main forms of privilege: common law and statutory. The first has developed over a long period of time and is governed by the applicable case law on the subject, whereas statutory privilege (or "privileged circumstances" as it is more generally referred to) is a more recent creation resulting from various international initiatives to develop common standards on the issue throughout participating jurisdictions. Legal privilege of the statutory kind has therefore been specifically written in to certain of the offences in the main Acts and the common law format has been ruled by the courts to apply to others.

The precise rules on privilege under the common law vary according to the nature of the instructions received. In relation to non-contentious work, "advice privilege" will cover "communications between a lawyer, acting in his capacity as a lawyer, and a client [...] if they are both confidential [and] for the purpose of seeking legal advice".[8] This, in turn, is based on the House of Lords decision in *Three Rivers District Council and others v Governor and Company of the Bank of England* 2004[9] at para 111. The Law Society practice note (LSPN) takes a wide view of the application of advice privilege for these purposes so as to include not just instructions received and advice provided but all other communications as well, provided that they are relevant to the performance of the solicitor's retainer.

Litigation privilege arises wherever litigation has started or is reasonably in prospect. This extends beyond communications in this context between a lawyer and a client to cover also communications between that lawyer and agent of the client, or a third party, as long as the communication is for the sole or dominant purpose of litigation. This in turn is not limited to seeking or giving advice, but also obtaining evidence or information for such evidence. Litigation privilege is generally seen as being wider than advice privilege, both in terms of the people and the information that can be involved.

In determining when privilege arises a principle which has proved to be highly problematic for reporting officers is that documents that have already been created other than for the legal process will generally fall outside the scope of privilege. This principle appears in the LSPN thus:

> "An original document not brought into existence for these privileged purposes and so not already privileged, does not become privileged merely by being given to a lawyer for advice or other privileged purpose." (para 6.4.4)

This is in line with the generally established principles of privilege and could therefore be taken to suggest that even though the issue upon which the client seeks advice or representation might be confidential and privileged, the benefit of that privilege could be lost as soon as a pre-existing document clarifying the issue is shown to the adviser. This is perhaps one of the starkest examples of a failure by the law and guidance to distinguish between privileged knowledge or information, as opposed to documentation. The logic of the advice would seem to be that if a client provides oral information to an adviser that is relevant to the issue on which they seek advice it will be protected by privilege, but if they then make the mistake of providing the same lawyer with a pre-existing document that clarifies the issue the same information will no longer be privileged, and a disclosure could therefore become necessary. It would be interesting to know if, on this basis, any firms decline to accept background documentation from clients when asked to advise on the legitimacy of certain actions.

There are ways in which common law privilege might be lost and other factors might mean that it does not arise in the first place. First, there may well be limitations to the range of individuals within a client organisation with whom the adviser can communicate under the ambit of privilege. This principle was one of the central issues in the leading case on advice privilege – *Three Rivers District Council and Others v Bank of England*. This principle appears in the LSPN at para 6.4.4 and this might suggest that once information has been too widely disseminated in a client organisation it is no longer privileged, and there is therefore no longer a defence to non-disclosure.

Second, the "crime/fraud" exception limits privilege where the adviser becomes, in effect, the means by which a crime will be committed, but this is not so much an exception to the usual rules of evidence as a failure for it to arise in the first place.[10] More recently this has been termed the "iniquity exception" which is preferred by many on grounds that it is not in fact limited to criminal or fraudulent activities. Although the Police and Criminal Evidence Act 1984 is often quoted on this rule the Act merely consolidates earlier common law principles, and from the case of *R v Cox and Railton* 1884[11] in particular. Cox and Railton were convicted of conspiring to defraud a third party, who was successful in a libel action against Railton. Cox had not been sued, and in an attempt to escape enforcement Railton effected a disposal of partnership assets to Cox. The prosecution alleged that the bill of sale that effected this disposal had been fraudulently backdated. More recently the nature of this defence was examined in detail in *Kuwait Airways Corporation v Iraqi Airways Co (no 6)* [2005] 1 WLR 2734 where Longmore L.J. confirmed, inter alia, that it extends to litigation privilege and is not limited, as once thought, to advice privilege.

It should be noted that this principle applies even if, as in the Cox and Railton case, the adviser does not realise that they are involved in a criminal scheme. Notwithstanding the crime/fraud exception the adviser is permitted to provide advice in order to prevent a crime, most obviously by their client, or to warn of the risks of prosecution, but not in order to enable them to commit a crime. It need not be the client that has intentions of committing a crime through the adviser – the same would apply if the client were being used as an innocent agent by another.

In respect of the state of knowledge required under the crime/fraud exception the adviser should clearly disclose if they know that they are being used to commit an offence, but the position if the adviser merely suspects that this is the case is, as the LSPN acknowledges, "more complex".[12] Based on case law decisions such as *O'Rourke v Darbishire* 1920[13] it suggests that the adviser must have *prima facie* evidence for their suspicion, or privilege will not be displaced. It does, however, helpfully quote the Crown Prosecution Service guidance for prosecutors which suggests that if a solicitor forms a genuine, but mistaken, belief that they are covered by privilege the alternative defence of "reasonable excuse" should apply. Its conclusion is therefore that it recommends that reporting officers should not make a disclosure unless they know of prima facie evidence that the firm is being used in the furtherance of a crime.

Statutory privilege – Privileged circumstances
Legal professional privilege can be found as a concept in most jurisdictions, but with numerous variations. Given the importance of privilege in the trial process in particular on issues of international concern such as money laundering and terrorist financing, a number of treaty requirements have arisen which have had to be addressed in domestic legislation. Thus the importance of privilege has been recognised under Articles 6 and 8 European Convention on Human Rights, covering the right to a fair trial and to privacy respectively, while the EU Charter of Fundamental Rights recognises "legitimate interests of confidentiality and of professional and business secrecy" (Article 41(2)). These requirements have taken shape within the UK as the defence of "privileged circumstances". This form of privilege has been described by Passmore as being a "very limited form of privilege"[14]. Whereas common law privilege is described in the LSPN at para 6.4.1 as "an absolute right" which "cannot be overridden by any other interest", the privileged circumstances defence is described as being "merely an exemption from certain of the provisions of POCA" (para 6.5). In line with common law privilege the statutory format also has variations between advice privilege and litigation. The main differences between this version of the defence and its common law equivalent are:

- Protection of advice – Under common law, advice privilege communications between an adviser and a third party will not be covered by common law privilege (although it does apply in litigation privilege), but privileged circumstances can extend to junior personnel within a client organisation or to other professionals that are involved in the matter, such as surveyors or accountants.

- Loss of privilege – Common law privilege is not lost when shared with those with a common interest, such as co-defendants, whereas privileged circumstances is limited to the actual exchange of information. The rather confusing example provided in the LSPN at para 12.3.2 is that it is therefore possible to preserve common law privilege if putting information into a data room by stipulating that privilege is not lost, but this would not apply to the statutory form of the defence and so this would be lost when enquiries are received from interested parties.
- Seizure – It has also been suggested that only common law privilege will mean that documents are immune from seizure in pursuance of a court order and that this immunity will not apply to privileged circumstances.

In practice, the scope of privilege is likely to cover most lawyers, whatever their discipline, when taking instructions in the great majority of cases. The only major likely exception is where there is an attempt to perpetrate a crime/fraud through the adviser, as in sham litigation or mortgage fraud. The more likely reason to make a disclosure is information received on the activities of another party in a transaction. In the circumstances where an adviser is provided with details of tax irregularities in a commercial transaction, for example, privilege might not extend to those acting for a purchaser or a lender.

There have also been important developments in relation to who may claim the benefit of this defence. At first it was confined to lawyers, but it did seem anomalous that whereas a taxation solicitor was generally exempted from having to make disclosures in relation to advice provided by virtue of privilege the same did not apply to an accountant providing advice to their client on exactly the same point.[15] Eventually the logic of their case was recognised and the extension of privilege to other professionals duly became one of the main tenets of the Third EU Directive, which provides that:

> "Member States shall not be obliged to apply the obligations laid down in Article 22(1) to notaries, independent legal professionals, auditors, external accountants and tax advisors with regard to information they receive from or obtain on one of their clients, in the course of ascertaining the legal position for their client or performing their task of defending or representing that client in, or concerning judicial proceedings, including advice on instituting or avoiding proceedings, whether such information is received or obtained before, during or after such proceedings." (Article 23(2))

The necessary changes from this provision were addressed in the Terrorism Act 2000 and Proceeds of Crime Act 2002 (Amendment) Regulations 2007 ("the Amendment

Regulations"). The defence to non-disclosure of "legal professional privilege" was extended to "other professional advisers" in those offences where it appears. Given the subsequent extension of the concept to other professional groups, such as accountants, the continued use of the term "legal professional privilege" in the context of money laundering and terrorist financing could now be seen to be confusing.

Which form of privilege applies?
Failure to disclose
The failure to disclose offences in relation to the regulated sector found at sections 330 POCA and 21A TA both attract the statutory "privileged circumstances" defence. The like wording for the defence in both provisions is that the belief or suspicion of the prohibited activity came to the person in privileged circumstances, and there must be no intention to further a criminal purpose. It applies where information is communicated to the adviser:

- By the client or their representative in connection with the giving of legal advice;
- By the client or their representative in connection with their seeking legal advice; and/or
- By any person for the purpose of or in connection with contemplated legal proceedings.

The scope of this defence has now been extended to other "relevant professional advisers" and the explanation of who qualifies as such is to be found at s.330(14):

".... An accountant, auditor or tax adviser who is a member of a professional body which is established for accountants, auditors or tax advisers (as the case may be) and which makes provision for –

(a) testing the competence of those seeking admission to membership of such a body as a condition for such admission; and

(b) imposing and maintaining professional and ethical standards for its members, as well as imposing sanctions for non-compliance with those standards."

It is not clear whether normal common law privilege also applies to the failure to disclose offences or if privilege has to apply to this defence in its statutory format only. The Court of Appeal ruled in *Bowman v Fels* (quoting Lord Hoffman in *R v the Home Department, ex parte Simms* 2000[16]) that "fundamental rights cannot be overridden by general [...] words" and on this basis it might be assumed that both common law privilege and the statutory format of the defence apply. This much seems to be suggested by the LSPN at para 6.5 where it states that in many instances common law privilege will also apply where the statutory format appears.

It is also possible that a lawyer working outside the regulated sector might become subject to the other format of the failure to disclose offence in the TA relating to those acting in the course of a "trade, profession, business or employment" if they suspect that "another person has committed an offence under any of sections 15-18". Here the defences are as set out within s.19(3-7) as being:

- Reasonable excuse;
- If an employee has made a disclosure in accordance with a procedure established for that purpose; and
- Privileged circumstances, which will only arise where there was no intention to further a criminal purpose.

Principal offences

Whereas the statutory privileged circumstances defence was written in to the POCA offences of failure to disclose (s.330) and tipping off (s.333) it was conspicuous by its absence from the principal offences at ss.327-329. This led to the conclusion that privilege, of both the common law format as well as the statutory, did not apply to these offences. This much was confirmed in the first major case on solicitor liability under the Act: *P v P* 2003.[17] In this case the wife's solicitors formed doubts as to the legitimacy of some of the funds forming the proposed ancillary settlement and had therefore disclosed to NCIS, as it then was, to protect themselves from liability for entering an arrangement under s.328. In relation to the issue of privilege Dame Elizabeth Butler-Sloss ruled that:

> "Issues of legal professional privilege do not seem to me to arise under sections 327, 328 or 329 and there is no professional privilege exemption in these sections." (para 50)

This approach was reviewed in the later case of *Bowman v Fels*. The most significant aspect of that judgment was that a lawyer does not enter an arrangement with their client when acting in the normal course of litigation, and so does not need to make an authorised disclosure to protect themselves from possible liability for the principal offences (paras 83-84). The Court of Appeal also considered whether privilege did apply to the principal offences. The conclusion was that, just because Parliament had not referred to statutory privilege in the principal offences, it could not be inferred from this that normal common law privilege had been removed from them. In the view of the court, much clearer wording would have been needed to overrule the normal application of legal professional privilege to any given offence. It followed, therefore, that if common law privilege did apply to the principal offences then a waiver of such privilege by the client would be needed before a disclosure could be made to the authorities, privilege "belonging", as it were, to the client. The Law Society thus duly amended its guidance on this point to state that if the information on which a solicitor would be making a disclosure were privileged then a client waiver of that common law privilege would be needed before a disclosure could be made. Confusing though this seems to remain, the position remains that when the reasons for disclosing to the NCA would involve information subject to common law privilege the client must waive their privilege and, in effect, consent to a disclosure being made. If consent is not forthcoming then the legal adviser would have no authority to disclose the privileged information and would in effect be obliged to cease to act.

The obvious concern in relation to this point is that raising such issues with clients sounds very much like an offence of tipping off – a point conceded in the *Bowman v Fels* judgment itself and the Law Society advice on the implications of that decision provided at the time. At para 104 of the judgment the observation was made that tipping off can only arise when a disclosure has been made, though it was conceded that the similar offence of "prejudicing an investigation" could still be a risk. Much the same would apply notwithstanding the changes to these offences in the Amendment Regulations 2007, with the new offence of "disclosing an investigation" which replaced "prejudicing an investigation" for those in the regulated sector. If the lawyer needs the waiver of privilege from their client – in effect their consent to make a disclosure so that the lawyer can continue to act – no disclosure will have been made at that point, although care is needed as the point at which a disclosure is deemed to have been made is when a formal report is made internally to the reporting officer.

Clearly, many clients will decline the suggestion that a disclosure should be made to the NCA (some, no doubt, in unsurprisingly blunt terms), in which case there is no need to disclose to gain a defence to the arrangements offence of s.328, as the solicitor will not then proceed to enter that arrangement because (s)he will cease to act in the transaction. Furthermore, in most cases, the information received to date will still be immune from disclosure under the "failure to disclose" offences on grounds of the statutory privilege that will usually apply to that section. The parties therefore go their separate ways and the lawyer will be left to rue the loss of the instructions, and might also struggle to be paid for their recorded time to date, but no report will be needed.

Where the client does consent to the disclosure it will often be appropriate to suggest that they join in on the communication, along with counsel if they are involved, in order that all concerned gain a defence to liability under the main Acts. The client will be left with the risk of liability for their predicate offence, but both they and their advisers should be immune from anti-money laundering liability once the NCA grants consent to continue with the matter. For most it will seem odd to have to obtain client consent in these circumstances even if it does accord with legal logic.

It should also be added that where the adviser is considering making a disclosure on grounds that, although confidential, it is not privileged the need for the waiver of privilege would clearly not arise and there would be no justification for not disclosing. This might arise, for example, in cases of sham litigation or where the crime/fraud exception arises. Quite how the solicitor's duty to act with integrity and in the best interests of the client, as required by Principles 2 and 4 of the SRA Handbook, should be interpreted in such circumstances is unclear. A material consideration where a future offence beyond money laundering or terrorist financing is involved is that obtaining consent through making an authorised disclosure to the NCA merely provides a defence to money laundering or terrorist financing charges, and so will not extend to an immunity for any illegal action subsequently undertaken by the client and any assistance provided by the lawyer in so doing – a point stressed in the NCA guidance on seeking consent. In any such case, withdrawal from acting would seem to be the only sensible option.

Tipping off

Initially the privileged circumstances defence applied to the main offence of tipping off at s.333 POCA in like terms to failure to disclose at s.330, but this was removed by the Amendment Regulations 2007. This was largely in response to the FATF recommendation that a lawyer should only be able to reveal to their client that a disclosure has been or will be made if they do so to dissuade the client from engaging in illegal activity. This specific defence can be found at s.21F TA and s.333D(2) POCA and provides that a professional adviser does not commit the offence of tipping off if the disclosure is made to the adviser's client and it is made for the purpose of dissuading the client from engaging in conduct amounting to an offence. The other defences introduced by the Amendment Regulations to the offence of tipping off are:

- Disclosures within a group or undertaking, i.e. internally within the firm (s.333B);
- Disclosures between institutions, including "by a professional legal adviser to another professional legal adviser" or by "a relevant professional adviser of a particular kind to another professional adviser of the same kind" but only in relation to a shared client or service or a transaction involving them both and the disclosure is "for the

purpose only of preventing an offence under this Part of the Act" (s.333C); and

- Disclosures to the regulatory body under the MLR 2007 (the SRA on behalf of the Law Society) (s.333D).

Disclosing an investigation

The scope of the wording of these defences remains untested and has yet to be reviewed in case law. Likewise, we have little guidance at all on how the "disclosing an investigation" offence might arise and the position of a lawyer who inadvertently hinders an investigation of which they were unaware. For the time being the LSPN deals with these provisions as a sub-set of the statutory privileged circumstances defence.

Prejudicing an investigation

Although the offence of prejudicing an investigation under s.342 POCA has now been taken beyond the ambit of the regulated sector by the Amendment Regulations 2007, the defence of privileged circumstances remains part of it (at subsections 4-5) and would be relevant for those lawyers who are, by virtue of their work type, outside the regulated sector.

Summary

The application of privilege to what the lawyer knows, as opposed to the documents they handle, has led to considerable uncertainty as to whether to disclose or not. The problems have been compounded by there being two separate formats of privilege – common law and statutory, each having its different rules as between advice and litigation. The offences of tipping off and disclosing an investigation in money laundering and terrorist financing have a different set of statutory defences again, but only in relation to situations involving the regulated sector. When acting outside the regulated sector, liability for the offence of prejudicing an investigation remains a possibility.

One of the striking examples of just how much confusion can arise from the current regime can be found in the LSPN dealing with the duty to disclose at s.330 POCA. The guidance provides that the instructions received from the vendor client in a corporate transaction will usually be privileged and then goes on to deal with the communication with potential buyers thus:

> "The information may be put into a data room and the purchaser, as part of the due diligence inquiries, may raise questions of the vendor's solicitors which, in effect, result in the information being received again by the vendor's solicitor.

"That second receipt from the purchaser, or their solicitor, would not be protected by privileged circumstances. It will lose its exemption from disclosure unless the information was also subject to LPP which had not been waived when it was placed in the data room (eg a letter of advice from a solicitor to the vendor)."

The implications would seem to be that the adviser is able to take instructions without fear of having to reveal any irregularity to the authorities, but this might cease to be the case as soon as they receive questions on exactly the same information from enquiries from another party.

If there is a case to overhaul the entire disclosure regime in relation to money laundering and terrorist financing then it would have to be hoped that the development of more readily intelligible guidance on the application of privilege must be a priority within the process.

Notes

1   *R v Special Commissioner and Another, ex parte Morgan Grenfell & Co Ltd* [2002] UKHL 21.
2   Quoted in *Bowman v Fels* [2005] EWCA Civ 226 at para 80.
3   Passmore, C. *Privilege*, 3rd edition. Sweet & Maxwell, 2013. See para 1.001.
4   Passmore, C. *Ibid*, para 7.003.
5   Guidance note 11 to Rule 4, Code of Conduct 2007.
6   *Hilton v Barker Booth & Eastwood* [2005] UKHL 8.
7   *Bowman v Fels* [2005] EWCA Civ 226.
8   Law Society practice note, 22nd October 2013, paras 6.4.2-3.
9   *Three Rivers District Council and others v Governor and Company of the Bank of England* [2004] UKHL 48.
10 Passmore: *Ibid*, para 8.002.
11 *R v Cox and Railton* (1884) 14 QBD 153.
12 Law Society guidance, para 6.4.5.
13 *O'Rourke v Darbishire* [1920] 1 AC 581.
14 Passmore C. *Ibid* paras 1.233-235.
15 This remains the case in general common law privilege, on which see Passmore c. at paras 1.145-1.146.
16 *R v the Home Department, ex parte Simms* [2000] 2 AC 115.
17 *P v P* [2003] EWHC Fam 2260.

CHAPTER 4

Making disclosures and handling investigations

Although the responsibilities of the MLRO are confined to judging whether disclosures are required from within their organisation, and then processing them if so, most reporting officers are likely to assume a wider role which will include responding to investigations and other such requests for information from the authorities. In this chapter we therefore consider the role of the MLRO in making disclosures and handling investigations, and also consider the possible civil liability that might arise for non-compliance with the firm's obligations, as by improperly releasing confidential or privileged information.

Disclosures

In most of the problem situations that arise under POCA/TA, lawyers have a choice as to what to do next. Having developed a suspicion or knowledge of illegal activity from instructions received they might deal with their responsibilities under the Acts by simply declining to act or refusing to proceed further. In this way they will not then risk entering any criminal arrangement and the operation of advice and litigation privilege will usually mean that they will be immune from the need to disclose their concerns to the authorities in relation to the knowledge already gained. In situations where privilege does not excuse a "failure to disclose" under s.330 POCA or s.21A TA, however, or where the client and lawyer are not best served by abandoning the retainer, a disclosure will be needed as a defence for actions then to be taken.

Disclosures are defined differently according to their context. A disclosure that is made out of the duty to do so under the various "failure to disclose" offences under s.330 is referred to as a "required disclosure". In relation to the principal offences s.338 POCA talks instead of the need for an "authorised disclosure" under which it will probably be necessary to seek permission to continue to act. Finally, disclosures are also referred to as being "protected" under s.337 POCA for the sake of immunity from professional liability or related contractual duties. The TA does not examine the disclosure regime in anything like the same amount of detail but requires authorised disclosures to be made to the NCA through the amendments made to section 21 of that Act by the Serious Organised Crime and Police Act 2005.

Whatever the statutory label given to them, all disclosures follow much the same principles. An individual, regardless of their status, gains a defence to any of the money laundering offences by making a disclosure to their reporting officer. Most firms will encourage personnel to discuss situations with the reporting officer before triggering a formal report to them. This is in part a practical view of how the regime can best be made to work, but is also a consequence of the rather curious arrangement whereby the statutory privileged circumstances defence does not appear in the separate offences at ss.331-332 POCA for reporting officers, which has been taken to mean that privilege fails as soon as the MLRO receives a formal internal report. The Law Society's view on this point is that the reasonable excuse defence which appears in POCA should apply in such circumstances.[1] Quite what the position is in relation to privilege where the MLRO forms a suspicion of reportable circumstances in the course of their own fee earning work (sole practitioners, most obviously), and whether they then flit from ss.330 to 331 as they change hats from fee earner to reporting officer, is one of the many points of uncertainty to remain from the regrettable standard of the drafting of part 7 of POCA and (fortunately, perhaps) the dearth of case law that has followed. In the normal course of events, however, on receipt of a report form from a partner or colleague the buck will pass to the reporting officer who has to decide whether or not they need to refer the information on to the NCA. If the reporting officer does not report on in circumstances where they should have done, it is they who will be potentially liable for failure to disclose under s.331 and not the colleague who made an internal report to them.

Most of the 4,000 or so lawyer reports made each year will require consent to continue with a transaction, in which case express consent should usually be forthcoming, or it might be necessary to wait for up to seven working days to elapse after which implied consent will arise. While waiting for such consent the firm is placed in a difficult position: if it effects a transaction before it has consent to do so the persons concerned risk liability under the principal offences, and if the reporting officer gives permission for anyone in the firm to do so they face the risk of liability for the separate offence of granting consent when they were not entitled to do so under s.336. Each aspect of the disclosure structure requires further consideration.

Required disclosures

A disclosure made in pursuance of the duty to disclose is referred to as a "required disclosure" and its format is described in some detail in s.330 POCA, as amended. The key ingredients are that the person knows or suspects, or has reasonable grounds for knowing or suspecting, that "another person" is engaged in money laundering, where:

- That knowledge or suspicion derives from their work in the regulated sector; and
- They can identify the person concerned or they believe, or have reasonable grounds for believing, that the information would be useful in identifying the property or identifying that other person.

The required disclosure is then defined by s.330(5) as being a disclosure of the identity of the other person and/or the whereabouts of the property, if they know it, and any other information that they have reason to believe will be useful. The disclosure is required by s.330(4) to be made to the nominated officer in the firm or, so far as the reporting officer is concerned, to the NCA "as soon as practicable" after the information comes to them. In this respect it should be borne in mind that the Law Society has expressed the view that a delay attributable to the firm seeking professional advice on its position will have the "reasonable excuse" defence available to it as long as the firm acts promptly[2]. Much the same regime is applied to terrorist reports under the revised s.21 TA.

Authorised disclosures

The more common reason for disclosures to be made to the NCA will be to gain a defence to the principal offences at ss.327-329 POCA and ss.15-18 TA. Again, POCA is more detailed and provides that the authorised disclosure will need to be made in accordance with the requirements of s.338. This provides that the disclosure should be made to "a constable, a customs officer or a nominated officer", but in effect to the NCA (the reference to "constable" having been taken to apply to the civilian personnel at the agency concerned since the regime was first introduced[3]). Although the provisions allow the making of a disclosure before, during or after the "prohibited act" some good reason will be needed for not doing so before the transaction is conducted. As to disclosures that are not made beforehand, s.338(2A) was inserted by SOCPA and covers disclosures "while the alleged offender is doing the prohibited act". Under such circumstances the adviser may have to show why they did not know or suspect at the time they started to do the prohibited act that anything untoward was involved. Where the prohibited act has already happened, a disclosure can nonetheless be authorised where there was a reasonable excuse for their earlier failure to make a disclosure under s.338(3). In both of these cases the disclosure should be made "as soon as is practicable after he first knows or suspects that the property constitutes or represents a person's benefit from criminal conduct" (s.338(2A)(c)).

The point at which a disclosure can be said to have been made is important in judging possible liability under this section and also in assessing whether potential liability for tipping off has arisen. This is as a result of the wording of s.333 to the effect that the main offence of tipping off can only be committed when a person knows or suspects that a disclosure falling within ss.337 or 338 has been made, though care is also needed in relation to the thus far largely unexplained ancillary offence of "disclosing an investigation" at s.333(A)3, which is not restricted in time in the same way as the main tipping off offence. The main definition of an authorised disclosure includes the provision at s.338(5) that the internal disclosure should be made to the nominated officer in the course of the alleged offender's employment. Taking the procedure in SOCPA of an informal discussion not amounting to a disclosure, the point at which a disclosure should be taken as having been made arises when the formal report is made internally to the reporting officer.

Dealing with the NCA

Disclosures, whether of the "required" format under failure to disclose or "authorised" in relation to the principal offences, have to be made to the NCA unless a defence applies. As dealt with in Chapter 3, the client's waiver of privilege will be needed if the firm's reasons for making a disclosure are as a result of privileged information. It follows that a disclosure can only be made where a waiver of privilege is obtained from the client (in effect, their consent to the disclosure) if common law privilege applies, or where the crime/fraud exception arises.

Having overcome any privilege hurdle a suspicious activity report (SAR) will be required. The alternative and simpler procedure under SOCPA of "limited information value reports" (LIVRs) was never of any great relevance to lawyer disclosures and has now been abolished in any event.

The preferred method of making reports to the NCA is now online; the alternatives of downloading the report forms and submitting them by post or by fax do remain, but as if to encourage online reporting only this form of report will prompt an acknowledgement. The 2014 Suspicious Activity Reports Annual Report revealed that over 99% of the disclosures received were electronic, but it could be that those received by more traditional means are disproportionately from professionals with just 1.39% of the total number of SARs for the year (354,186) being from accountants and 1.02% from lawyers. Confusingly there are provisions at s.339(1A) POCA for a prescribed method of reporting to be stipulated, but although this states that an authorised disclosure must be in the specified format this has not yet been implemented. There was a consultation in 2007 on the potential criminal liability that would then arise if a particular format were to be ordained but the Home Office indicated that this should await a more thorough review of the law. To apply criminal sanctions for what would be a reporting method anomaly would be in keeping with the general "sledgehammer to crack a nut" principle that is such a feature of anti-money laundering law, which the Home Office assurances given at the time – that prosecution would only be likely in more extreme cases – did little to allay: quite what sort of conduct would amount to an "extreme" failure to use the correct reporting methodology is difficult to imagine. Either way, it is to be hoped that professional people will not be placed at risk of acquiring a criminal record through such extraordinary legislative pedantry.

The confidentiality of disclosures has also received attention from time to time. Sadly, it has to be taken into account that disclosures might concern organised crime or dangerous individuals and this is not without risk to the firms and the advisers concerned. In the early years of the regime the Law Society received a number of representations from firms that felt let down by the law enforcement or trial processes where the source of disclosures had been revealed. This prompted a Home Office response – 'Money Laundering: The Confidentiality and Sensitivity of Suspicious Activity Reports (SARs) and the Identity of those who make them' (Circular 53/2005) – which arguably did little more than to acknowledge the issue. In relation to this Home Office advice the NCA recorded just two cases of concerns over confidentiality lapses in its operations in the 2014 SARs Annual Report. It is clearly in the interests of all concerned to ensure that the identity of those making disclosures are protected and the Home Office circular provides that disclosures should be regarded as "restricted" information, with breaches of this obligation being a potentially disciplinary offence.

Obtaining consent
The NCA's SARs Annual Report for 2014 reported that the average response time where consent to continue had been requested had increased to 4.3 days, the main explanations for the increase being a greater number of requests received and an alleged decline in the quality of reports. The number of situations where consent is withheld has remained about one in ten for some time, so in the majority of cases where consent to continue to act is granted the reporting officer may then give the "appropriate consent" to the partner or colleague to continue, this being defined as the "consent of the nominated officer to do a prohibited act". The reporting officer's position is set out in similar terms at s.336 where the statutory consent regime is to be found, with the main principle being that

the reporting officer must not give such consent unless they themselves have gained consent to do so. Although express consent to continue will be the norm there is the alternative process of implied consent, which was added to the regime in POCA to ensure that the difficulties faced by organisations while they awaited a reply were minimised. Clearly an organisation, and its reporting officer in particular, is placed in a difficult situation while it is awaiting a response from the NCA and could have increasing difficulties fending off enquiries from the client the longer this delay continues. The provisions on implied consent are to be found at s.336(3), which states that if the reporting officer has not heard from the NCA "before the end of the notice period" that consent will be refused, then they may assume that consent has been granted. The relevant notice period is defined by s.336(7) as being "seven working days starting with the first working day after the nominated officer makes the disclosure." Working days are defined so as to exclude weekends, bank holidays, Christmas day and Good Friday.

There is a third and very much more complex option, which is that within the seven working days period the NCA withholds consent, in which case the "moratorium period" arises. This is set at 31 days (not working days), starting at the day on which the refusal of consent is stated. In effect this gives the authorities one month to make an application under the Act, and if they have not done so in that time the firm may continue as if it had consent to do so. The actual situation for the firm unlucky enough to find itself in this position is, of course, very much more complicated than as described by statute. A firm might stall on a matter for a few days and perhaps continue with its preparatory work in the matter, but to put a matter off for a month will clearly need much more by way of explanation to the client and others. In these circumstances the reporting officer will have to consider carefully what they can tell their client under the tipping off provisions and will probably attempt to agree with the authorities concerned what may be revealed. Failing this they might need to apply to court for an order setting out what they should do in these circumstances. This would be unfamiliar territory for most reporting officers and would be one situation where advice from one of the firms listed by the Law Society as offering professional compliance advice would probably be advisable.

Arising from its concerns about the quality of SARs received, the NCA issued guidance on the disclosure process and then effected some important changes to the process. These changes were originally due to take effect on the 15th September 2014 but were then postponed to the 1st October. First, clarification was provided on the implications of consent to continue to act to the effect that consent under part 7 of POCA does not oblige or mandate the reporter to take the action thus permitted or imply NCA approval in any way. There is therefore no compulsion to continue to act, and withdrawal from acting further would remain an option. More importantly the guidance stresses that consent does not provide a defence to other criminal offences arising from the proposed act or excuse any breach of professional duties or other regulatory requirements. Taking this into account it was prudent to stress that continuing judgement is required in firms notwithstanding the receipt of consent to continue from the NCA.[4]

The major change of process was in relation to the rejection of consent requests. There had been growing criticism by the authorities of the quality of consent requests for some time and the NCA will accordingly no longer treat a disclosure as having been made if it shows what it regards as inadequate information for its processes. For these purposes the NCA lists the "five essential elements of a submission" if dealing with the regulated sector as being:

- The information or other matter giving rise to the grounds for knowledge, suspicion or belief;
- A description of the property which is known, suspected or believed to be criminal property;
- A description of the prohibited act for which consent is being applied;
- The identity of the person(s) known or suspected to be involved in money laundering; and
- The whereabouts of the property that is known or suspected to be criminal property.

Whereas previously the NCA would process all disclosures and make follow-up enquiries to complete the information it requires, it will now reject the disclosure, meaning that the firm will be treated as still not having met its obligation under POCA or TA to report its concerns or request permission to continue to act. The NCA encourages reporting officers to identify specific categories of suspicious activity in its report as listed on its website.[5]

The position of the firm that is awaiting consent has been examined in case law and is now also covered in the Law Society guidance. So far as Dame Elizabeth Butler-Sloss was concerned in *P v P* 2003, "no further steps" should be taken while a firm was awaiting a reply from the authorities. This part of the judgment caused considerable problems at the time, for it might have worked well enough in the context of a long-running dispute on the ancillary elements of a divorce (as in this case), but it would clearly cause problems when applied to a fast-moving transaction with a completion date looming large in the lawyer's concerns. The situation was reviewed further in *Bowman v Fels* 2005 where it was held that a lawyer taking any steps to issue or pursue legal proceedings would not be entering an arrangement, nor would an arrangement arise through "any intermediate step" that they were to take in the matter (paras 66-69). Although these remarks were made in the context of litigation, they enabled the

Law Society to issue revised guidance to the effect that as long as an adviser ensures that they are not entering an arrangement, they could continue with preparatory steps as if completion were still on track. In practical terms this was taken to mean that although the mortgage funds could be requested, they could not be used as completion monies, for example. Although the critical point at which an "arrangement" can be said to arise remains partly unclear, it will usually be the point at which the transaction is effected – completion, in most cases. Being able to continue on the basis that this will occur lessens significantly the practical problems of awaiting consent.

Unfortunately the degree of confidence that firms might have in this line of advice has diminished in recent years, especially in relation to criminal clients of the firm. On this see *Fitzpatrick v Metropolitan Commissioner of Police* 2012 (see page 30)[6]. Although in this case no prosecution followed, let alone a conviction, it should strike a cautionary note since reporting officers will be understandably concerned to avoid the stress and potential reputational harm that can result from the mere threat of legal proceedings. Furthermore, although reliable figures may not be available on how often partners and others have found themselves bailed pending further enquiries, anecdotal evidence suggests that it is very much more commonplace than prosecution trends might suggest.

Civil liability

There are, of course, professional issues in relation to making disclosures of confidential information outside the firm and the extent to which solicitors risk liability by doing so. Within POCA this is addressed at s.337 through the concept of "protected disclosures", which provides that there will be immunity from civil liability if three conditions are satisfied:

- The information disclosed came to the discloser in the course of their trade, profession, business or employment;
- This information "or other matters" caused them to know or suspect, or to have reasonable grounds for knowing or suspecting, that another person is engaged in money laundering; and
- They then disclose their suspicions.

Where these conditions, as slightly amended by SOCPA, are met, the discloser will be taken not to have breached "any restriction on the disclosure of information (however imposed)". This would clearly include disciplinary charges under the principles in the SRA Handbook, such as to act in the best interests of each client (P4) and to provide a proper standard of service (P5), and the more specific obligations found in chapter 4 of the Code of Conduct such as the duty to maintain the confidentiality of client information at O(4.1). The position on breach of contract is, however, more complex. The authors of *Blackstone's Guide to the Proceeds of Crime Act 2002*[7] are robust in their view that the wording of s.337 would be wide enough to "provide immunity from any action based, for example, on a breach of contract or confidentiality" in which respect it would seem to remain to be seen whether this would include liability for interest payments on delayed completion. Given the uncertainty on this point, many firms include such terms in their terms of business to the effect that they will not accept liability for losses sustained in this way. Whether these would be acceptable to a court if challenged under the Unfair Contract Terms Act 1977 remains uncertain, and they do not form part of the current Law Society "client care information" practice note.[8] It is also relevant to add that the feasibility of a "POCA clause" was discussed in the *Bowman v Fels* decision – namely one whereby "an arrangement might be made but expressly not to take effect until authorised disclosure has been made pursuant to s.328 of the Proceeds of Crime Act 2002 and appropriate consent is given or deemed to be given" (para 103). The judgment left open the issue of whether such clauses would be permissible but expressed reservations about them, mostly on grounds of potential tipping off.

The leading case in relation to the tricky issue of how much suspicion a reporting officer requires to be able to justify the inevitable breach of confidentiality in reporting to the authorities is *Shah v HSBC Private Bank* 2012.[9] More than just a legal decision, the "Shah case" represented a remarkable long-running legal saga involving no fewer than seven separate decisions and three visits to the Court of Appeal. The eventual decision in this case – much to the relief of all reporting officers, no doubt – was that the amount of suspicion needed to be able to justify a disclosure to the NCA is quite low. The firm does not have to have "reasonable grounds" for its belief or suspicions, but there must be something specific to trigger the suspicion rather than merely a "vague feeling of unease".

The facts of the case were no less extraordinary. Mr and Mrs Shah were wealthy entrepreneurs with business interests in Africa. In July 2006 they made an initial transfer of US$28m from their Geneva-based Credit Suisse account to their HSBC Private Bank account in London, explaining in so doing that they suspected that somebody was attempting to steal from the Swiss account. During the course of 2007 they made four large scale transfers from a Geneva-based Credit Suisse account to their London HSBC account, but on each occasion there was a delay explained to the Shahs as resulting from the Bank complying with "UK statutory obligations" – an oblique reference to avoid possible liability for tipping off to the Bank having made a SAR to the then SOCA on each occasion as it was unsure as to the legitimacy of the source of funds.

Unfortunately the delay in processing the payments had disastrous consequences. The funds were required for business dealings in Zimbabwe and the delay in processing payments resulted in an inability to pay a debt of some US$7,000 to a Mr Kabra, an ex-employee based there. This individual therefore took it upon himself to report Mr Shah to the authorities locally, adding that his former employer was suspected of money laundering in the UK. The Zimbabwean police duly obtained a warrant to search the Shahs' property and demanded further explanation. When HSBC refused to assist with these enquiries a seizure of the Shahs' assets in the country ensued.

Faced with losses of over US$300m the Shahs launched their claim for breach of contract for the Bank's failure to process payments. The Bank contended that it could not be blamed for the need, as the Bank saw it, to obtain the approval of (then) SOCA for receiving the funds and would have been behaving illegally had it not done so, nor could it give a full explanation at the time to its customers for fear of liability for tipping off under s.333 POCA. The Shahs countered that the Bank's actions had been "irrational, negligently self-induced and mistaken".

Unsurprisingly, in the view of most expert commentators at the time, the Court sided with the Bank and found against the claimants, notwithstanding that it was wrong for all concerned to have seemingly been more concerned with the destination of the funds – Zimbabwe – rather than their source. The Bank had been entitled to follow its processes and not to explain to the Shahs what it was doing and why. In the absence of an express contractual term permitting it to proceed as it had done, and not to incur liability for having done so, there was an implied term to this effect in any event. In its advice on the implications of this decision for MLROs in law firms the Law Society advised that there must be some real grounds for making a disclosure and not simply (in one of the most refreshingly down-to-earth pieces of guidance that it has issued on this topic) that the client is "a bit fishy". Most usefully of all it has advised that:

"existing criminal property (must be) involved in the transaction or in a person's possession, before you can form a suspicion of money laundering".

This would therefore seem to exclude from the ambit of money laundering criminal plans that a client has shared with their adviser, including attempted mortgage fraud, where no gain has yet accrued. In most such cases the firm will be taking the right course of action in its competing duties to comply with the AML and CTF provisions on the one hand, but to respect client confidentiality and privilege on the other, by advising the client on the inappropriateness of their plans and the possible consequences if they do persist. Furthermore there would be no liability for tipping off in so doing since at that stage no disclosure would yet have been made.

Some other practical points arise from the judgment. The Bank's MLRO – Mr Wigley – endured a lengthy spell of cross investigation which was made all the more uncomfortable by his failure to have made contemporaneous records of his actions. Such records need to display if later questioned that there was – as held by Longmore L. J. in the Da Silva case – "a possibility, which is more than fanciful, that the relevant facts exist". It should also be borne in mind that such records might become disclosable once the immediate concerns over tipping off have been overcome, in which case they should be anonymised before being released.

A further theme of the case law in this area is the desire of the courts to ensure that the proceeds of crime are recovered when possible. In *National Crime Agency v Amiz Azam and Others (No 2)* 2014[10] it was held that an innocent owner of property would have a high hurdle to overcome to overturn a civil recovery order under s. 266(3) POCA.

Fortunately the position of the MLRO in making a report has now been made much clearer through s.37 of the Serious Crime Act 2015, which amends s.338 POCA to provide civil immunity for any disclosure made in good faith.

Trustee liability

The risk of a civil award against the firm should also be taken into account, either through the firm becoming a constructive trustee or through the creation of a resulting trust. The firm might become liable as a constructive trustee through its interference with trust property or where there has been a breach of its fiduciary duties, and will thereby be at risk of an order of the civil courts to compensate any claimant for their losses. Liability might also arise through the concept of "knowing receipt" under which people who receive trust property or in the course of fiduciary duties owed by them can be liable for any misuse of the assets. Critically, the defendant must be shown to have known that they were misapplying the funds, this area being based, in part at least, in the equitable doctrine of "unconscionability".[11] Although there is some debate as to the precise operation of these rights it is clear that some degree of wrongdoing is a requisite for liability, in which respect the extent of the vicarious liability of the firm for the actions of its personnel might also be a factor.[12]

The case of *Armstrong DLW GMBH v Winnington Networks Ltd* 2012[13] provides a helpful illustration of how civil liability might arise from a failure to manage an organisation's AML responsibilities. The case involved the trade of stolen carbon credits, which were worth over €250,000, and the failure of the recipient to conduct the required CDD before then trading them on. Even the most cursory of checks would have triggered concerns: the initial contact had been made by way of a free web-based email account;

there was no company information on the fraudster's letters; and there was also no official company website. Winnington had asked for the usual CDD on a number of occasions but this had not been forthcoming, but had nonetheless taken delivery of the carbon credits, paid for them and then traded the credits on to a regular client. In so doing it was held that it became a constructive trustee of the carbon credits, thereby enabling the victim to pursue a civil claim for the wrongful receipt of trust property against it.

Recovery orders

The primary objective of POCA is to deprive wrongdoers of their criminal gains rather than to provide compensation for the victims in the civil courts. In keeping with this principle part 5 of the Act ("Civil recovery of the proceeds etc. of unlawful conduct") is stated to enable "the enforcement authority to recover, in civil proceedings before the High Court or Court of Session, property which is, or represents, property obtained through unlawful conduct", and also for the forfeiture of cash through civil proceedings in the magistrates' courts (or the sheriff in Scotland).

The usual object of proceedings under this part of the Act is the making of a "recovery order" which can also be ordered on an interim basis. Such orders are possible where the property in question has been obtained through "unlawful conduct", as defined by s.241. Since these proceedings are civil in their nature there is no need for a prior criminal conviction or even a criminal investigation to have occurred, and there have even been applications for such orders following acquittals (though not necessarily against law firms). If served with such an order in relation to client funds the effect will be to prohibit "any person to whose property the order applies from dealing with the property" and most firms would need professional advice as to how to deal with their conflicting duties to the client on the one hand, and compliance with any such order on the other. This would also apply to the more recent device of the "freezing order" that was added by SOCPA, which prohibits "any person to whose property the order applies from in any way dealing with the property".[14]

Handling investigations

The non-criminal practitioner, and the unfortunate reporting officer in particular, is more likely to encounter the general workings of the Act in relation to part 8 of POCA dealing with "Investigations". Confiscation orders under part 2 of the Act (in England and Wales) are only available when a conviction has been recorded, but there is a wide range of statutory devices that are open to the authorities in advance of such a finding. Investigations into alleged money laundering offences are governed by the Act, as opposed to the normal principles of criminal enquiries, and take a number of forms as set out at s.341, including "confiscation investigations" and "money laundering investigations". These processes attract their own investigative powers, of which the most significant for law firms are:

- Production orders;
- Search and seizure warrants; and
- Disclosure orders.

The purpose of production orders is to compel the disclosure of material on a named person or business and will usually concern bank statements or other such documentation. Search and seizure warrants are a more extreme tool and are available when the investigating authorities do not know what they are seeking or cannot describe the desired evidence with sufficient precision. They will authorise entry to stated premises with a right to seize and retain any material thereby uncovered, while a disclosure order requires a named individual to attend an interview to answer questions.

A law firm served with a production or disclosure order should withhold any information that is privileged, but will not be able to use the professional duty of confidentiality as an excuse for non-compliance with its provisions. The material might be removed where the privileged information is inextricably linked to other material which is merely confidential in which case a review might be required. A further complication arises where material has been received by the firm under an express undertaking to the court that the material will not be used for any purpose other than the civil proceedings in question. Here an application to the court might be needed for the lawyer concerned to be discharged from that undertaking as the order from the criminal court might not overrule the undertaking provided to the civil court.

The same safeguard on the non-disclosure of privileged material applies to search and seizure warrants, with the consequence that any privileged documents should not therefore be removed from the premises. Where there is a dispute as to the status of the material, as where the investigating authority claim that the crime/fraud exception applies but this is disputed, there is a "blue bag" process whereby the material may be removed without being inspected and independent counsel may then rule on the matter. The distinction between what is merely confidential as opposed to privileged is critical in many regards to the AML regime and especially so here.

There are other investigative powers that are limited to the banks and other financial institutions in the format of "customer information orders" and "account monitoring orders". There is also a specific offence of "prejudicing an investigation" set out in this part of the Act at section 342 which is aimed at these processes, and which is dealt with in greater detail in Chapter 2 in relation to the tipping off offences. Most lawyers and their staff will now be excluded from this offence in relation to their work within the firm as a result of amendments that took effect in late 2007, though there is a broad equivalent under the revised provisions in relation to the main tipping off offence at s.333.

Finally, the Law Society has issued helpful advice on how a firm should deal with requests or orders to produce client files or other documents. This takes the form of a practice note of the 14th March 2013 "Responding to a financial crime investigation" and can be found under the Practice Notes tab on the Law Society website. This provides a helpful summary of the other more general criminal provisions which can also be used to order the production of documents or other investigations.

Notes

1   LSPN 5.7.1.
2   LSPN 5.6.2.
3   See the Pilot Guidance of the Law Society on Money Laundering (January 2004) at 2.21.
4   See 'Submitting a Suspicious Activity Report (SAR) within the Regulated Sector', NCA, revised May 2014.
5   See 'SAR glossary codes: Revisions explained', NCA, October 2013.
6   *Fitzpatrick v Metropolitan Commissioner of Police* [2012] EWHC 12 QB.
7   Rees QC, E., Fisher, R, and Bogan, P. *Blackstone's Guide to the Proceeds of Crime Act 2002*. Oxford: Oxford University Press, 2011. Page 148.
8   Law Society practice note: Client care information (26th March 2013 edition), see 4.2.8.
9   *Shah v HSBC Private Bank* [2012], EWCA 1283 (QB).
10 *National Crime Agency v Azam & Ors (No. 2),* [2014] EWHC 3573 (QB).
11 *BCCI v Akindele* [2001] 1 Ch 437.
12 *Dubai Aluminium Co Ltd v Salaam* [2002] 3 WLR 1913.
13 *Armstrong DLW GMBH v Winnington Networks Ltd* [2012] EWHC 10 (Ch).
14 POCA s.245A(2).

PART B

The Money Laundering Regulations

Introduction

The Money Laundering Regulations 2007 ("MLR 2007") took effect on the 15th December of that year and represented something of a step change in the approach that regulated concerns would have to adopt to ensure compliance. Compliance under the previous regime was seen for the most part as a series of mechanical steps that had to be taken to be permitted to undertake the activities that were then regulated, but the Third EU Directive and the resulting MLR 2007 would be "risk-based". The new regime would take into account that not all clients or new instructions pose the same level of threat and a "one size fits all" approach was therefore no longer appropriate. Also, in line with the "40 Recommendations" laid down by FATF in 2003, "risk" would now be central to the AML compliance regime.

As we will see, the risk-based approach is fundamental to the main client checking or "customer due diligence" process, which represents the main obligation for law firms and all other types of institutions covered by the regulations. More generally, the firm will need to adopt a relevant policy and accompanying procedures to address its responsibilities not just under the MLR 2007 but also to be able to make disclosures to the authorities when required.

We examine the regulatory requirements in general in Chapter 5, then explain the risk-sensitive approach in more detail in Chapter 6 and the steps that can be taken to identify and verify clients in Chapters 7 and 8. Finally, we examine the fuller implications of addressing CDD requirements in relation to the three main client types: individuals, corporations and other forms of organisations such as educational establishments, charities and public sector bodies.

CHAPTER 5

The Money Laundering Regulations 2007

The MLR 2007 apply to most, but not all, law firms in the UK. Regardless of the status of the firm, however, all practices will need to adopt a suitable policy for the purposes of its AML and CTF profile, even if only to assert that the practice as a whole, or certain distinct parts of it, are outside the scope of the regulations. The range of appropriate policies might vary from a short statement that the MLR 2007 do not apply to the work of the firm, to a highly complex set of guidelines and forms in the large international firm undertaking cross-border transactions and private client work.

For the majority of firms where the MLR 2007 do apply, at least in part, there is a direct obligation to adopt "policies and procedures" at r.20. However, even where the firm is entirely outside the ambit of the regulations those responsible for compliance would be well advised to have some form of arrangements in place for ensuring that there is a mechanism for making disclosures, if required, to the National Crime Agency ("NCA"). In providing the necessary internal controls to mitigate the firm's exposure to money laundering and terrorist financing, the policies and procedures that are adopted here also form part of the firm's overall approach to risk management. Outcome 7.5 of the Code of Conduct requires firms to address "legislation applicable to your business, including anti-money laundering [...] legislation". Those firms that have adopted the Lexcel standard will also have to adopt a policy to ensure compliance with anti-money laundering legislation (section 5.13: Lexcel version 6).

The scope of the MLR 2007

For law firms, the all-important definition of whether firms or particular departments are caught by the regulations is that relating to "independent legal professionals", who are stated to be:

> "..... a firm or sole practitioner who by way of business provides legal or notarial services to other persons, when participating in financial or real property transactions concerning –

(a) the buying and selling of real property or business entities;

(b) the managing of client money, securities or other assets;

(c) the opening or management of bank, savings or securities accounts;

(d) the organisation of contributions necessary for the creation, operation or management of companies; or

(e) the creation, operation or management of trusts, companies or similar structures,

and, for this purpose, a person participates in a transaction by assisting in the planning or execution of the transaction or otherwise acting for or on behalf of a client in the transaction." (r.3(9))

The full implications of the definition have been much debated but few firms argue that the work of any non-contentious department is exempt. Having at first recommended a "cautious" approach on the issue of exemptions and exclusions in its earliest pilot guidance, the Law Society now advises that "the broadest of the possible approaches" should be taken to the issue of which areas of practice are covered. The LSPN confidently asserts that the term "independent legal professionals" excludes solicitors employed by a public authority or working in-house, but in-house lawyers might need to consider whether the activities of their employers bring them back into the scope of the regulated sector as employees of organisations that are otherwise subject to the regulations. An in-house legal department in a financial institution would find itself in the regulated sector, for example, but under the auspices of the Financial Conduct Authority ("FCA") rather than the SRA.[1]

In cases of doubt private practice firms should consult the Law Society Anti-Money Laundering practice note and this provides that "managing client money" is more than simply having funds pass through client or office account, and that "opening and managing a bank account" is more than simply opening a client account. More specifically, the following activities have been agreed with the Treasury not to be "participation in financial transactions" (Law Society practice note 1.4.5) ("LSPN"):

- Preparing a Home Information Pack or any of its contents (r.4(1)(f) MLR 2007);
- Payments on account of costs or payment of the firm's bills;
- Provision of legal advice;
- Participation in litigation or a form of ADR;
- Will-writing; and
- Publicly-funded work.

The conclusion drawn by most firms seems to be that it is better to have one firmwide approach to the required checking process, regardless of which parts of the practice are actually covered by the regulations. This will have the advantage of consistency of approach, in that everyone in the firm will know where they stand. Others might apply exceptions in certain areas of the practice that are capable of being clearly ring-fenced, a common example being personal injury work where the clients are not locally based and so might be lost to the firm if they were to approach potential competitors nearer to home for certification of their identity.

So far as the general profile of firms is concerned, those that deal exclusively with litigation are the most likely to be exempt from the regulations – especially firms that deal exclusively with crime or personal injury work. The Law Society has declined to provide definitive guidance on the status of any specific areas of work, however, since all depends on what actually gets dealt with under any given firm's heading for the work type in question. This is particularly the case in areas that often combine contentious and non-contentious work, such as construction law, intellectual property and employment work. It is perhaps commercial litigation that is the most borderline case. If this is mere debt recovery it might well fall under the litigation exemption, but if negotiations are conducted in a litigious environment this might not be the case. Similar considerations apply to ancillary disputes in family law, where it is safer to regard the department as being within the regulations because of the ancillary financial and property elements that will usually arise in most such disputes.

The need for policies and procedures

Regulation 20(1) requires regulated bodies to:

> "establish and maintain appropriate and risk-sensitive policies and procedures relating to –
>
> (a)   [client] due diligence measures and ongoing monitoring;
>
> (b)   reporting;
>
> (c)   record-keeping;
>
> (d)   internal control;
>
> (e)   risk assessment and management;
>
> (f)   the monitoring and management of compliance with, and the internal communication of, such policies and procedures."

Regulation 20(2) sets out certain issues that have to be covered as part of the policies and procedures. They are:

- Identification and scrutiny of complex, unusually large or unusual patterns of transactions or any other activity likely to be related to money laundering or terrorist financing;
- Taking additional measures in relation to products or transactions which might favour anonymity;
- Determination of clients as politically exposed persons (PEPs);
- Appointment of a nominated officer;
- Internal reporting of suspicious activities; and
- Consideration by the nominated officer as to nature of reported activities.

If the firm fails to comply with any provisions set out in r.20(1) then it will be liable to a fine (r.45(1)). Individual partners will also be liable if the offence is committed with the consent or connivance of the partner or is attributable to neglect on his or her part (r.47(2)). This will generally apply to senior management and the firm's MLRO. It is advisable for the firm to follow the guidance set out in the LSPN in developing its policies and procedures. If it does this, then this must be taken into account by the courts in determining whether the firm, or any of its partners, have committed an offence as a result of formal Treasury approval having been obtained to the guidelines. (See r.45(3) MLR 2007 in relation to this point and the LSPN para 1.5).

The nature of the policies and procedures to be adopted are not absolute but are determined by factors such as:

- The nature, scale and complexity of the firm;
- The diversity of the firm's operations, including geographical diversity;
- The firm's client, service and activity profile;
- The degree of risk associated with each area of the firm's operations; and
- The services being offered and the frequency of client contact.[2]

These factors indicate that the size of the firm and its risk profile will dictate the complexity of procedures that it needs to adopt. Smaller firms with lower risk clients require simple procedures, whereas large firms with higher risk clients or transactions will require more complex arrangements.

It is suggested that the areas that should be considered to form part of the firm's policies and procedures include:

- The responsibilities of the firm/senior management;
- The appointment, role and function of the nominated officer;

- The method of risk assessment adopted;
- The risk profile of the firm;
- Risk indicators at client and matter level;
- The application of CDD measures and ongoing monitoring;
- Use of client account and cash payments;
- The disclosure procedure;
- Training;
- Record keeping; and
- Monitoring and audit.

A sample AML/CTF policy can be found at Chapter 18.

Appointment, role and function of the nominated officer/MLRO

The senior management of the firm needs to undertake the firm-wide risk assessment and appoint a nominated officer. They also need to establish the firm's AML/CTF policies and procedures, including the nature of CDD and ongoing monitoring. Other aspects they need to consider are the training of relevant personnel and an appropriate record-keeping system.

It is a requirement of the regulations (r.20(2)(d)(1)) for a nominated officer to be appointed to receive internal suspicious activity reports (SARs) and to decide whether to notify the NCA of such reported activities and obtain consent where appropriate. Sole practitioners do not need to appoint a nominated officer, provided they do not employ or act in association with any other person, as permitted by r.20(3), so it may be useful to draw the distinction between sole practitioners who operate completely solo, as opposed to sole principals who have at least one colleague, whether fee earning or administrative.

Although the disclosure obligations on organisations that are outside the regulated sector are much reduced, the LSPN suggests at para 3.3.1 that a reporting officer should still be appointed to enable the firm to comply with its compliance obligations which may nonetheless arise under POCA and TA. To do so might therefore be seen to be part of the general obligation to "run your business or carry out your role in the business effectively and in accordance with proper governance and sound financial and risk management principles" as required by Principle 8 of the SRA Handbook. It is important that the nominated officer is of sufficient seniority to make decisions relating to reporting matters to the NCA as this carries important consequences for the firm, both with regard to client relationships and in exposing the firm to criminal or civil liability. Such a person also needs to be able to access all relevant information in order to decide whether a report should be made in accordance with the obligations to do so.

The nominated officer is generally called the Money Laundering Reporting Officer (MLRO). This function emanates from the financial services sector as regulated by the FCA. This is the title given to the person who is responsible for the oversight of the firm's compliance with the rules on systems and controls against money laundering and not just limited to making disclosures to the NCA. These rules are set out in the FCA handbook.[3] The Fourth EU Directive also provides for the appointment of a compliance officer at managerial level, so we may see a move towards different and complementary roles of MLRO and Money Laundering Compliance Officer ("MLCO") as already seen elsewhere, as in Jersey.[4]

It is common practice for non-FCA regulated firms to appoint an MLRO whose role and function is wider than that of a nominated officer and includes the various functions required by the FCA. Most firms take the view that the MLRO should be a partner, though this is not a requirement as such and it is a role performed by a number of risk directors in major firms. The more usual arrangement, however, is for many of the compliance functions to be delegated to personnel in employed risk positions and for them to be designated one of the deputy nominated officers with a partner or director still in overall charge and with ultimate responsibility. If the MLRO is given further duties, in addition to those of a nominated officer, such duties will carry with them criminal liability if any failure in such duties gives rise to non-compliance of the requirements set out in r.20(1) (see r.47(2)).

The duties of the MLRO are likely to include:

- Ensuring that satisfactory internal procedures are maintained, including risk assessment, CDD checking and the keeping of records;
- Arranging for periodic training for all relevant members of the firm;
- Providing advice when consulted on possible reports and receiving reports of suspicious circumstances;
- Reporting such circumstances to the NCA, if appropriate, on behalf of the firm;
- Directing colleagues as to what action to take when suspicion arises and a report is made;
- Monitoring and managing compliance with, and the internal communication of, policies and procedures relating to anti-money laundering; and
- Keeping full and accurate records of the above.

Risk assessment and management
The requirements for risk assessment are set out in Chapter 6. It is advisable to document the way in which the risk profile of the firm and those of clients and matters are assessed.

It is also important to document the actual risk profile of the firm as this will be important evidence to demonstrate to the SRA that the measures the firm has taken are appropriate in accordance with the requirement laid down in r.7(3)(b).

CDD and ongoing monitoring

The procedures should outline the system of CCD and ongoing monitoring that needs to be applied to new clients, existing clients and their matters. A CDD system may include:

- The method of risk assessment for both clients and matters and the level of personnel permitted to undertake such risk assessment;
- Any escalation procedure if a client or matter is deemed higher risk;
- The types of CDD that need to be undertaken in respect of individual, corporate or other client types and beneficial owners;
- CDD for existing clients and ongoing monitoring;
- The methods of verification that may be undertaken, such as inspection of original documents, certification, assurance by an authorised person, reliance, or electronic or other web-based searches;
- Steps to be taken in cases of simplified or enhanced due diligence;
- The procedure for identifying if a client is a PEP and the need to refer to senior management; and
- Timing of CDD and ability to continue with a matter if CDD checks are not completed.

See Chapter 7 for more details.

Disclosure

The firm's procedures should provide that members of the firm are to make a disclosure to the nominated officer if they are aware of money laundering or terrorist financing activity. This should be the case even if the suspicion is slight, in which case they should be encouraged to speak with their nominated officer on an informal basis.

The procedures should also outline the steps to be taken by the nominated officer on receipt of a disclosure, which will include making further enquiries to determine whether a report needs to be made to the NCA and, if so, whether privilege applies, preventing such disclosure.

The nominated officer needs to ensure that all those involved in the particular case understand the concept of tipping off and are aware of what they can and cannot say to the client following the formal disclosure to the nominated officer. It is advisable that the nominated officer retains possession of the matter file so that no one can carry on work on the file whilst the nominated officer is considering the position and before (s)he has had a chance to outline what further steps, if any, can be taken while consent is being sought from the NCA.

Training

According to r.21, the firm must take appropriate measures so that all "relevant employees" are:

> "(a) Made aware of the law relating to money laundering and terrorist financing; and
>
> (b) Regularly given training in how to recognise and deal with transactions and other activities which may be related to money laundering or terrorist financing."

The firm has to take "appropriate measures" in relation to the "relevant employees" but no guidance is given as to the meaning of these two phrases. The self employed status of partners was probably not uppermost in the draftsperson's considerations when this was taking shape and it would be wise to include partners within the definition. In accordance with the overall risk-based approach, the firm needs to consider the role and activities of staff and decide which of them are exposed to greater risk of money laundering activities. Those with client-facing roles require more intensive training, whereas staff in lower-risk environments, such as clerical and administrative roles, may need a more general awareness and understanding of the issues. The categories of staff that require training will include:

- Lawyers/partners (including the MLRO);
- Secretaries;
- Finance staff;
- Receptionists; and
- Compliance staff.

All relevant staff need to be trained initially as part of any induction programme and also on an ongoing basis. The LSPN note states at para 3.9.3 that refresher training should take place every two years, although it is suggested that in areas of higher risk, or where there are important changes or developments in the AML/CTF arena, such training should be more frequent.

There are many ways of presenting training. The obvious way is face-to-face but there are several providers who have produced bespoke e-learning products for the legal profession, including the Infolegal website where the sample AML policy at chapter 18 is available for download (www.infolegal.co.uk). Most such programmes also provide tracking systems to monitor progress and an assessment process so that the compliance department or the MLRO can ascertain that individuals have undertaken the training. There are also frequent external conferences on developments in the field which are appropriate for MLROs and compliance staff. Of late the FCA has started to favour face-to-face training in place of electronic packages and it remains to be seen if the SRA will follow suit.

Failure to conduct the required training can provide staff members with a defence for non-disclosure under s.330(7) POCA. If invoked it would no doubt increase the interest of the authorities as to the apparent breach of the regulations by their employer. The same defence does not appear in the equivalent provisions dealing with terrorist financing.

Record keeping

There is a need for certain records to be maintained under r.19 in relation to evidence of client identity and supporting records in respect of a business relationship or an occasional transaction which is the subject of CDD or ongoing monitoring. There are also requirements for record keeping where the firm has been relied on under r.17. Other records, such as risk assessment, internal disclosures, suspicious activity reports to the NCA and training records are not covered but should also be maintained.

Regulation 19(1) also provides that the firm needs to keep a copy of, or reference to, the evidence of the client's identity obtained in relation to rr.7, 8, 10, 14 or 16(4). These may be hard copies or they can be scanned and held electronically. The records must be kept for five years from the date on which the occasional transaction was completed or the business relationship ended (r.19(3)). It is not easy to determine when the business relationship with a client ends, as new instructions may come years after a transaction was completed, so it is therefore preferable to keep the records separate from the matter file. This will mean that they will not be subject to the firm's archiving rules for storage of matter files which are often kept for six to 15 years from the date the file was closed, the business relationship often continuing for much longer than this period. In the Fourth Directive member states are able to allow further retention of records without exceeding an additional five years.

In place of documents, the firm can keep references to documents, such as the number of a client's passport. This may be useful if, for example, the lawyer visits the client in his or her own home. However, it does mean that the firm will not have copies of the original document and it may not be able to obtain a copy if required at a later date.

The firm also has to keep supporting records in respect of a business relationship or occasional transaction which is the subject of CDD or ongoing monitoring. This will generally be information relating to ongoing monitoring of the matter file in which case the record needs only to be stored for five years from the date on which the transaction was completed (r.19(3)(b)). Such information can therefore be stored on the matter file, as the time limit for storage will be in line with most firms' general rules for retention of matter files.

If the firm has permitted another regulated body to rely on its CDD checks under r.17 it will have to keep a record of such checks for five years from the date of reliance. This means that a separate system will need to be set up to record the name of the regulated body, the date of reliance, a copy of the reliance letter and copies of the relevant documentation. If a request is made, the firm has to make available information about the client and forward copies of the documents to the regulated party as soon as reasonably practicable (r.19(5)).

Although not required by r.19, it is advisable to keep records of other documents that will be useful if the firm has to demonstrate to the SRA that it has adopted appropriate measures in relation to its obligations under r.7(3)(b) or that it has not committed an offence under POCA or TA. Such records might include:

- Risk assessments both at client and matter level;
- Internal disclosures – this relates to copies of the relevant internal SARs and any notes made in relation to such suspicion or advice sought from the MLRO prior to a formal disclosure being made, including reasons not to disclose to the NCA; and
- SARs made to the NCA and notes of any conversations with the NCA or other law enforcement agencies.

Clients may make a subject access report to the firm in relation to documents held by the firm for AML/CTF purposes under the Data Protection Act 1998 (DPA), and this could include disclosures made to the NCA. However, there is a defence in s.29 DPA which states that personal data need not be provided if the provision of such data would be likely to prejudice the prevention or detection of crime, or the apprehension or prosecution of offenders. The Information Commissioner has stated that the provision of such data would be likely to prejudice an offence only where disclosure to the client would amount to tipping off.

Monitoring

Although commonly overlooked it is a requirement under r.20 for the firm to have a monitoring and audit system in place to establish whether its procedures are working effectively. This will also include whether the risk assessments at firm, client and matter level are effective, and whether the risk profile at any of these levels has changed and as a result further or different checks need to be undertaken. Monitoring could include:

- Regular audits of files – This could be included within any quality audits the firm operates;
- An analysis of the internal SARs made to the MLRO, to see if there is any pattern emerging;
- An analysis of the types of clients or transactions the firm is taking on; and
- The adequacy of staff training and awareness.

The FCA rules require the MLRO to make an annual report to senior management as part of the monitoring process. Although this is not required of firms that are not FCA regulated, it is suggested that the collation of such a report is a useful exercise in determining whether the firm is using appropriate measures as required by r.7(3)(b).

Looking forward, the Fourth EU Directive provides for an independent audit function depending on the size and nature of the business (Fourth EU Directive, Chapter 1, Section 2, Article 8(4)(b)).

Notes
1   See SRA Practice Framework Rules and in particular 4.7 (Related Bodies), 4.12 (Associations) and 4.14 (Commercial legal advice services).
2   Financial Action Task Force, 'RBA Guidance for Legal Professionals', 23 October 2008, para 125.
3   Financial Conduct Authority handbook, SYSC 3.2.6I R, see https://www.fca.org.uk/ handbook.
4   The Fourth EU Directive, Chapter 1, Section 2, Article 8 (4)(a).

CHAPTER 6

The risk sensitive approach

As we have seen, the CDD processes are required to be risk-based under r.20 MLR 2007. The checking process should be risk-based so as to ensure the greatest possible protection from the risks of liability for the firm and all personnel under POCA and TA. In order to satisfy this principle all firms should first assess risk at a number of levels and then ensure that this risk assessment is used to shape the right policies, processes and procedures for them.

No system can prevent all money laundering or terrorist financing activities, but the objectives of a risk-based approach are to:

- Recognise that the threat of money laundering and terrorist financing to firms varies according to the type of client, business relationship or transaction;
- Allow firms to differentiate between their clients in a way that matches the risk to their particular business;
- Allow firms to apply their own approach to their procedures, systems and controls, in accordance with their size and risk profile; and
- Help to produce a cost-effective system.

Although the MLR 2007 require a risk-sensitive approach to be adopted they do not specify what steps this might entail, nor is the Law Society practice note ('LSPN') entirely clear on this point. It is therefore suggested that a firm should undertake a risk assessment at three levels:

- A general risk assessment in relation to the services provided and the clients that are represented ("firm risk");
- Client identity ("client risk"); and
- The legitimacy of the instructions received ("matter risk").

The Fourth EU Directive requires further levels to this risk checking process with a new requirement for checking at EU and national levels. This will presumably then be used to shape the proposals for a revised set of Money Laundering Regulations and the professional requirements of the various supervisory bodies in due course.

At present it is necessary to assess the risk profile of the firm as a whole, or perhaps in relation to its constituent departments, especially where they operate for different client types or groups. This will need to be supplemented by the everyday risk assessment process at client and matter level.

It is perhaps not sufficiently apparent from the MLR 2007 or the LSPN that the three levels of the risk assessment process are inextricably linked. If a firm, or any given department within it, has a high risk profile, it will need a more thorough risk assessment at client and matter level with more detailed forms to probe into all possible issues. The same may not be true of other firms, however, or even certain departments within a mixed practice, with the result that different levels of checking and perhaps a variety of forms of differing complexity might validly be in use within the same firm. Where there is a good deal of cross referral between departments, however, it might be preferable to have one type of form for the process and not a choice of them. It is also likely to be easier for management to enforce the correct use of forms and procedures where one version is in use throughout the practice.

Before looking at the three levels of risk assessment – firm, client and matter – it is useful to consider how a risk assessment might be undertaken. The following sets out how to undertake a risk analysis at firm, client and matter level.

Risk assessment

In carrying out a risk assessment it is advisable for the firm to follow the commonly adopted process of risk analysis, risk mitigation and risk monitoring.

Risk analysis

The firm has to identify, describe and estimate the level of risk it faces from money laundering and terrorist financing activities. This can be drawn up by the use of a risk matrix identifying the level of risk as high, standard or low. The nature of the risks presented will depend on the type of clients the firm has, its business relationship with those clients, the nature of the legal work it undertakes and any ancillary services it provides.

Risk mitigation

The firm needs to look at the risks identified and the level of those risks (high, standard or low) and decide the type of CDD measures and other controls that need to be implemented by the firm to control and mitigate those risks.

> *Risk monitoring*
>
> The firm needs to establish a system of reviewing its procedures to ensure that they remain adequate to mitigate the risks presented to the firm by its client base and the nature of the retainers and transactions it undertakes. This system should identify changes to the risk profile of the firm through, for example, changes to the client base or types of practice areas/transactions undertaken. An annual risk reassessment will indicate whether there are additional or different risks presented that are not covered by the firm's established CDD measures.

Firm level risk analysis

The first step is to undertake the risk analysis, either on a firm-wide or a departmental basis. The requirement for a firm-wide risk analysis can be found at r.7(3) MLR 2007, which provides that regulated bodies must:

> "(a) determine the extent of customer due diligence measures on a risk-sensitive basis depending on the type of customer, business relationship, product or transaction".

The factors the firm should consider when undertaking its risk analysis include:

- The size of the firm;
- The type of clients it has, including their geographical location, legal structure and ownership;
- The legal work it undertakes; and
- Any services it provides which are ancillary to its legal practice, particularly relating to the use of its client account.

In its "Guidance for Legal Professionals", FATF states that the "identification of the money laundering and terrorist financing risks associated with certain client or categories of clients, and certain types of work will allow legal professionals to determine and implement reasonable and proportionate measures to mitigate these risks."[1]

A useful starting point for the firm is set out in chapter 2 of the LSPN. It lists factors which are indicative of a higher risk legal practice, shown in Table 1.

In drawing up its own risk matrix the firm must decide, in relation to each risk identified, the level to which it is exposed given its own client base, areas of practice and associated services. Each risk identified should be accorded a level – low, medium/standard or high. The firm will then have estimated the level of its exposure to identified risks, which should in turn enable it to establish its overall risk profile. An example of a risk matrix, which is based on the Law Society's list of risk factors, is shown in Table 2 at the end of this chapter.

Table 1: Factors indicative of a higher risk legal practice

Client demographic	<ul><li>High turnover of clients;</li><li>Acting for politically exposed persons;</li><li>Acting for clients who are not met in person;</li><li>Practising in locations with high levels of acquisitive crime, or with a client base that has such convictions;</li><li>Accepting instructions from clients based in suspect territories;</li><li>Acting for entities with complex ownership structures; and</li><li>Difficulty in determining issues of beneficial ownership.</li></ul>
Services and areas of law	<ul><li>Complex financial or property transactions;</li><li>Setting up companies or trusts to obscure ownership;</li><li>Payments to be made to or from third parties;</li><li>Cash payments; and</li><li>Transactions with a cross-border element.</li></ul>

It probably follows from the list of high risk factors above that a high risk profile is more likely in the larger commercial firm undertaking transactional and other financially related work, or a firm that undertakes higher value private client, property or tax work. The great majority of law firms, and certainly most that are of a 'high street' nature serving a local clientele, will be lower risk. It follows that relatively simple forms and procedures will suffice for most firms, as reflected by the sample policy and procedures set out in Chapter 18. Firms with a more complex profile may need more advanced systems that are more bespoke in their nature.

Client level risk analysis

The next step in the risk assessment process will be to identify the level of risk presented by the firm's client base. Such risk indicators will enable the firm to determine the level of risk presented by individual clients based on their client type – such risk is generally categorised as high, standard or low. This follows the system adopted by the MLR 2007, which identify certain types of clients as low risk and so being subject to simplified due diligence (r.13) or higher risk and so subject to enhanced due diligence (r.14). This analysis should form part of the client acceptance process.

Clients can be broadly divided into three main types – individual, corporate and other legal bodies. The level of risk presented by each of these client types depends on factors such as their structure, ownership, geographical location and whether the client or its representative has been met in person. For example, a firm that deals with UK owner-managed businesses may decide that it should adopt standard due diligence for this type of client. A firm acting for more complex corporate structures or clients based in high risk jurisdictions will generally need to undertake enhanced due diligence. Table 3, at the end of this chapter, identifies client types and the general level of risk which firms may attribute to those clients. A more detailed explanation of the categorisation of client types and the nature of identification and verification checks for those client types, which need to be carried out as part of CDD, is given in Chapters 9 to 11. An overly formulaic approach should be avoided, however, and it is important that individual judgement is retained in the due diligence process. For example, a client met in person may generally present a standard risk, but it may be that the documentation provided or other factors lead the firm to decide that they present a higher risk, in which case enhanced due diligence should be preferred.

The firm must also examine the purpose and intended nature of the business relationship between the firm and the client as part of the client acceptance procedure (r.5(c)). This is based on the need to "know your client" (often abbreviated to KYC). The following are examples of factors which may indicate that the nature of the business relationship presents a higher risk:

- The client is a legal entity that has been recently established;
- The nature of commercial activity undertaken by the client is unclear;
- The source of wealth/funds is not apparent;
- There are undue levels of secrecy; and
- The client's business involves significant amounts of cash.

KYC will involve obtaining information to investigate the risk factors identified in order to determine whether the purpose of the client, in entering in a business relationship with the firm, is legitimate.

Matter level risk analysis

Finally, as part of the matter opening process there will also need to be an analysis of the risk presented by the instructions given or the nature of the transaction being undertaken. This can also be seen as part of "ongoing monitoring" required by r.8 MLR 2007: the better the firm knows its clients, the better it is able to assess ongoing risks and detect any suspicious activities.

Risk factors identified at matter level may include: certain types of transactions in financially based areas such as property, corporate, tax or trusts; unusual instructions; cash payments; unknown source of funds; the use of client account; or connection with a high risk jurisdiction.

There is also a useful series of money-laundering warning signs in the LSPN at chapter 11, which can be used as criteria to assist the firm in deciding if a matter presents a higher risk. A summary of these signs is set out in Table 4 at the end of this chapter. In addition, FATF has issued a report on 'Money laundering and terrorist financing vulnerabilities of legal professionals', June 2013 which categorises warning signs or 'red flags' into four categories: client; source of funds; choice of lawyer; and the nature of the retainer. Within these categories are 42 red flags that can be used when identifying risks at matter level.

The publication "A Lawyer's Guide to Detecting and Preventing Money Laundering" (October 2014) also deals with red flags in Chapter IV. This influential guide has been produced by the International Bar Association, the American Bar Association and the Council of Bars and Law Societies of Europe.

General risk assessment

In addition to risk assessment for AML and CTF purposes, many firms also conduct a more general risk assessment at the outset of matters as a core element of their overall risk management processes. This might be viewed as an element of the obligation to conduct all the activities of the firm in accordance with Principle 8 of the SRA Handbook and the need to run the practice "in accordance with ... sound financial and risk management processes" or, more specifically, the requirement in the Lexcel quality management standard to undertake file opening risk management checks. The separate assessments are, of course, interlinked. The lawyer needs to evaluate the instructions received to assess if the firm may validly accept the work, or if it might involve illegal or unprofessional conduct contrary to the SRA Handbook. Failure to evaluate instructions in this way would lead to the risks of censure from the SRA and potential involvement in an "arrangement" under s.328 POCA or s.18 TA. It makes sense, therefore, to harmonise general risk assessment and matter evaluation processes with the other issues that arise under the AML regime. Where this is the case it is likely to be preferable to integrate the general and AML/CTF assessments.

Risk mitigation

The firm must decide the measures it needs to take to mitigate the risks it has identified. Such internal controls should be documented in the AML/CTF policy and procedures of the firm (see Chapter 5 for more details) and should include such details as:

- The level of personnel who are allowed to carry out risk assessments;
- The documentation and other checks required to undertake CDD, depending on whether the client or matter is classified as simplified, standard or enhanced CDD;
- Whether the firm is to accept outsourcing of CDD or reliance on another regulated body;
- The circumstances in which the firm will accept a delay in completing the relevant checks;
- When payment of cash will be accepted;
- Whether the firm will accept payments made to or from a third party; and
- The procedure for making disclosures to the nominated officer.

(LSPN para 3.5)

Ongoing monitoring will also be needed under r.8 in order to be able to identify retainers or transactions that may present a higher risk of money laundering or terrorist financing activities, rather than simply carrying out investigations at the beginning of the client relationship or on acceptance of the instructions given. Ongoing monitoring should be carried out on a risk-based approach, with higher-risk client/retainer combinations being subject to an appropriate frequency and depth of scrutiny, which is likely to be greater than where a lower risk profile applies.

Risk monitoring

The firm needs to monitor compliance so that it can update policies and procedures to meet new and emerging risks or to ensure current measures are sufficient to mitigate known risks. The higher the risk profile of the firm, the more active a monitoring process is likely to be needed. The types of monitoring activities the firm should consider undertaking are:

- Using checklists to assist in completion of risk assessments and CDD;
- Undertaking regular audits to ensure that the systems and controls are being implemented;
- Analysing suspicious activity reports made to the MLRO to ensure that such risk indicators are taken into account when conducting CDD;
- Checking understanding and awareness of the firm's policies and procedures by use of online testing;
- Reviewing the firm's risk profile to see if there are changes in client types, services or areas of work, which might give rise to a higher risk of money laundering or terrorist financing; and
- Keeping up to date with external reports (NCA, SRA, etc.) indicating areas of increasing risk to the legal profession.

The Fourth EU Directive

The whole concept of risk assessment features heavily in the changes introduced by the Fourth EU Directive, with a process required at three levels: EU level, national level and that of the "obliged entity", or regulated body.

At EU level, the Commission will conduct an assessment of the money laundering and terrorist financing risks affecting the internal market within two years from the date of entry into force of the Fourth Directive.[2] This report will be made available to the member states to assist them in drawing up their own risk assessment.

At national level, each member state will have to take appropriate steps to identify, assess, understand and mitigate the money laundering and terrorist financing risks affecting it, and keep the assessment up to date.[3] The assessment is to be used to:

- Improve its AML/CTF regime, in particular by identifying any areas where obliged entities shall apply enhanced measures and, where appropriate, specifying the measures to be taken;
- Identify sectors of lower and greater risks;
- Assist in the allocation and prioritisation of resources;
- Ensure that appropriate rules are drawn up for each sector or area;
- Make information available to obliged entities to carry out their own AML/CTF risk assessments.

At the level of obliged entities, they are to take appropriate steps to identify and assess their AML/CTF risks taking into account risk factors including clients, countries or geographic areas, products, services, transactions or delivery channels.[4] Such risk assessments are to be documented and kept up to date and must be made available to the competent authorities. They are also to have policies, controls and procedures in place to mitigate and manage risks identified at EU, member state and obliged entity level. Such policies shall include customer due diligence, reporting, record keeping, internal control, compliance management and employee screening. Where appropriate, given the size and nature of the obliged entity, they must appoint a compliance officer and carry out an independent audit function.

Notes
1   Financial Action Task Force, 'RBA Guidance for Legal Professionals', 23rd October 2008.
2   The Fourth EU Directive, Chapter 1, Section 2, Article 6.
3   *Ibid*, Chapter I, Section 2 Article 7.
4   *Ibid*, Chapter I, Section 2 Article 8.

Table 2: Risk matrix for firm-wide risk assessment

Factor	Low risk	Medium/standard risk	High risk	Risk assessment (high, standard or low)
		Client demographic		
Client turnover	• High level of new instructions emanate from existing clients.	• Even mix of instructions from existing and new clients.	• High turnover of clients; • Majority of instructions are one-off (over €15,000 limit); or • Very transient client base.	
Client wealth base	• Individual clients with low asset and income base; • Fixed income – employed or state benefits; or • Regular identifiable source of income.	• Identified source of income/asset base.	• Individuals with unidentifiable/obscure source of personal wealth; or • Politically exposed persons.	
Client interface	• Regulated bodies (for example, the FCA); • Listed on regulated	• Individuals met in person; or • Private companies/other	• Individuals/directors/other key individuals not met in person.	

Table 2 (continued)

Factor	Low risk	Medium/standard risk	High risk	Risk assessment (high, standard or low)
	market; • Public authorities in the UK; • Professional bodies; • Long-established clients; or • Appointment subject to court approval.	legal entities where key individuals are met in person – for example, trusts, partnerships or charities.		
Potential for acquisitive crime	• Client base not linked to local area which has high level of acquisitive crime; or • National client base.	• Local client base in area not linked to higher than average acquisitive crime.	• Local client base in area of high acquisitive crime; or • Client base has convictions for acquisitive crime.	

Table 2 (continued)

Factor	Low risk	Medium/standard risk	High risk	Risk assessment (high, standard or low)
Client location/jurisdiction	• Local/national client base; or • Clients from EEA countries with high Corruption Perceptions Index (CPI) rating.	• International client base situated in countries which have equivalent AML/CTF legislation/medium CPI rating.	• Clients based in countries with high levels of corruption/acquisitive crime; • Clients based in countries without equivalent AML/CTF legislation; or • Clients based in countries with low CPI rating. Note: you cannot act for clients on HM Treasury consolidated list of financial sanctions.	
Complexity of structures	• Individuals; or • Simple legal structures.	• Owner-managed companies; or • Structures that are standard, with clearly identifiable ownership.	• Complex structures; • Offshore trusts; or • Ownership unclear.	
Identification of beneficial owners	• No beneficial owners.	• Easily identifiable beneficial owners.	• Ultimate control not readily identifiable/unable to obtain	

Table 2 (continued)

Factor	Low risk	Medium/standard risk	High risk	Risk assessment (high, standard or low)
			details of beneficial owners.	
Services and areas of law				
Number and complexity of financial/property transactions	• Limited transactional work; • Limited corporate, financial, property, trusts and tax work; or • Predominantly legal advice/contentious/non-regulated activities.	• Non-specialised or commodity-based services within regulated areas; • Low transactional values; • Cross-selling between contentious/non-regulated areas of practice and regulated/transactional areas of practice; or • Full service firms.	• Highly specialised work in areas of property, finance, corporate, trusts and tax.	
Setting up legal	• Not involved in the	• Setting up simple	• Setting up complex trusts or	

Table 2 (continued)

Factor	Low risk	Medium/standard risk	High risk	Risk assessment (high, standard or low)
structures	setting up of legal entities.	legal structures with limited layers and easily recognisable ownership.	corporate structures.	
Payments from client account	• No payments to third parties.	• Occasional payments to third parties with clear legitimate purpose.	• Reasons for payment unclear; or • Payments to third parties more than occasional.	
Handling cash	• No cash received.	• Limited/low levels of cash received, and from clients directly.	• Clients in cash-based activities; • Cash is main method of payments for transactions; or • Payments of cash received from third parties.	

Table 2 (continued)

Factor	Low risk	Medium/standard risk	High risk	Risk assessment (high, standard or low)
Cross-border transactions	• Within EEA countries with high CPI ratings.	• Involves other FATF countries with equivalent AML/CTF legislation/medium CPI ratings.	• Involves countries with high levels of corruption /acquisitive crime; • Involves countries without equivalent AML/CTF legislation; or • Involves countries with low CPI ratings.	

Table 3: Client types and associated risk levels

Individual client types	Corporate client types	Other bodies or client types
Low risk • Long-established clients; • Member of recognised professional body; or • Well-known individuals. *Medium/standard risk* • Client seen in person (UK resident); or • Client seen in person (non-UK resident). *Higher risk* • Client not seen in person (UK resident); • Client not seen in person (non-UK resident); • Clients not able to produce standard documentation; • Agent; • Politically exposed person; • Initial client ID raises issues/suspicion; or • Client based in high risk jurisdiction/jurisdiction without equivalent AML/CTF legislation. *Banned individuals* • HM Treasury sanctions list; or • Jurisdiction subject to FATF counter-measures.	*Low risk* • Household name/well-known in industry sector; • Public company (listed in UK including AIM) or majority owned subsidiary; • Public overseas company listed on regulated market in EEA or with similar disclosure requirements to that required by EC legislation; • Regulated utility companies; • Bank, credit or financial institution (regulated within UK/EEA or equivalent jurisdiction); or • Subsidiary of existing client. *Medium/standard risk* • Private company with key directors met in person and clear ownership structure with identifiable beneficial owners; or • Regulated bodies under MLR 2007. *High risk* • Private company with complex structure, obscure ownership or unidentified beneficial owners; • Private overseas company in high risk jurisdiction/ without equivalent AML/CTF legislation; or • Initial client ID raises issues/suspicion.	*Low risk* • Public authorities in UK; • Community institutions; • State schools, colleges and universities; or • Occupational pension schemes. *Medium/standard risk* • Governments, public authorities in EEA/equivalent jurisdictions; • Trusts with standard structure and identifiable beneficial owners; • Partnerships/UK LLPs; • Estates of a deceased person; • Independent schools and colleges; • Charities; • Churches/places of worship; or • Clubs and associations. *High risk* • Governments, public authorities in high risk jurisdictions; • Trusts/partnerships with complex ownership structure/situated in high risk jurisdictions; • Other arrangements and legal entities with complex structures/situated in high risk jurisdictions; or • Initial client ID raises issues/suspicion.

Table 4: Risk assessment at matter level – warning signs
Based on chapter 11 of the Law Society practice note

General warning signs	Property work
Secretive clients	*Ownership issues*
Unusual instructions	• Multiple owners;
• Outside the firm's area of expertise;	• Use of nominee companies; or
• Change instructions unexpectedly; or	• Sudden or unexplained changes in ownership, flipping.
• Involve asking for return of money deposited in client account, payments to third parties or unexplained changes in source of funds.	*Funding*
	• Private funding;
	• Funds from a third party; or
Unusual retainers	• Direct payments between buyers and sellers.
• Disputes easily settled which may indicate sham litigation;	*Valuing*
• Loss-making transactions;	• Unusual sale price;
• Transfers of property which may be to avoid seizure by relevant authorities;	• Sale at an undervalue; or
	• High valuation.
• Payments in cash;	*Lender issues*
• Payment directly between parties;	• Discrepancies over buyer's stated income; or
• Complex or unusually large transactions; or	• Transactions not at arm's length.
• Unusual patterns of transactions which have no apparent commercial purpose.	*Tax issues*
	• Tax irregularities, for example, abuse of stamp duty procedures.
Use of client account	
• Cash paid directly into client account;	**Corporate**
• Payments made into client account and return requested without transaction having taken place; or	• Complex ownership structures;
	• Affiliation with high risk jurisdictions;
	• Source of funds unclear;
• Using the client account as more of a banking service.	• Complex financial transactions;
Source of funds	• Formation of companies or subsidiaries without any apparent commercial purpose (front or shell companies);
• Funds from source other than client; or	
• Obscure or unidentified source of funds.	• Request to appoint a solicitor as a director of the firm with little or no apparent involvement;
Suspect territory	
• Without equivalent AML/CTF legislation;	• Large payments to third parties for unknown services;
• Low CPI rating; or	• Transactions above or below market price; or
• Known to be connected with high levels of drug production, drug trafficking, or terrorism.	• Lengthy delays in production of company accounts.
Multiple advisers	**Private client**
• Several law firms acting for same client in similar transactions.	• Client with background of acquisitive crime/benefit fraud/tax evasion;
	• Unusual trust structures;
	• Trust based in high risk jurisdictions;
	• Purpose of trust not clear;
	• Unclear source and control of funds; or
	• Formation of trust with no apparent purpose.

CHAPTER 7

Client due diligence measures

The MLR 2003 had required relatively simple identity checks to be made by those organisations that were subject to their provisions, but the 2007 regulations introduced the more complex concept of "customer due diligence" (CDD). In addition to the verification of client identity at the outset of each matter or engagement, a firm would now have to obtain information on the purpose and intended nature of the business relationship between it and its client, and identify any beneficial owners involved in the ultimate ownership or control of that client (r.5).

In pursuance of the risk principle, and in recognition that not all clients present the same degree of risk, the MLR 2007 also introduced the concepts of simplified and enhanced CDD. Simplified due diligence (r.13) requires minimal checks for a prescribed list of clients who present a low risk; for example, because they are already subject to a regime of disclosure regulations required by law, such as banks and public companies. Enhanced due diligence, by contrast, relates to areas of higher risk, including individual clients who are not physically present at the time of verification (r.14(2)) and those who are regarded as being "politically exposed persons" (PEPs) (r.14(4)).

The need for ongoing monitoring was also introduced by the MLR 2007 and can be found at r.8. The CDD process is no longer confined to one point of time and needs to be subject to some degree of continued checking, not just in relation to changes in the key information on the client, such as their address details, but also whether the instructions from the client remain consistent with the firm's expectations of that client to date.

Application of CDD measures

Regulation 7(1) provides that the law firm, if it is a regulated body[1], must apply CDD measures when it:

"(a) establishes a business relationship;

(b) carries out an occasional transaction;

(c) suspects money laundering or terrorist financing;

(d) doubts the veracity or adequacy of documents, data or information previously obtained for the purposes of identification or verification."

The concepts of "business relationship" and an "occasional transaction" are not particularly helpful to law firms, being based instead on banking activities and representing the difference between opening an account and making a one-off investment. The terms are defined as follows in r.2:

- Business relationship: "a business, professional or commercial relationship between a [regulated body] and a [client], which is expected by the [regulated body] at the time when contact is established, to have an element of duration"; and
- Occasional transaction: "a transaction (carried out other than as part of a business relationship) amounting to 15,000 euro or more, whether the transaction is carried out in a single operation or several operations which appear to be linked."

Of these two main headings the business relationship is the more significant within the legal profession. In relation to the "element of duration" it may, of course, be difficult to anticipate whether any given client relationship will extend beyond the initial retainer, but it would seem that this relates more to the expectation of the firm than the client. A firm may find it difficult, at the point of initial contact, to anticipate whether the client will give the firm further instructions, although it is a well accepted principle that most business comes from existing clients. In addition, the initial retainer may involve non-regulated activities such as pure legal advice or contentious work, but the client may then instruct the firm in relation to areas that do fall within the MLR 2007. The common practice of most firms is therefore to carry out CDD at the point of acceptance of a new client, regardless of the element of duration or the nature of the work involved. This will ensure that the firm has complied with its obligations and it does not have to ask for information or documents at a later stage when it might be more difficult to collect them, and should also help to prevent delays in executing the client's instructions.

The one exception to the general concept of "across the board" checking which might be helpful to firms lies in the application of the €15,000 limit to most cases of one-off transactions where CDD will not need to be conducted. Some firms will want to take advantage of this exception where they have a supply of work that is very limited in its scope – advice on settlement agreements in employment law being one common example.

CDD measures also need to be undertaken if the firm "suspects money laundering or terrorist financing" (r.7 (1)(c)) or if it "doubts the veracity or accuracy of documents, data or information previously obtained" (r.7(1)(d)). This will not only satisfy the CDD requirements under r.7(1) but it will also help to highlight any liability for the failure to disclose offences under s.330 POCA and s.21A TA by ensuring that any suspicious circumstances are clarified or a report is made to the NCA.

Meaning of CDD measures

CDD measures are designed to control and mitigate the level of risk that has been identified and assessed through the firm's risk assessment procedures. Regulation 5 MLR 2007 sets out the measures the firm needs to undertake:

> "(a) identifying the [client] and verifying the [client's] identity on the basis of documents, data or information obtained from a reliable and independent source;

> (b) identifying, where there is a beneficial owner who is not the [client], the beneficial owner and taking adequate measures, on a risk-sensitive basis, to verify his identity so that the [firm] is satisfied that [it] knows who the beneficial owner is, including, in the case of a legal person, trust or similar arrangement, measures to understand the ownership and control structure of the person, trust or arrangement; and

> (c) obtaining information on the purpose and intended nature of the business relationship."

There is therefore a three-stage procedure that the firm has to carry out when undertaking CDD.

Stage one: Client identification and verification

Identification is explained by the Law Society practice note at para 4.3.2 as establishing or "coming to know a client's identifying details, such as their name and address". Verification is then described as obtaining evidence to support that claim of identity – in other words, establishing that the client who presents him or herself is indeed the person they claim to be. The identification and verification evidence can take the form of documents, data or information, which is "from a reliable and independent source" (r.5(a)). This usually takes the form of examining original documents, but might alternatively be obtaining certified documents from others, undertaking electronic searches, or relying on information obtained from others if they are sufficiently reliable.

Stage two: Identification and verification of any beneficial owners, and understanding ownership and control structure

It is also necessary to identify any beneficial owners under r.6 of the MLR 2007. In the case of corporate entities and partnerships a beneficial owner is a natural person who owns more than 25% of the entity or its voting rights, a threshold which is retained in the Fourth Directive. For trusts the threshold is "a specified interest of at least 25% of the capital of the trust property".[2]

The general principle is that there is a lower test of verification for beneficial owners than that which applies to a client. The obligation to verify the identity of a beneficial owner is for the firm to take "adequate measures" on a "risk-sensitive basis" so that it is satisfied it "knows who the beneficial owner is" (r.5(b)). There is, however, no specific requirement for the firm to rely on documents or any particular type of evidence, or that such evidence has to be from a reliable and independent source, so it is for the firm to decide what it will regard as adequate measures, with the LSPN suggesting that it might be limited to gaining assurances from the client as to the names and addresses of the beneficial owners if the overall risk is considered to be low. This is an area that is likely to change under the Fourth Directive, which currently uses the words "reasonable measures" instead of adequate, a phrase which is derived from the FATF Recommendation 10(b).[3]

In relation to legal (rather than natural) persons, trusts or similar arrangements, the identification of beneficial owners extends to understanding the ownership and control structure of that body. This necessitates an understanding of not just immediate ownership and control but also who has ultimate control, which may prove to be difficult to assess in certain complex structures, especially in relation to corporate structures involving different jurisdictions and offshore territories where a greater degree of secrecy is an accepted part of the business culture. The LSPN advocates a "reasonable and proportionate" approach at para 4.7.4 so as to gain an overall understanding of the ownership and control structure.

Stage three: Purpose and intended nature of the business relationship

In addition to identification of the client and verification of that identity, it is also necessary to obtain information on the purpose and intended nature of the business relationship. This requires an analysis, on a risk-sensitive basis, of the underlying purpose of the client in engaging the services of the firm. The LSPN observes that it is "good practice" to obtain information on such purposes in order to fully understand the instructions given and monitor the development of each retainer and should be applied to both business relationships and occasional transactions (para 4.3.2). The view should also be taken that the need to obtain information about the intended business relationship also forms an important component of the firm's more general professional obligations.

The information that should be gathered when looking at the purpose and intended nature of the business relationship includes:

- The nature of the business activity of the client;
- The source and origin of any funds;
- Information relating to the financial standing of the client; and
- The length of time the client's business has been established.

The level of detail of information gathered will depend on the risk profile of the client and the extent to which the characteristics of the business relationship give rise to a higher risk of money laundering and terrorist financing activities. The types of questions the firm may consider relevant in determining the nature of the business relationship in the case of a corporate body are:

- Why is the client seeking the services of the firm?
- What are its business activities and industry sector?
- Who are its auditors and are the accounts qualified?
- What are the key sources of income (trading, investment, etc.)?
- What are the key sources of capital?
- What are the scales of the client's turnover, profits/losses and net assets?
- Why is it connected to a particular jurisdiction? And
- What is the history of the client since incorporation?

The types of questions the firm might consider relevant in relation to individual clients are:

- Why is the client seeking the services of the firm?
- What is its purpose for entering into any specific transaction?
- What are the scale and sources of capital and income? And
- Why is there a connection to any particular jurisdiction?

Particular warnings have been given about clients who seek relatively straightforward work from firms that are based some distance away, where the same service could easily be obtained closer to home, and situations where the client is anxious to involve a solicitor as a director or trustee. In this latter case the risk is that the adviser is being duped into giving a criminal scheme greater credibility through their status as a professional person.

Timing of CDD

The firm has to carry out CDD in accordance with the provisions on timing set out in r.9 MLR 2007. Regulation 9(2) states that the firm "must verify the identity of the [client] (and any beneficial owner) before the establishment of a business relationship or the carrying out of an occasional transaction." This means that, as a general rule, no retainer can be agreed before the necessary identity checks have been completed. The firm does not, however, have to gather information on the purpose and intended nature of the business relationship before accepting the client.

Given that O(7.5) of the SRA Code of Conduct requires firms to "comply with legislation applicable to your business, including anti-money laundering ... legislation" the common problem of CDD checks not being completed, or not completed in time, is potentially an issue for the firm's COLP which will often need to be recorded as a breach and, where it is widespread within the firm, reported to the SRA as one that is material[4].

Regulation 11(1) sets out the consequences if the firm is unable to apply CDD measures as required. They are:

- Not to carry out a transaction with or for the client through a bank account;
- Not to establish a business relationship or carry out an occasional transaction with the client;
- Terminate any existing business relationship with the client; and
- Consider whether there is a need to make a disclosure to the nominated officer or the NCA.

It should be noted that payments on account of costs and payments of a solicitor's bill are not included in the prohibition on the use of bank accounts as such activities do not fall within the scope of being part of the regulated sector.[5]

It is, of course, not always practicable to obtain all of the necessary information or documents before taking instructions or giving preliminary legal advice. This is recognised in the regulations, which provide two limited exceptions to the general rule – the first being if it "is necessary not to interrupt the normal conduct of business" (r.9(3)(a)), and the second if a lawyer or other professional adviser "is in the course of ascertaining the legal position for his client or performing his task of defending or representing that client in, or concerning, legal proceedings, including advice on the institution or avoidance of proceedings" (r.11(2)).

The first exception

CDD may be completed during the establishment of a business relationship if it is necessary not to interrupt the normal course of business and there is little risk of money laundering or terrorist financing occurring (r.9(3)(a)-(b)), but subject to the proviso that the verification should be completed as soon as practicable after contact is first established (r.9(3)). In order to rely on the exception it is necessary to complete a risk assessment before entering the business relationship to ensure that there is little risk of money laundering or terrorist financing. If the risk is low and there is a business necessity to continue, then the firm may carry on working for the client whilst the necessary checks are completed. It is important to stress, however, that the checks must be completed as soon as practicable. In addition, the LSPN states at para 4.3.5 that no funds or property may be transferred or any final agreements signed before relevant checks have been carried out in full. It must also be remembered that any delay or refusal on the part of the client in providing documentation might make it necessary to consider whether a disclosure is needed if the failure to produce the required evidence itself raises suspicions (r.11(1)). The firm must also consider whether it has an obligation under r.11(1)(c) to cease to act for the client.

Some firms have imposed a maximum period of time – either days or number of chargeable hours – before the adviser is no longer permitted to continue to act without CDD requests having been complied with. It is also worth noting the Law Society's advice in the practice note at para 11.2.3 that firms should "think carefully" about providing their client account details and this should not be done until the client has provided the necessary ID evidence. If a cheque is received from a client in advance of CDD being completed, it should usually be returned, but the position on a bank transfer is more complicated and might require a disclosure to the NCA to protect the firm's position if there is a suspicion that the firm is being used to process a suspect payment.

Conveyancing could produce particular problems with these provisions. Speed of response is critical in gaining the work and providing the level of service the client is likely to expect. If the transaction is seen as a business relationship (on grounds that the firm's relationship with that client is expected to have an element of duration) it may well be that the firm could collect fees on account and commission searches before completing CDD, but only if it has no doubts as to the instructions, not least as the money will immediately be spent on defined activities and so will not be available for a client refund in any event. Nonetheless, the firm would be well advised if doing so to insist on production of the required evidence within a stated period of time as a condition of continuing to act. The safest course of action in the normal course of events is to insist on receipt of the ID evidence before taking money into client account and to limit the fees collected at the outset of the matter to the level of search fees that will be commissioned. This will at least mean that funds do not have to be repaid to the client if the ID evidence is not forthcoming or if the matter is abortive.

The second exception

A lawyer or other professional adviser can act for a client even though they are unable to complete CDD measures whilst "in the course of ascertaining the legal position for his client, or performing his task of defending or representing that client in, or concerning, legal proceedings, including advice on the institution or avoidance of proceedings" (r.11(2)). This covers legal advice and litigation and applies if there is a delay or even if the client refuses to provide the necessary information or evidence.

The definition of "other professional adviser" is set out in r.11(3) as an auditor, accountant or tax adviser who is a member of a professional body which is established for any such person and which makes provision for:

"(a) testing the competence of those seeking admission to membership of such a body as a condition for such admission; and

(b) imposing and maintaining professional and ethical standards for its members, as well as imposing sanctions for non-compliance with those standards."

Ongoing monitoring

There is an obligation to continue the CDD process through r.8(1), which requires the firm to undertake ongoing monitoring of both the verification of client ID and also of the current matter or transaction provided there is a business relationship. The Joint Money Laundering Steering Group (JMLSG) guidance states that the key elements of any system of monitoring are: "having up-to-date customer information, on the basis of which it will be possible to spot the unusual, and asking pertinent questions to elicit the reasons for unusual transactions or activities in order to judge whether they may represent something suspicious."[6]

The level of monitoring will depend on the client risk profile, so if the firm acts for clients that are generally considered higher risk then greater monitoring needs to be undertaken than for clients who are considered to have a lower risk profile. It will also be relevant to consider whether the retainer itself falls into a higher risk category, and whether the retainer is similar to other similar instructions received or whether there are features which require closer monitoring and more detailed instructions.

Regulation 8(2) defines "ongoing monitoring" of a business relationship as:

"(a) scrutiny of transactions undertaken throughout the course of the relationship (including, where necessary, the source of funds) to ensure that the transactions are consistent with the [firm's] knowledge of the [client], his business and risk profile; and

(b) keeping the documents, data or information obtained for the purpose of applying client due diligence measures up-to-date."

Scrutiny of transactions

A firm should ensure a risk assessment is carried out at the beginning of each new retainer and require its lawyers to be vigilant throughout the course of the matter. This will not only satisfy the requirements of the MLR but should also help to safeguard against criminal liability due to the failure to disclose under s.330 POCA. In this respect it is necessary to remind many advisers that it is not just identity risk that they are monitoring for but also, and more importantly, the "matter risk" emerging from the instructions and the circumstances of the transaction: copious amounts of identity evidence will not allay fears about the source of funds or the client's wealth. The actual level of ongoing monitoring that is required is determined on a risk-sensitive basis depending on the type of client, business relationship or transaction (r.8(3) and r.7(3)). Chapter 6 has already outlined the issues that need to be considered when establishing the risk assessment at matter level and the warning signs that may be indicative of higher risk when dealing with a particular matter or transaction.

One important area which is often overlooked is that of source of funds. Regulation 8(2)(a) MLR 2007 states that ongoing monitoring specifically includes the source of funds as an area that needs to be kept under review "where necessary". It is common practice to ascertain the source of funds as part of matter inception or at a point in the transaction where the identity of the funds needs to be established. The test is whether the source of funds is consistent with the risk profile of the client, the retainer and their business. Although there is no obligation to seek documentary evidence of the source of funds it is common practice to do so. Such items might include bank statements, recent filed company accounts, or documents showing evidence of funds such as the sale of a house, redundancy payment, savings accounts or receipt of personal injury damages. Although bank statements are used as evidence of source of funds it must be remembered that the fact that funds are in a bank account does not mean they are clean. It might be prudent to look behind the bank statement to find the origin of the funds – the "source of wealth" as opposed to merely the "source of funds". It is usually a matter of judgement as to when to question the client further as to the source of their wealth.

Keeping CDD documents up to date
The LSPN states at para 4.4 that to keep CDD material up to date, a firm should consider reviewing it:

- "when taking new instructions from a client, particularly if there has been a gap of over three years between instructions
- when [the firm] receive[s] information of a change in identity details".

Again, the risk principle applies and the three year period is merely a suggestion. In higher risk situations the checking should be more frequent and it follows that in other cases the checks might be less so. Changes in identity details may include:

- Name, for example due to marriage or divorce;
- Address or jurisdiction; or
- Business activity or structure.

There is no general obligation, as many seem to think, to update documents if the only reason is that the documents are no longer valid, for example if a passport has expired since the holder's details were taken, but it is regarded as good practice to be reliant on documents that are up to date in terms of the data protection principles. The LSPN states at para 4.4 that the firm, when conducting ongoing monitoring, is not required to repeat the entire CDD process again every few years or conduct random audits of files, nor is it obliged to suspend or terminate a business relationship until the CDD evidence has been updated, as long as there are no real doubts as to the client's identity. There is also a reference to not having to use sophisticated computer monitoring programmes, this being the standard practice in banks. The firm should, however, keep any request for updated documents under review and to simplify the process many firms opt to permit partners (and sometimes others) to give written assurance as to the identity of known clients in accordance with the guidelines at para 4.6.1 of the LSPN – see also chapter 8.

Simplified due diligence
Prescribed categories
Regulation 13 MLR 2007 sets out the concept of simplified due diligence for certain types

of client. The categories of bodies that qualify for these provisions are:

- Credit or financial institutions which are subject to the Third Directive (r.13(2)(a));
- Credit or financial institutions situated in a non-EEA state which imposes requirements equivalent to those laid down in the Third Directive and which are supervised for compliance (r.13(2)(b));
- Companies listed on a regulated market subject to specified disclosure obligations (r.13(3));
- Beneficial owners of pooled accounts held by notaries or independent legal professions (r.13(4));
- Public authorities in the UK (r.13(5));
- Certain EEA public authorities which are subject to the conditions set out in Schedule 2 para 2 MLR 2007 (r.13(5));
- Certain life assurance and e-money products (r.13(7)(a), (b) and (d));
- Certain pension funds (r.13(7)(c));
- Certain low risk products (r.13(8) and Schedule 2, para 3); and
- Child trust funds and junior ISAs (r.13(9)).

The firm does not have to apply CDD measures provided it "has reasonable grounds for believing that the [client], [or] transaction" falls within one of the stated categories (r.13(1)). Actual knowledge is not required, the test being instead that the belief must be reasonable, meaning that reasonable evidence has to be obtained indicating that the client falls within one of the stated categories. Where this exception applies the firm will not have to obtain any ID on the client itself, nor will it have to verify the identity of any beneficial owners or obtain information about the nature and purpose of the business relationship with the client at the acceptance stage. It must be remembered, however, that simplified due diligence only applies in respect of client identification and does not exempt the firm from carrying out ongoing monitoring of the business relationship with the client, nor does it provide immunity from the relevant offences under POCA and TA. It should also be borne in mind that simplified due diligence also does not apply if there is a suspicion that the client might be involved in money laundering or terrorist financing activities.

Credit or financial institutions – Equivalent jurisdictions
Credit or financial institutions benefit from simplified due diligence if they are subject to the requirements of the Third Directive or requirements equivalent to the Third Directive. As such they are said to be subject to a presumption of equivalence if they are situated in:

- EU/EEA member states; or
- Countries on a list of equivalent jurisdictions issued by the EU Committee on the Prevention of Money Laundering and Terrorist Financing.

Some care is needed on this issue as the JMLSG guidance states that where there is "substantive information which indicates that a presumption of equivalence cannot be sustained" then it is necessary to consider whether procedures should be enhanced to take account of that information.[7] For the up to date position of the implementation of the Third Directive across the EEA, reference should be made to the Europa website[8] or the website of the International Bar Association Anti-Money Laundering Forum.[9] In relation to equivalent jurisdictions outside the EU/EEA, the EU Committee on the Prevention of Money Laundering and Terrorist Financing has drawn up a list of such countries – "Common Understanding on third country equivalence under the Anti-Money Laundering Directive". The list is voluntary, non-binding and subject to review.[10]

The countries set out in this list as at 26 June 2012 were:

Australia, Brazil, Canada, Hong Kong, India, Japan, South Korea, Mexico, Singapore, Switzerland, South Africa, the United States of America.

The list also includes the French and Dutch overseas territories. Jersey, Guernsey and the Isle of Man may also be considered as equivalent.

The Common Understanding produced by the EU Committee also states that the countries on the list only benefit from a refutable presumption of the application of simplified due diligence. It does not obviate the need to apply enhanced due diligence where the circumstances present a higher risk of money laundering or terrorist financing.

It should be noted, however, that HM Treasury has stated that it does not consider that applying simplified due diligence on a country-wide basis is appropriate or consistent with the risk-based approach. This is only one of the factors to be taken into account when deciding on the appropriate level of due diligence.[11]

In relation to non EU/EEA countries, as well as being situated in an equivalent jurisdiction, it is also necessary for the firm to check that the credit or financial institution is supervised for compliance. It is suggested that extreme care must be taken when relying on CDD carried out by third parties in countries with equivalent jurisdictions, unless the firm has a working relationship with the third party and can easily ascertain that it is supervised for compliance with provisions equivalent to that of the Third Directive. A list of regulators in FATF countries can be found on the JMLSG website.[12]

Credit and financial institutions – Non equivalent jurisdictions
In relation to those countries which are not listed by the EU Committee, the JMLSG guidance states:

"A majority of countries and territories do not fall within the lists of countries that can be presumed to be 'equivalent jurisdictions'. This does not necessarily mean that the AML/CTF legislation, and standards of due diligence, in those countries are lower than those in 'equivalent jurisdictions'. However, standards vary significantly, and firms will need to carry out their own assessment of particular countries. In addition to a firm's own knowledge and experience of the country concerned, particular attention should be paid to any FATF-style or IMF/World Bank evaluations that have been undertaken".[13]

The factors to be taken into account when assessing other jurisdictions include:

- Membership of groups that set a minimum admission standard;
- Contextual factors, such as political stability, the level of endemic corruption, etc;
- Evidence of relevant public criticism of the jurisdiction including by such advisory bodies as FATF, and independent and public assessments of the AML regime within that jurisdiction;
- How recent any assessment is and any implementation standards adopted; and
- Trade patterns with the jurisdiction, but proportionately so where very small.

Pooled client accounts
Pooled client accounts held by law firms are currently subject to simplified due diligence but this will cease to be the case under the Fourth EU Directive. It has been decided, however, that member states should be permitted to determine which arrangements should qualify as low risk and be suitable for simplified due diligence. The Law Society will lobby H.M. Treasury to list pooled accounts as being appropriate for exemption from the full requirements.

Enhanced due diligence
Whereas simplified due diligence permits less checking than the norm in some cases, a greater degree of checking is required in other instances under the provisions dealing with enhanced due diligence. The main situations relevant to law firms which arise under this heading involve individual clients who are not met in person and PEPs under r.14.

These requirements are therefore examined in Chapter 9, which deals with how the CDD process is undertaken with individuals.

The other situation of enhanced due diligence is stated to be where a credit institution proposes to establish a correspondent banking relationship with a respondent institution from a non-EEA state, which is outside the remit of this publication. It should also be borne in mind, however, that the need for enhanced due diligence also arises in any other situation which by its nature can present higher risks of money laundering or terrorist financing under r.14(1)(b).

Beneficial owners

Regulation 5(b) MLR 2007 extends the requirement for verification of the identity of clients to beneficial owners to include: "identifying, where there is a beneficial owner who is not the [client], the beneficial owner and taking adequate measures, on a risk-sensitive basis, to verify his identity so that the [firm] is satisfied that [it] knows who the beneficial owner is, including, in the case of a legal person, trust or similar arrangement, measures to understand the ownership and control structure of the person, trust or arrangement". A beneficial owner will always be an individual but the precise range of those involved does depend on the list of definitions at r.6 of the MLR 2007, dealing with:

- Corporate (r.6(1));
- Partnership (r.6(2);
- Trusts (r.6(3)-(5));
- Other legal entities or legal arrangements (r.6(6)-(7));
- Estate of a deceased person (r.6(8)); and
- Any person who ultimately controls or owns the client or on whose behalf a transaction is being conducted (r.6(9)).

The general principle is that a beneficial owner is any individual that owns or controls more than 25% of a corporate body or partnership, or at least 25% of any trust or other legal entity, or otherwise ultimately owns or exercises control over the management of the entity. For a more detailed explanation, see Chapter 10 (corporate bodies) and Chapter 11 (other bodies).

In the case of trusts and other legal entities, the definition is extended to include the class of persons who may benefit from the trust or entity. It is sufficient in such cases for the firm to ascertain and name the scope of the class as opposed to identifying every individual member of the class.

In the case of the estate of a deceased person, the executor or administrator is stated to be the beneficial owner, which means that the beneficiaries of the estate do not have to be identified and their identity verified. If there is a will trust, the rules for identifying beneficial owners under a trust will apply once the administration of the estate is complete.

In the case of agency, the principal is the beneficial owner as the person on whose behalf the transaction is being conducted.

CDD for beneficial owners

Only "adequate measures" on a "risk-sensitive" basis need to be taken to verify the identity of a beneficial owner, whereas verification for a client must be on the basis of documents, data or information obtained from a reliable and independent source, meaning that there is a wider range of methods available for identifying and verifying the identity of beneficial owners. In addition, in the case of a legal person, trust or similar arrangement, it is necessary to understand the ownership and control structure of that body. This will include, but will not be limited to, the identification of beneficial owners. The range of measures which could be considered include:

- Written assurance from the client confirming the identity of any beneficial owners;
- A Companies House search detailing the names of shareholders and their percentage shareholdings;
- A copy of the partnership, trust or other deed detailing the names and shares of the individuals concerned;
- Electronic search; and
- Full identity checks using passport and other independent documents.

Further details of such measures can be found in the relevant sections of Chapters 9, 10 and 11, depending on whether the client is an individual, corporate or other body.

English law has pre-empted this by the passing of the Small Business, Enterprise and Employment Act 2015 which introduces a public register in Companies House with effect from June 2016. The register covers people with significant control – i.e. those who own or control more than 25% of the shares of voting rights.

In relation to corporate and other legal entities the Fourth EU Directive provides that member states are required to ensure that all such entities hold information on their beneficial ownership and provide it to obliged entities when they are undertaking CDD activities[14].

In addition, the Directive requires there to be a central register containing beneficial ownership information on corporate bodies. Access to the register will be given to:

- Competent authorities and FIUs;
- Obliged entities when undertaking CDD; and
- Anyone else with a legitimate interest in its contents[15].

In relation to trusts member states are required to ensure that information on beneficial ownership is held by the trust concerned and provided to obliged entities when undertaking CDD measures[16]. In addition, the Directive requires there to be a central register containing beneficial ownership information of trusts[17], but only if they generate tax consequences and so have to file annual returns with HMRC. Access to the register will be made available to competent authorities and FIUs. The Law Society's Money Laundering Task Force lobbied during the passage of the Directive against central registers for trusts and some success was achieved in the various restrictions that will apply. There is a provision, however, for obliged entities to have access to the register only if the member state concerned so permits and it is likely that the Task Force will continue to lobby against this level of access as the revised Money Laundering Regulations take shape.

Jurisdictional issues

More generally, one of the factors when dealing with overseas clients is whether they are situated in a jurisdiction that is higher risk. FATF issues a list of jurisdictions which it considers to be higher risk and so requiring enhanced due diligence to be undertaken.[18] The list is regularly updated – 26th June 2015 being the current version at the time of going to press. The Financial Conduct Authority published a more comprehensive list of high risk jurisdictions comprising 95 of the 196 countries in the world, but this did understandably attract protests from some of those shown in an unfavourable light and it has been withdrawn. Another useful source, however, is the website maintained by Transparency International, 'Corruption Perception Index'.[19]

In addition, in the Fourth Directive there is a provision for the identification of jurisdictions which are judged to have strategic deficiencies in their national AML/CTF regimes. The Commission will identify such high risk territories and this will be taken into account when determining enhanced due diligence under annex III of the Directive.[20]

Sanctions

Although it does not form part of the AML regime as such, all MLROs should be aware of the sanctions regime which is also in place within the UK. Whereas the AML regime seeks to prevent or disrupt the flow of illicit funds, the sanctions regime seeks to prevent the use of any funds – whether legitimate in their source or not – for the use of certain designated individuals or organisations.

The Law Society has issued various warnings as to the low level of awareness amongst the profession on the issue of sanctions, including reports of a survey in 2009 that 48% of respondents did not check their clients against sanctions lists. It is not, as has sometimes been suggested, a strict liability offence to deal with someone appearing on one of the sanctions lists, but liability could arise if the firm has not taken adequate steps to make the required checks in circumstances where it should reasonably have done so. Under the Terrorism (United Nations Measures) Order 2006, for example, it is an offence to knowingly or intentionally participate in activities which would circumvent the financial restrictions in place, or to facilitate dealing with the funds of designated persons or making funds available to them, directly or indirectly.

Sanctions and embargoes are mostly imposed by the UN and the EU, but can also emanate from the UK or other national governments. There can be various reasons for sanctions being imposed; those generated by the UN have the aim of ensuring international peace and stability and the EU will seek to further its common foreign and security policy objectives. The full and consolidated list of all sanctions is open to public inspection on the Treasury website at www.hm-treasury.gov.uk/ financialsanctions. Since the records are open to the public there is no equivalent of the tipping off offences found in both the AML and CTF regimes and there is no prohibition against discussing the circumstances that might arise with a client as such, though complications may arise where the listing is a result of terrorist activities which might give cause for concern as to terrorist financing in relation to the current matter.

The practical effect of the regime for law firms is the need to add to the risk assessment process on this topic at the firm-wide level as covered in Chapter 6, not least as the Law Society has confirmed that firms may adopt a risk-based approach to sanctions checking. Since there are British citizens on the list also it should not be assumed that the firm is only at risk if it deals with international work or clients. On the other hand, there are a number of regimes to which financial sanctions have been imposed; since this list is subject to change at any time in response to political developments worldwide it should be kept under review and can be found through the link to "regime specific lists and releases" on the main financial sanctions site. It is therefore suggested in the Law Society guidance that case by case checking is likely to be appropriate only where the risk of sanctions involvement is low and perhaps then confined to situations where one of the higher risk regimes is involved as one of the parties or where the client seems unable to access the banking system. Where there is a need to check for this issue the various electronic ID checking agencies have obvious advantages in that they will automatically check against the various listings in any event, therefore making the task that much simpler for all firms. A policy of conducting an e-check against all new clients at least is therefore likely to meet the compliance needs of most firms in this regard.

Beyond screening, the other issue that might arise within firms is that they are notified or discover that they are dealing with someone who appears on the sanctions list. In these circumstances it should be possible to explain to the client what is happening and the implications of the development and it should then be possible to apply to HM Treasury for permission by way of a licence to proceed and for the firm to be paid. This is likely to take at least eight weeks and so it is likely that the firm will put the instructions into abeyance until a positive outcome is achieved.

In addition to the Law Society advice notes on this topic and the information on the Treasury website listed above, there is also a helpful HM Treasury "frequently asked questions" booklet from 2013 which can be downloaded from its website. The application of the regime to legal services is dealt with right at the end of this publication where it suggests that the provision of legal services does not require an export licence, but the payment of legal fees from frozen funds will require permission by way of a licence since it will constitute the use of frozen funds. It also warns that the Legal Aid Agency or other third party funders should require a licence since they might otherwise breach the prohibition on making funds available to solicitors, as unlisted persons, whereby a financial benefit is made available to someone appearing on the list.

The Fourth EU Directive

Simplified due diligence

Not surprisingly, given the significance of CDD processes to the AML regime, the draft Fourth Directive will have some important ramifications for the regulated sector. So far as simplified due diligence is concerned the Directive states that "where a Member State or an obliged entity identifies areas of lower risk, that Member State may allow obliged entities to apply simplified customer due diligence measures", meaning that no longer will there be prescribed lists of simplified due diligence as at present.[21] There will also need to be a risk assessment in such circumstances whereas at present if a client falls into a prescribed category no risk assessment needs to be undertaken. There is nonetheless a list of potentially lower risk situations which are set out in the Fourth Directive and which are likely to be taken into account when assessing whether a client is subject to simplified due diligence.[22] These include:

- Public companies listed on a stock exchange subject to requirements to ensure adequate transparency of beneficial ownership;
- Public administration or enterprises;
- Other EU member states; and
- Third countries having effective anti-money laundering/combating terrorist financing systems.

The Fourth Directive also provides that obliged entities should carry out sufficient monitoring of the transaction or business relationship to enable the detection of unusual or suspicious transactions.[23] In addition, the European Supervisory Authorities are to issue guidelines on the risk factors to be taken into consideration, and/or the measures to be taken in situations where simplified due diligence measures are appropriate. Such guidelines are to be issued within two years of the date of entry into force of the Fourth Directive.[24]

Enhanced due diligence
The Fourth Directive places more emphasis in relation to enhanced due diligence on the assessment of the risk rather than laying down prescribed categories. There are, however, two categories to which enhanced due diligence is automatically attributed, one of them being PEPs. The requirement for persons not seen in person to automatically qualify for enhanced due diligence will no longer exist.

When assessing if there is a higher risk situation regard must be had to the non-exhaustive list of factors and types of evidence set out in the Fourth Directive.[25] These include:
- The business relationship is conducted in unusual circumstances;
- The ownership structure of the company appears unusual or excessively complex given the nature of the company's business;
- Non face to face business relationships or transactions;
- Payment received from unknown or un-associated third parties; and
- Countries identified by credible sources as having significant levels of corruption or other criminal activity.

The Fourth Directive also states that "Member States shall require obliged entities to examine, as far as reasonably possible, the background and purpose of all complex, unusual large transactions, and all unusual patterns of transactions, which have no apparent economic or lawful purpose."[26] In particular they should increase the level of ongoing monitoring to determine whether the transaction is unusual or suspicious. In addition, the European Supervisory Authorities are to issue guidelines on the risk factors to be taken into consideration, and/or the measures to be taken in situations where enhanced due diligence measures are appropriate. Such guidelines are to be issued within two years of the date of entry into force of the Fourth Directive.[27]

Notes

1   See r.3(1) for a list of bodies regulated by the MLR 2007.
2   MLR 2007 6(3)(a).
3   See 'International standards on combating money laundering and the financing of terrorism & proliferation – The FATF Recommendations', FATF, February 2012. Available at http://www.fatf-gafi.org/media/fatf/documents/recommendations/pdfs/FATF_Recommendations.pdf.
4   SRA Authorisation Rules: 8(5).
5   LSPN 1.4.5.
6   'Prevention of money laundering / combating terrorist financing: Guidance for the UK financial sector', JMLSG, 2014 Revised Version, part I para 5.7.8.
7   *Ibid*, part III para 2.2(a).
8   See: http://ec.europa.eu/internal_market/company/docs/official/080522web_en.pdf.
9   http://www.anti-moneylaundering.org/globalchart.aspx.
10   'Common Understanding between Member States on third country equivalence under the Anti-Money Laundering Directive (Directive 2005/60/EC)', June 2012. http://ec.europa.eu/internal_market/company/docs/financial-crime/3rd-country-equivalence-list_en.pdf.
11   *Ibid (6)*, part III para 2.2(b).
12   See http://www.jmlsg.org.uk/other-helpful-material/article/regulators-in-fatf-countries.
13   *Ibid (6)*, part III para 2.2(b).
14   The Fourth EU Directive, 2015, Chapter III, article 30(1).
15   *Ibid*, Chapter III, article 30(5).
16   *Ibid (14)* Chapter III, article 31(2).
17   *Ibid (14)* Chapter III, article 31(4).
18   See http://www.fatf-gafi.org/topics/high-riskandnon-cooperativejurisdictions/.
19   http://www.transparency.org/cpi2013.
20   *Ibid(14)* Chapter 1, Section 3, article 9.
21   *Ibid (14)*, Chapter II, section 2 article 15(1).
22   *Ibid (14)*, Chapter II, section 2 article 16/annex II.
23   *Ibid (14)*, Chapter II, section 2 article 15(3).
24   *Ibid (14)*, Chapter II, section 2 article 17.
25   *Ibid (14)*, Chapter II, section 3 article 18(3)/annex III.
26   *Ibid (14)*, Chapter II, section 3 article 18(2).
27   *Ibid (14)*, Chapter II, section 3 article 18(4).

CHAPTER 8

Client verification – Checking and processes

Identification is defined by the Law Society AML practice note as "simply being told or coming to know a client's identifying details, such as their name and address" and verification the process of "obtaining some evidence which supports this claim of identity". Verification can be conducted in various ways – "on the basis of documents, data or information obtained from a reliable and independent source" according to r.5(a) MLR 2007. Whatever the evidence used it will need to provide evidence of certain key attributes of the client; for example, with regard to individuals, their full name and either their home address or date of birth. The verification process involves obtaining an independent check of these identifying features and retaining records for future reference.

Verification will usually take the form of the inspection and copying of original documents, but alternatives include:

- Certification by a third party;
- Electronic verification;
- Annotation of independent information gained other than from the client;
- Reliance on information used by certain other regulated persons; or
- Written assurance by an authorised person from within the regulated sector.

Inspection and copying original documents

In the normal course of events the client's identity will be verified by someone from the firm viewing original documents which support the identification details supplied by the client and which come from "a reliable and independent source" as required by r.5(a) of the MLR 2007. It is important that the firm's representative considers the evidential strength of the documents supplied and they will need to request additional documentation or commission an electronic search if in doubt. Sometimes there will be doubts as to the validity of documents such as passports, on which the Law Society practice note states, at para 4.3.3, that "you should not ignore obvious forgeries, but you are not required to be an expert in forged documents."

In relation to documents that are in a foreign language, the requirement in the Law Society's earlier practice notes to obtain a translation has been relaxed and is now limited to an obligation to "take appropriate steps to be reasonably satisfied that the documents in fact provide evidence of the client's identity" (LSPN para 4.6.1). Depending on the circumstances it may be advisable for a translation of any document to be attached to the evidence to prove to the SRA, or another body, that the document was understood at the time it was accepted as reliable evidence.

A representative of the firm must check the copy against the original document, and then sign and date the copy as a true copy of that original. In the case of photographic evidence, the certifier should confirm that the individual is the person shown in the photograph. When copying a passport or national identity card, only the personal details pages need to be copied and retained. The certified copies must then be kept in accordance with the firm's procedures on record keeping.

Certification by a third party

If it is not possible to obtain original documents, for example where the firm does not see a client in person, the most likely alternative is to obtain copy documents as certified by a third party. There is no prescribed list of individuals or bodies that may provide certification in this way, but the following are suggested categories of certifiers and are listed in order of ease of verification of their identity.

Within the UK:

- The Post Office's Identity Checking Service.[1] This is readily available for a reasonable fee and can be instantly verified because the official Post Office stamp will be placed on each document;
- A credit or financial institution, auditor, insolvency practitioner, external accountant or independent legal professional as defined in r.3; or
- Other professional person, for example, MP, JP, GP, local councillor, minister of religion, officer or teacher.

Outside the UK:

- A British Embassy, Consulate or High Commission official or a notary; or

- A credit, financial institution, auditor, insolvency practitioner, external accountant or independent legal professional as defined in r.3.

To certify a copy document the certifier, if external to the firm, should be required to state on the document that it is a true copy of the original and sign and date the certification with name, occupation and contact details. If there is a photograph on the copy document then an additional declaration should be made which states that this is a true likeness of the client, quoting their name.

It is good practice to verify the identity of the certifier by consulting a professional directory or by some other independent method – this check should also be noted in some way and kept as part of the firm's anti-money laundering records. This has become all the more important in the light of the warnings by the SRA of the increased incidence of bogus firms forming part of fraud conspiracies, with the Risk Outlook of 2015/2016 reporting 701 such known incidents in the first eight months of 2014 alone. The certifier should always be a named and identifiable individual in order that they can be contacted if required.

Electronic verification

Verification by electronic means is becoming increasingly popular amongst law firms and is recognised as being sufficient evidence of an individual's identity in itself under the LSPN at para 4.6.1 – "Electronic verification may be sufficient verification on its own as long as the service provider uses multiple sources of data in the verification process." There remains, however, an apparent contradiction within the practice note in that it also states at para 4.3.3 the rather obvious limitation to the use of electronic identification in that it does not confirm that the client the firm is dealing with is actually the person they claim to be, in which respect the same section suggests mitigating this risk by combining the electronic verification with some other CDD material.

In practice, the approach which appears to be taken by most firms is that electronic verification can be used where the risk identified requires standard due diligence or can also be used as a useful supplement for situations of enhanced CDD where more checking than the norm is required. It is also a useful expedient when the risk is low, for example in relation to existing clients who have already been subject to standard due diligence, or in the case of verification of the identity of directors or beneficial owners where the standard of verification is lower. There are other firms, however, that take the view that this is a more thorough means of checking for the necessary information and use it as a matter of course and in preference to checking the client's documents.

There are several providers of electronic search databases which can be accessed via the internet for a subscription. Most electronic search providers only access data which is available for residents within the UK but certain of the more specialist databases provide access to global lists of higher risk individuals, including PEPs.

It is important to distinguish electronic searches for the purposes of money laundering checks from the more standard credit checks. Credit checks require consent under the Data Protection Act 1998 and access detailed financial information. Money laundering checks access publicly held information and leave a different 'footprint' on the client's electronic file to that left by a credit check and do not therefore affect a client's credit rating.

The Law Society's position as to whether the consent of the client is required for the undertaking of the electronic search has also changed from the earlier guidance and practice notes. Whereas client consent used to be a requirement for the use of electronic searches, the current provision at para 4.3.3 of the practice note is that "you are not required to obtain consent from your client, but they must be informed that this check will take place." Although there is no guidance on the point, the safer view is that merely covering the notification in the terms of business may not be sufficient communication on this point, and that this is therefore one of the issues that should be brought specifically to the client's attention in an early consultation with them or in the retainer letter.

When considering a supplier for electronic checks, a firm should be satisfied that the information provided by that data provider is considered to be reliable and accurate. This judgement may be assisted by considering whether the provider meets the following criteria:[2]

- It is registered with the Information Commissioner's Office to store personal data; and
- It offers services which use a wide range of positive data sources that can be called upon to link applicants to both current and historical data sources. Positive information relates to verification of the full name, address and date of birth of the client. The standard level of verification is usually:
  - One match on full name and current address; and
  - A second match on full name and either full address or date of birth.

Examples of databases which are accessed for positive information include:

- The electoral roll;
- Postal address file;
- Royal Mail address redirection;

- Fixed-line telephone data;
- SHARE records (of bank accounts, mortgage, loans and credit cards);
- FTSE 350 database of UK shareholders;
- 'Directors At Home' data; and
- Electricity supply data.

An agency should use negative screening services which include lists of individuals who are known to have committed identity or other fraud, registers of deceased persons and information relating to county court judgments or insolvencies.

It is also important that a wide range of alert data sources is used, including the identification of PEPs or persons on the HM Treasury list of individuals subject to financial sanctions[3] or specially designated nationals or blocked persons on the US Office of Foreign Assets sanctions list.[4]

The checking process should be transparent, meaning that the firm can know what checks were carried out, what the results of those checks were, and have an indication of how much certainty they give as to the identity of the subject.

Annotation

In certain circumstances the firm will gain independent evidence of identity from a source which is not provided by the client, such as through electronic database searches or copying extracts from a relevant website listing. Examples include:

- Companies House searches;
- Evidence of membership of a professional body, for example, Law Society; and
- Evidence of regulation by a supervisory body, for example, FCA membership.

A copy of such evidence should be kept and preferably be dated and signed by the person who made the copy. The evidence may be stored either as hard copy or in electronic format in accordance with the firm's rules on record keeping.

Reliance

In addition to the certification option, under which the firm secures the assistance of a third party in certifying the necessary information, there is also the procedure of "reliance", whereby the firm will rely on CDD that has been conducted by a third party as defined in r.17(2)(a)-(d). In these circumstances the firm will not be establishing CDD for itself but sharing in the checks undertaken by another organisation. The LSPN observes at para 4.3.4 that "reliance has a very specific meaning within the regulations and relates to the process under regulation 17 where you rely on another regulated person to conduct CDD for you." The distinction is between the firm relying on the third party's checks and thus not having to undertake such checks itself, as opposed to the more usual "certification" process, in which the firm enlists the assistance of another concern to conduct its checks remotely and, in effect, as its agent.

Although reliance may seem an apparently sensible option, a number of complications make this a complex procedure and one which many firms have therefore discounted. The MLR 2007 state at r.17 that the firm, as a regulated body, may rely on a third party's CDD measures provided that the third party consents to such reliance and keeps appropriate records, but the major snag for many is that the firm requesting reliance remains liable for any failure to apply such measures. The firm therefore has not only to seek consent to take the benefit of reliance but also remains liable for any failures in how the process has been conducted down the line.

If a request from another organisation is received there is no obligation for the law firm to permit reliance on its own CDD measures even though it is one of the relatively few organisations upon which reliance can be made. The use of an outsourcing agency – for example, the provider of an electronic database – is not considered to be reliance, searches of this nature being seen instead as a means by which the firm may carry out its own CDD measures through an external agency.

The prerequisites for reliance are:

- The third party is a person defined in r.17(2);
- Consent of the third party;
- Liability is retained by the firm as a regulated body;
- CDD measures are appropriate for reliance;
- The third party is suitable for reliance; and
- The third party confirms that it will provide, on request, copies of verification material and will store such material for a period of five years.

Definition of third party

It is important to note that only certain regulated bodies can be relied on and that this process does not therefore extend to all organisations that are within the regulated sector. A third party is defined at r.17(2)(a)-(d). The definition depends on whether the third party is situated in the UK, EEA or a non-EEA state.

UK

In the UK a firm can rely on r.17(2)(a)(aa)(b):

- A credit or financial institution (excluding a money service business) (r.3(2)(3));
- A consumer credit financial institution (r.22(1)); or
- An auditor, insolvency practitioner, external accountant, tax adviser, or independent legal professional (r.3(4)-(9)).

The credit or financial institution has to be authorised under the Financial Services and Markets Act 2000 by the FCA, with the term "authorised person" defined at s.2(1). It is readily possible to check whether a body is authorised by the FCA as the Financial Services Register can be accessed through the FCA website.[5]

The reference to the consumer credit financial institution was inserted into the MLR 2007 by the Money Laundering (Amendment) Regulations 2012. A definition can be found in r.22(1) MLR 2007.

UK auditors, insolvency practitioners, external accountants, tax advisers or independent legal professionals must be supervised for compliance by one of the bodies set out in a list in Schedule 3 MLR 2007, for example the Law Society, or the Institute of Chartered Accountants in England and Wales. To rely on any member of these bodies, the firm needs to obtain evidence of their membership by accessing the relevant professional website. Interestingly, the list does not include the Institute of Legal Executives.

EEA
The third parties that can be relied on in the EEA (other than the UK) (r.17(2)(c)) are:

- A credit or financial institution (excluding a money service business); or
- An auditor (or equivalent), insolvency practitioner (or equivalent), external accountant, tax adviser, or an independent legal professional.

In relation to such third parties they must be:

"(ii) subject to mandatory professional registration recognised by law; and

(iii) supervised for compliance with the requirements laid down in the [Third Directive] in accordance with section 2 of Chapter V of that directive" (r.17(2)(c)).

A third party will only be supervised for compliance in accordance with the Third Directive if it has been implemented within the member state in question, on which there is a table setting out the extent to which EEA states have implemented the Directive on the Europa website.[6] The International Bar Association Anti-Money Laundering Forum website also lists those member states that have implemented the Third Directive.[7]

Non EEA states

The third parties that can be relied on in non-EEA states are:

- A credit or financial institution (or equivalent) (excluding a money service business); or
- An auditor (or equivalent), insolvency practitioner (or equivalent), external accountant, tax adviser, or an independent legal professional.

In relation to such third parties, according to r.17(2)(d) they must be:

"(ii) subject to mandatory professional registration recognised by law;

(iii) subject to requirements equivalent to those laid down in the [Third Directive]; and

(iv) supervised for compliance with those requirements in a manner equivalent to section 2 of Chapter V of the [Third Directive]."

It is therefore necessary to check that the third party is subject to mandatory professional registration, is situated in an equivalent jurisdiction, and is supervised for compliance with equivalent anti-money laundering legislation. The list, issued by the EU Committee on the Prevention of Money Laundering and Terrorist Financing, of those jurisdictions outside the EEA which are considered to have equivalent anti-money laundering legislation to the Third Directive, is applicable here and has been discussed in Chapter 7. Extreme caution must be taken when relying on CDD carried out by third parties in countries with equivalent jurisdictions, but might be more feasible if the firm has a working relationship with the third party and can easily ascertain that it is subject to mandatory professional registration and is supervised for compliance.

Consent/Letter of reliance

Consent is not defined in r.17 but it is suggested that such consent should be made in writing, so that it is clear to both parties that consent has been given. In actual fact it is advisable to obtain a letter of reliance signed by the third party, stating:

- The identity of the client or beneficial owner, including their full name and address;
- A statement that the CDD measures undertaken meet the requirements of the MLR 2007/Third Directive;
- An indication of the documentary or other evidence obtained;
- Confirmation that the third party will make available, on request, copies of the

relevant documents, data or information obtained or preferably supply copies with the letter; and

- Confirmation that the third party gives consent to reliance being made on the CDD checks undertaken.

Liability
Regulation 17(1)(b) states that the firm, as a regulated body, remains liable for any failure of the third party in applying CDD measures. This means that reliance itself presents a risk and it is advisable that the firm asks for copies of any documents or other information which the third party has used in verifying the client's identity.

Appropriate CDD measures
There are limitations on the type of CDD measures which can be relied on. Such verification must be at the level of standard due diligence. Reliance cannot be placed on measures taken in respect of simplified due diligence or where there is "other exceptional form of verification, such as the use of source of funds as evidence of identity".[8] If a client is higher risk then the firm should carry out its own checks rather than rely on those carried out by a third party. In any event, ongoing monitoring means that reliance is restricted in time and the firm should be alert to the need to carry out its own CDD as part of its ongoing monitoring procedures.

It must be noted that reliance can only be placed on CDD measures carried out by the third party. Reliance cannot take place if the third party has not carried out the checks itself but is relying on checks carried out by another regulated body.

Suitability of a third party
It is necessary to give careful consideration to the suitability of a third party before relying on its CDD measures. In addition to verifying that the third party falls within the definition of persons who can be relied on, careful consideration must also be given to:

- Any public disciplinary record;
- The nature of the client, the service sought and the sums of money involved;
- Any adverse experience of the third party's general efficiency in business dealings; and
- Any other knowledge that the firm has regarding the standing of the third party.[9]

Retention of CDD material and production on request
It is the responsibility of the third party to keep records of the CDD checks for a period

of five years from the date of reliance (r.19(4)). Within that five year period, if requested by the firm the third party has to:

> "as soon as reasonably practicable make available to [the firm] any information about the [client] (and any beneficial owner) which [the third party] obtained when applying [client] due diligence measures" (r. 19(5)(a) and r.19(6)(a)); and

> "as soon as reasonably practicable forward to the [the firm] copies of any identification and verification data and other relevant documents on the identity of the [client] (and any beneficial owner) which [the third party] obtained when applying those measures" (r.19(5)(b) and r.19(6)(b)).

Passporting

Many law firms have offices or networks in other jurisdictions and so reliance on such bodies is advisable. This form of reliance is called "passporting" and it might take a number of different formats:

- The firm may maintain a central database of checks which have been carried out in other jurisdictions. In these circumstances, the firm must ensure that the central database is monitored carefully to ensure that the evidence is compliant with the Third Directive. If this is not the case, the firm must obtain the necessary additional information and add it to the central database;
- A letter of reliance can be sent from the office that carried out the checks to the office that is currently acting for the client. This can only be undertaken if the provisions relating to reliance are met; and
- The office that has carried out the CDD can send the material it has obtained to the office that wishes to carry out checks. This will not be reliance as the receiving office is merely obtaining the evidence in order to carry out its own checks. Such a process is called outsourcing and is similar to certification or electronic searches where evidence is being received via a third party.

Written assurance by an authorised person

It has always been possible for someone in the firm, or even someone from another concern in the regulated sector, to "sign in" a client from their personal knowledge of them. In the earliest Law Society guidance it was suggested that the person giving the assurance needed to have known the new or existing client for at least two years, but the provision in the current LSPN is more general and talks about "a member of the firm or other person in the regulated sector" having known the client "for a number of years" and who is therefore able to attest to their identity (para 4.6.1). The knowledge seems to be in either a personal or professional capacity and only applies to individual clients including directors, trustees or partners.

Different approaches are taken to this option. There are some firms that see it as an eminently sensible way of not having to trouble close contacts and relatives with the need for standard documentation, but others are more cautious. There is a caveat in the Law Society practice note at para 4.6.1 to the effect that the person giving the assurance may not be available if the identity is questioned at a later stage, but this does not seem to trouble most firms unduly. Most firms seem to make a distinction between certification by someone in the firm as opposed to outsiders. Where assurance is adopted, it is often limited to internal certification – and then perhaps for partners only. There are clear benefits in this process, for example when the firm needs to verify the identity of existing clients. Some firms confine this process to checks on existing clients rather than permitting them at the outset of the client relationship. Where the process does include outside organisations, it should be distinguished from reliance, where the firm relies on the identity checks carried out by another regulated body.

Where this option is employed, a certificate of assurance should be given stating the name and address of the client, the number of years that the certifier has known the client and whether in a professional or personal capacity, and the certificate should be signed and dated. If given by someone outside the firm, the person should belong to a regulated body (see the LSPN at 4.6.1) and preferably also belong to a professional body. The certificate should also state their professional status and contact details. It is also necessary to ensure that the person and his firm are listed on the relevant register of the professional body in question.

Notes

1   See http://www.postoffice.co.uk/document-certification-service?intcampaignid= MNidentitydoccert.
2   'Prevention of money laundering / combating terrorist financing: Guidance for the UK financial sector', JMLSG, 2014 Revised Version, part I para 5.3.40; Law Society practice note at 4.3.3.
3   See https://www.gov.uk/government/publications/financial-sanctions-consolidated-list-of-targets.
4   See http://www.treasury.gov/ofac/downloads/t11sdn.pdf.
5   See http://www.fsa.gov.uk/register/firmSearchForm.do.
6   http://ec.europa.eu/internal_market/company/docs/official/080522web_en.pdf.
7   http://www.anti-moneylaundering.org/globalchart.aspx.
8   *Ibid (2)*, part I para 5.6.11.
9   *Ibid (2)*, part I para 5.6.14.

CHAPTER 9

Individual client identification procedures

Individuals seen in person

In order to verify the identity of an individual client, the firm needs to obtain "documents, data or information obtained from a reliable and independent source" (r.5(a) MLR 2007) which relate to the name, address and/or date of birth of the client. A client seen in person will generally be considered to fall within the standard risk category and, as there is a face to face meeting, the most likely option is that they will be asked to bring documentary evidence with them to verify their name and address or date of birth. In all such cases the firm should see the originals and not copies of the documents supplied. A member of the firm – a lawyer or suitably trained secretary or member of reception staff – should make copies of the originals and certify them as true copies of the documents that have been seen. For more details on the certification process see Chapter 8.

Documentary evidence

When a client is met face to face it is easier for the firm to verify the identity of the client, most obviously by comparing the photographic evidence with the person physically present. The former guidance requiring two pieces of evidence – one to prove the name and the other the address – was relaxed in the February 2008 version of the Law Society practice note ("LSPN"), so that in cases of face to face verification it is now permissible to rely on:

- One government document with a photograph which verifies either the full name and address or full name and date of birth; or
- A government document without a photograph which verifies the client's full name, and another supporting document which verifies his full name and address or date of birth (para 4.6.1).

Table 1: Identification documents with photographic evidence

- Current signed passport;
- Current photo-card driving licence (full or provisional);
- Firearms certificate or shotgun licence;
- Current identity card issued by the Electoral Office for Northern Ireland; or
- Residence permit issued by the Home Office.

Notwithstanding this relaxation, most firms continue to request two pieces of evidence, often on grounds that this system is understood by most clients and staff members alike. It is, however, one example of the risk-based approach permitting a lower level of documentation which firms might wish to consider.

A government document is one issued by a government department or agency, or by a court. A supporting document is one that has been issued either by a government source, a judicial authority, a public body, a regulated utility company or an FCA regulated body or similar regulated body in an equivalent jurisdiction.

The types of government documents which contain photographic evidence, and so can be used on their own to verify the client's full name and either his/her address or date of birth, are shown in Table 1.

Table 2 shows examples of government documents without photographic evidence which provide verification of the client's full name (List A) and supporting documents which verify both the client's name and their residential address (List B). Where possible, one document from each list should be obtained.

Other methods of verification

Although obtaining documentary evidence may be the norm when the client is met in person there are alternatives, which include:

- Electronic verification – The LSPN states at para 4.6.1 that, where it is not possible to obtain documentary evidence, the firm will need to "consider the reliability of other sources and the risks associated with the client and the retainer". It states that "electronic verification may be sufficient on its own as long as the service provider uses multiple sources of data in the verification process". It is commonplace for firms to use electronic databases to confirm the identity of the client. In addition, electronic verification could be used where no Table 2 List B documentation is available to support the document obtained from Table 2 List A. For further information on electronic verification see Chapter 8;

Table 2: Identification documents without photographic evidence

List A Government documents showing full name	List B Supporting documents showing residential address
• Valid old style full driving licence; or • Recent evidence of entitlement to a state or local authority benefit (including housing benefit and council tax benefit), tax credit, pensions, educational or other grant.	• Current bank, building society or credit union statement or passbook containing current address; • Local council tax bill for current year; • Recent utility bill or statement (not mobile telephone bills); • Recent mortgage statement; • Solicitor's letter confirming recent house purchase or land registry confirmation of address; • Local council or housing association rent card or tenancy agreement; • HMRC self-assessment statement or tax demand; • House or motor insurance certificate; • Cheque or electronic transfer drawn on an account in the name of the client with a regulated financial institution; or • Instrument of a court appointment (for example, grant of probate). Note: None of these documents may have been obtained from the internet. The assumption is that hard copies will have been delivered to the client at the address given.

- Reliance – The firm may rely on a third party's CDD checks. Third parties are credit or financial institutions, a consumer credit financial institution, an auditor, insolvency practitioner, external accountant, tax adviser, or an independent legal professional in accordance with the provisions set out in r.17 MLR 2007 (for further information on reliance see Chapter 8); or
- Written assurance – This is given by a member of the firm, preferably a partner, or a member of another regulated body and states that they have known the client personally or professionally for a number of years. For further information see Chapter 8.

If a client who is met in person is considered to be higher risk the firm should obtain additional documentation corroborating their name and address or date of birth. This may include additional documentation from the lists above or conducting an electronic search as a supplement to the standard documentation requirements.

Individuals not seen in person
Enhanced due diligence is required when an individual client is not met in person.

> "Where the [client] has not been physically present for identification purposes, [the firm] must take specific and adequate measures to compensate for the higher risk" (r.14(2)).

The explanation provided by the Law Society for this approach is that clients who are seeking to engage in criminal activity will often try to limit the amount that a solicitor knows about them and their transaction, which is clearly easier when the client is not met in person. There are also advantages in being able to interview the client face to face and gauge their reactions to questions that are put to them. In the normal course of events the same documentary evidence should be obtained as if the client had been met in person, but further checking should also be undertaken such as:

- Obtaining evidence which is additional to that required of a client seen in person, for example, additional identification documents from Table 1 or Table 2 Lists A or B;
- Undertaking an electronic search;
- Asking the client to produce certified copies of the standard documents; or
- Ensuring the first payment in the retainer is made through an account opened in the client's name with a bank. This is because EU regulations that came into force on 1 January 2007 require that credit institutions must provide the payer's name, address and account number with all electronic fund transfers.[1] As such, the firm would be able to check whether the account details are the same as the identity details provided by the client.

Politically exposed persons
The other situation where EDD will be required for individuals can be found at r.14(4) in relation to PEPs. This is on the basis that those who hold or have recently held high political office present a higher money laundering risk as their position brings with it greater opportunity for corruption. The fact that someone is a PEP does not, of course, necessarily mean that any money laundering activity has occurred, but the client will be placed in a higher risk category and additional steps must therefore be taken in conducting the CDD process with them.

In order to comply with these requirements a firm should, as part of its overall risk analysis, determine the extent to which clients may be PEPs. It should consider the existing client base, taking into account the general demographics, and how many clients are currently known to be PEPs. Where the firm has a higher risk of having PEPs as clients, it should introduce measures that are designed to determine whether clients are PEPs and what kind of investigations should be made to satisfy the requirement to undertake enhanced due diligence, including the steps set out in r.14(4). The higher the risk of money laundering activities, the greater the measures the firm needs to undertake to identify PEPs in its client base. The highest risk is generally presented by individuals who are linked to corrupt jurisdictions, in which respect the Corruption Perception Index (as referred to in Chapter 6) is useful to assist in determining the level of corruption in a jurisdiction and so the level of risk presented.

The LSPN states at para 4.9.2, "If the risk of you acquiring a PEP as a client is low, you may simply wish to ask clients whether they fall within any of the PEP categories." In practice, asking most clients in most firms if they have in the last year been in the sort of high profile international position described may seem very odd, and it is quite clearly the case that most fee earners do not do so most of the time, if ever. The design of compliance forms can therefore be of assistance by providing a prompt for the issue to be addressed as required.

Definition of a PEP

A PEP is defined at r.14(5) as "an individual who is or has, at any time in the preceding year, been entrusted with a prominent public function by (i) a state other than the United Kingdom; a Community institution; or an international body". This includes a non-exhaustive list of those who are:

"(i) heads of state, heads of government, ministers and deputy or assistant ministers;

(ii) members of parliaments;

(iii) members of supreme courts, of constitutional courts or of other high-level judicial bodies whose decisions are not generally subject to further appeal, other than in exceptional circumstances;

(iv) members of courts of auditors or of the boards of central banks;

(v) ambassadors, chargés d'affaires and high-ranking officers in the armed forces; and

(vi) members of the administrative, management or supervisory bodies of state-owned enterprises" (Schedule 2, para 4(1)(a)).

As to the level of seniority required, the definition of a PEP does not cover middle-ranking or junior officials or individuals who hold office below national level, but the JMLSG guidance states that "when their political exposure is comparable to that of similar positions at national level [...] firms should consider, on a risk-based approach, whether persons exercising those public functions should be considered as PEPs."[2] Currently, domestic PEPs are not subject to EDD but the Fourth Directive extends the definition of PEP to include domestic PEPs, meaning that the local MP will no longer escape from the rigours of enhanced due diligence once the new Directive is enacted into English law.[3]

Although under the definition of PEP an individual ceases to be regarded as one after he has left office after 12 months, it may also be advisable to undertake checks on individuals even if they have left office longer ago than the 12 month period. The 12 month period appears to be an arbitrary cut-off point given the overall risk-based approach of the Third Directive. In the Fourth Directive, where the PEP has ceased to hold office the firm is required to consider the continuing risk posed by the PEP and to apply such appropriate and risk sensitive measures until such time as that person is deemed to pose no further risk. This period of time is stated to be for at least 12 months.[4] If a public authority outside the UK – rather than an individual – instructs a firm, this does not mean that the firm is entering a relationship with PEPs. However, it is necessary to apply CDD measures in relation to the public authority.

It is also important to bear in mind that family members (r.14(5(b)) and known close associates (r.14(5)(c)) also fall under the definition of PEPs, as is the case under the Fourth Directive also. Family members include the client's spouse, partner, children and their spouses or partners, and parents (Schedule 2, paragraph 4(1)(c)) and a partner is a person who is considered by their national law as being equivalent to a spouse (Schedule 2, paragraph 4(2)). The term "known close associates" includes:

> "(i) any individual who is known to have joint beneficial ownership of a legal entity or legal arrangement, or any other close business relations, with a person [who is a PEP]; and
>
> (ii) any individual who has sole beneficial ownership of a legal entity or legal arrangement which is known to have been set up for the benefit of a person [who is a PEP]" (Schedule 2, paragraph 4(1)(d))."

Unfortunately, getting to grips with just precisely who is to be regarded as a PEP is not straightforward, all the more so in relation to family members and close associates. As an alternative to simply asking the client about their status, firms might use internet search engines, databases and other electronic sources. Since the commercial databases that are available for these purposes operate primarily by scanning the media for the profile of individuals and their allegiances they are far from foolproof, but perhaps more importantly for the firm it will have met its responsibilities in this regard if it has made such searches and has considered the other evidence available to it from the instructions it has received.

In the case of close associates of a PEP, the firm does not need actively to research whether a person falls within that category – it only needs to have regard to information which is in its possession or publicly known (r.14(6)). This indicates that, even in high risk situations, the firm does not have to access specialist databases but may instead rely on internet search engines and other freely available material. Likewise, the firm does not need to actively investigate whether any beneficial owners are PEPs. If it is aware that any beneficial owner is a PEP, however, then it is necessary for the firm to decide what additional measures need to be taken. Looking forward, the Fourth Directive extends the definition of a PEP to include not just clients but beneficial owners too.[5]

Application of enhanced due diligence to PEPs

The enhanced due diligence measures the firm must undertake if a client is a PEP are to:

"(a) have approval from senior management for establishing the business relationship with that person;

(b) take adequate measures to establish the source of wealth and source of funds which are involved in the proposed business relationship or occasional transaction; and

(c) where the business relationship is entered into, conduct enhanced ongoing monitoring of the relationship." (r.14(4))

The term "senior management" is not defined in the Regulations but the Law Society practice note suggests at para 4.9.2 that senior management may be:

- "the head of a practice group
- another partner who is not involved with the particular file
- the partner supervising the particular file
- the nominated officer
- the managing partner".

The JMLSG guidance states that approval has to be sought "from a higher level of authority from the person seeking such approval."[6] The Fourth Directive defines senior management as "an officer or employee with sufficient knowledge of the institution's money laundering and terrorist financing risk exposure and sufficient seniority to take decisions affecting its risk exposure, and need not, in all cases, be a member of the board of directors".[7] The best arrangement might be to have to seek approval from the managing partner or nominated officer, both of whom will have had more direct experience of the firm's anti-money laundering practice and procedures and greater knowledge of the firm's overall risk profile, or from a specialist committee set up for client acceptance in these situations. This will also enable them to compile a list of known PEPs amongst the firm's client base for future reference.

Where a client has been identified as a PEP, the firm has to undertake measures designed to identify his/her source of wealth and the source of any funds which will be used in connection with the proposed business transaction. This will involve asking the PEP and consulting any relevant register of interests. Some jurisdictions expect senior public officials to file asset and income declarations. If the information received does not adequately explain the level of funds available then further investigation will need to be undertaken or the firm will be unable to act for that client.

Ongoing monitoring requires the firm to remain alert as to whether a client may be a PEP or, if a PEP, that the source of wealth/funds may be as a result of corruption or fraud. If funds are received from a government account, the client communicates with the firm from an official source or the firm gains certain information from the media about the client, this should be investigated as these might indicate that the client is a PEP.

Non-UK residents

The types of documentary evidence required for verification of the ID of non-UK residents met in person are the same as for UK residents but a national identity card can be used in the place of a passport. The JMLSG guidance suggests that this should be restricted to national identity cards from EEA member states or Switzerland.[8] The firm should not, however, rely on just one piece of documentary evidence from Table 1 such as a passport or national identity card; it is advisable for it also to request at least one supporting document from Table 2 List B. This is especially important in countries outside the EEA which do not have equivalent AML or CTF legislation.

If the firm is concerned that any documents may not be genuine, it should contact the relevant embassy or consulate in the UK. If documents provided are in a foreign language then it is necessary for the firm to be satisfied that they do provide evidence of the person's identity. A translation should be sought if required, but is no longer a requirement as such (see the LSPN at para 4.6.1). Commercial software is available which can check the validity of passports or national identity cards, provided they are machine-readable so that the algorithms used to generate passport numbers can be checked, which assists in countering the risk of identity fraud.

When the client is not met in person the usual documentary evidence should be sought, but the supporting address evidence (see list B in Table 2 above) is likely to become more important even if a passport or national identity card is provided. Suitable additional steps will be required in any event to meet the need for enhanced due diligence (r.14). One of the most common additional checks will be for the firm to ensure that copies of the standard documents are certified as set out in Chapter 8, but this might pose difficulties in relation to ensuring the authenticity of the firm or person providing this service. Ideally they should be registered with an appropriate professional body or similar and can be checked as such, but obtaining such evidence can sometimes be difficult. It is therefore suggested that one or more of the following checks should be considered in addition to those set out for standard due diligence:

- Obtaining evidence which is additional to that required of a non-UK resident seen in person, for example, additional identification documents from Table 1 or Table 2 Lists A or B;
- Certification of the foreign passports/identity card and any supporting documentation by the local British embassy or consulate or in accordance with its directions, or by a Notary Public; or
- The first payment in the retainer is made through an account in the client's name. Within EEA member states all credit institutions must provide payee name, and account number with all electronic fund transfers, along with address details if required.

In relation to the address details of clients based overseas the LSPN suggests at para 4.6.1 that evidence of the individual's address may also be obtained from an official overseas source or a reputable directory. It does not give any examples, however, and it can be difficult to ascertain whether a source is official or reputable. There are additional problems in states or territories where the address details consist of Post Office numbers rather than street names and numbers, with earlier Law Society pilot guidelines having suggested that "a post box number alone is not normally sufficient evidence of address".[9]

Professionals
If the client is a professional person subject to regulation by a recognised body such as the Law Society or the Institute of Chartered Accountants in England and Wales, the risk

presented is generally low since such persons are subject to an annual renewal of their practising certificates or membership. If such a person is acting in their professional capacity, it is acceptable to access the relevant professional directory to check their name and business address and there is no need to check their home address.

Much the same considerations apply to foreign professionals, provided the directory is maintained by their professional body and the information is translated if necessary. It may be advisable to restrict this method of verification to those professionals on whom the firm can place reliance in accordance with r.17 MLR 2007, because they can be traced more easily and are generally subject to professional codes of conduct. This includes banks, independent legal professionals and external accountants.

If a professional person is acting in their personal capacity, their identity needs to be verified as for any other private individual, and reliance on an entry in a professional directory alone is not sufficient for this purpose.

Well-known individuals

If a client is well-known, either nationally or internationally, then the firm may decide it is sufficient to make a file note to that effect, although this will need to include a residential address. It is important to bear in mind, however, that this does not negate the need to examine the business relationship, including the source of wealth of such individuals. If they hold an overseas government office they may be a PEP and should therefore be subject to the more stringent requirements set out in r.14(4) MLR 2007.

Existing clients

The MLR 2003 contained an exemption for clients already known to the firm as of the commencement date for those provisions – 1st March 2004 – but this exemption was removed when the MLR 2007 took effect with r.7(2) stating that CDD measures would have to be applied to existing clients as well as those who were new to the firm. Existing clients are defined as persons who were clients of the firm before 15th December 2007, when the MLR 2007 came into force. Such due diligence has to be carried out at "appropriate times" and "on a risk-sensitive basis". This could mean repeating the entire CDD process from time to time but a more limited form of verification should normally be possible, usually to be conducted when the client enters into a new retainer with the firm. In many cases the updating might be limited to address evidence only.

There are three possible forms of verification under this option:

- The firm may consider information already held on files, which would verify the client's identity;

- If a member of the firm, preferably a partner, or another person within the regulated sector, has known the client for a number of years, they can give a written assurance as to the client's name and home address (see Chapter 8 for more details); or
- The firm could consider undertaking an electronic search to confirm the name and address of the client. The search should comply with the requirements for electronic searches (see Chapter 8 for more details).

Individuals unable to produce standard documentation

Certain clients will not be able to produce standard documentation, although not for any reason associated with higher risk, and it is not intended to make access to legal services difficult to obtain for these people. In such circumstances it is necessary to decide whether the inability to produce the standard documentation is consistent with the client's profile and circumstances, or whether there are reasons giving rise to an enhanced risk of money laundering or terrorist financing. Some clients – the elderly, most obviously – may not have a passport or driving licence, or their name may not appear on utility bills.

Where it is decided that a client has a good reason for not meeting the standard verification requirements, the firm may accept alternative methods of verification. Examples of clients who may not be able to produce standard documentation and alternative methods of verification are:

Joint clients

In the case of joint clients, both individuals have to provide documentary evidence of their identity. In certain cases, one of them may not have evidence of address because, for example, all the household bills are in the name of the other person. In such circumstances the firm might rely on alternative proof of address such as an NHS medical card or a letter confirming receipt of child benefit.

Asylum seekers

The firm should be able to obtain the registration card of asylum seekers, but as an alternative the firm could seek a letter of assurance from an official authority, lawyer or member of the medical profession who has had dealings with the person.

Refugees

The refugee might be able to provide a letter from the Home Office confirming their refugee status and granting permission to work, or a Home Office travel document for refugees.

Students or minors
The firm should see their passport or photo driving licence, if possible. If they do not hold such documents they should be asked to provide their birth certificate or NHS medical card and confirmation of their parents' address. Alternatively, they could provide a letter of confirmation from their school or other place of study. Where a family member or guardian is acting on behalf of a child, their identity also needs to be verified.

Residents in care homes
The firm could obtain an entitlement letter from the Department for Work and Pensions confirming that the person is in receipt of a state pension. If this is not available a letter from an appropriate person – for example, the manager or matron of the care home – could be sought.

Clients with mental health problems
The firm should approach medical workers, hostel staff, social workers, or receivers or guardians appointed by the court who could locate appropriate identification documents or confirm the client's identity.

Clients with no permanent address
The firm should consider obtaining a letter from a householder named on a current council tax bill or a hostel manager, confirming temporary residence.

Agents
Agency falls within the concept of beneficial ownership. The agent is the client and it is the principal who is to be regarded as the beneficial owner. Regulation 6(9) states that "beneficial owner" means "the individual who ultimately owns or controls the [client] or on whose behalf a transaction is being conducted."

It is presumed an individual client is acting on his own behalf, unless there are aspects of the transaction which indicate he is in fact acting on behalf of someone else (see the LSPN at 4.7.3). The firm does not have to search for principals, but needs to make enquiries when it appears the client is acting as an agent for a third party. The agent is the client and as such their identity needs to be verified according to the type of individual concerned; for example, met/not met in person. Common examples of agency include:

- Exercising a power of attorney;
- Acting as a receiver, administrator or insolvency practitioner; and
- Acting as an appointed broker or other agent.

In such cases, appointment documents or signed letters of appointment will constitute adequate measures sufficient to establish the identity of the principal. The identity of the agent will need to be verified in the normal way according to whether or not they have been seen in person.

In determining whether the agent presents a higher risk, the risk assessment must address reasons why agency is being used. The LSPN suggests at para 4.7.2 that in assessing whether the risk is standard or higher a number of factors might be taken into account, such as the reasons for the client being represented and whether they are doing so in a personal or professional capacity, and any international implications in the arrangement. The most important point is that the principal should be treated as a beneficial owner and so the firm has to verify their identity accordingly.

Notes

1. Regulation (EC) No 1781/2006 on information on the payer accompanying transfer of funds, but from 26th June 2017 these regulations will be replaced by Regulation 2015/847.
2. 'Prevention of money laundering / combating terrorist financing: Guidance for the UK financial sector', JMLSG, 2014 Revised Version, part I, para 5.5.21.
3. The Fourth Directive, 2015. Chapter 1, section 1, article 3(9).
4. *Ibid (3)*, Chapter II, section 3 article 22.
5. *Ibid (3)*, Chapter II, section 3 article 20(a).
6. *Ibid (2)*, part I para 5.5.31.
7. *Ibid (3)*, Chapter I, section 1 article 3(12).
8. *Ibid (2)*, part I para 5.3.66.
9. Law Society Pilot AML Guidance, para 3.88.

CHAPTER 10

Corporate client identification procedures

In some respects it should be easier to establish CDD with corporations since they, unlike individuals or most other legal bodies, are subject to legal obligations to file records on a publicly available register. The greatest disclosure requirements apply to companies listed on a stock exchange or other regulated market but even the smallest of private companies are obliged to file certain documents at regular intervals with a central body, such as Companies House in the UK.

Public companies are subject to a high level of regulation and therefore present a low risk of money laundering or terrorist financing and are therefore subject to "simplified due diligence" under r.13 MLR 2007. Most private companies present a standard risk but may become higher risk if, for example:

- They are associated with higher risk jurisdictions;
- There is lack of transparency in their ownership or control structure; or
- The names of beneficial ownership are difficult to ascertain.

There may also be other factors, relating not so much to client identity but rather to the intended business relationship, which pose a higher risk. The most common examples in practice are where the business activities are unclear or the source of funding is unknown.

Although each client has to be assessed according to its own perceived risk, there are certain generic criteria which are outlined below. These provide guidance as to the level of risk associated with particular types of corporate bodies and the type of CDD measures which should therefore be undertaken.

Public companies

The MLR 2007 expressly state, at r.13(3), that simplified due diligence applies where the client "is a company whose securities are listed on a regulated market subject to specified disclosure obligations". Such companies are publicly owned and subject to strict disclosure obligations, which means they are already regulated by such regime and so no verification of identity is required. Regulation 13(1) states that, in these circumstances, a regulated body "is not required to apply [client] due diligence measures" provided there are "reasonable grounds for believing" that the client falls within the stated definition. As such, it is merely necessary to check that the company is actually listed on the relevant market and there is no need to obtain the evidence of the directors or shareholders. Any company listed on a market which is not subject to the required disclosure obligations will need to have its identity verified in accordance with the provisions relating to private companies.

Public companies listed in the UK or majority-owned subsidiaries
The regulated market within the UK is the London Stock Exchange. Although CDD is not required if a company is listed on this market, evidence of listing needs to be obtained, which can be:

- A copy of the listing page, dated, from the website of London Stock Exchange (www.londonstockexchange.com); or
- A photocopy of the listing from a reputable daily newspaper (dated).

Simplified due diligence can also be used to verify the identity of a majority-owned and consolidated subsidiary of a listed company. In addition to evidence that the parent is listed on the relevant market, evidence of the parent/subsidiary relationship is also required, such evidence being available from:

- The subsidiary's last filed annual return;
- A note in the last audited accounts of the parent or subsidiary; or
- Information from a reputable electronic verification service provider or online registry.

Both the latest annual return and audited accounts can be obtained from a search at Companies House, subject to a small charge.

No checks on shareholders or directors are required if the company is listed on a recognised exchange or is a majority owned subsidiary and although ongoing monitoring is required, this should usually be relatively limited as the risk presented is low.

AIM is not considered a regulated market (for reasons of price transparency), but both the LSPN (at para 4.6.3) and the JMLSG guidelines[1] indicate that it is probably sufficient to treat an AIM company in the same way as one listed on the Stock Exchange for the purposes of simplified due diligence. Details of the AIM market can be found on the London Stock Exchange website.

Public overseas companies – Within the EEA
Regulated markets within the EEA fall within the ambit of the Markets in Financial Instruments Directive[2] (MiFID) which was passed to ensure the development of a single securities market for both new issues and trading of securities in the EEA. For simplified due diligence to apply, the firm needs to check that the company is listed on a market which is regulated within the meaning of MiFID.[3] The firm must retain a copy of dated evidence of such listing from the website of the relevant exchange. Simplified due diligence also applies to any majority-owned and consolidated subsidiary of a listed company within the EEA, provided evidence is also obtained of the parent/subsidiary relationship.

Public overseas companies – Outside the EEA
Companies listed on markets outside the EEA can be subject to simplified due diligence provided the market is subject to "specified disclosure obligations", as defined in r.2, which provides that such obligations must be consistent with the relevant articles of the following directives:

- The Prospectus Directive (2003/71/EC) – this relates to prospectuses to be published when securities are offered to the public or admitted to trading. The relevant articles are 3, 5, 7, 8, 10, 14 and 16;
- The Transparency Obligations Directive (2004/109/EC) – this relates to the harmonisation of transparency requirements in relation to information about issuers whose securities are admitted to trading on a regulated market. The relevant articles are 4 to 6, 14, 16 to 19 and 30; and
- The Market Abuse Directive (2003/6/EC) – which relates to insider dealing and market manipulations. The relevant articles are 6(1) to (4).

If the market is consistent with the relevant articles of these Directives, then evidence of such listing is sufficient and, if a majority-owned subsidiary, evidence of the parent subsidiary relationship must also be obtained. Evidence of listing should be available from the website of the relevant market. Any copy should be dated and kept in accordance with the record keeping procedures of the firm and evidence of any parent/subsidiary relationship can be obtained from the relevant registry in the country of incorporation. A list of worldwide registries can be obtained from the Companies House website.[4]

Credit or financial institutions

Simplified due diligence is also applied to credit or financial institutions which are within the EEA and are subject to the requirements of the Third Directive or within a non-EEA state, provided they are subject to anti-money laundering requirements which are equivalent to those laid down in the Third Directive and are supervised for compliance with those requirements (r.13(2)(b)).

The definitions of a credit and a financial institution are set out in r.3(2) and 3(3), both definitions referring to the Banking Consolidation Directive 2006/48/EC. A credit institution has to fall within the definition as set out in Article 4(1)(a) of this directive but only "when it accepts deposits or other repayable funds from the public or grants credits for its own account" (r.3(2)).

A financial institution is one which falls within the list set out in r.3(3) and includes one which carries out one or more of the activities listed in Schedule 1 of the MLR 2007. These are:

- Lending (including consumer credit and mortgage credit);
- Financial leasing;
- Money transmission services;
- Issuing and administering means of payment (including credit cards and travellers' cheques);
- Guarantees and commitments;
- Trading in money market instruments, foreign exchange, financial futures and options, exchange and interest-rate instruments, and transferable securities;
- Participation in securities issues, advice to undertakings on capital structures;
- Money broking;
- Portfolio management and advice;
- Safekeeping and administration of securities; and
- Safe custody services.

Credit or financial institutions within the UK/EEA

In order to qualify for simplified due diligence, credit or financial institutions within the UK/EEA must be subject to the requirements of the Third Directive. Member states within the EEA benefit from a presumption that they comply with these provisions and as such, institutions in those countries benefit from the application of simplified due diligence. See Chapter 7 for further details.

Although all member states of the EEA were supposed to have implemented the Third Directive by 15th December 2007, this was not universally the case. Where there are doubts to suggest that a presumption of equivalence cannot be sustained it will be necessary to consider whether their procedures should be enhanced to take account of this information. For the up-to-date position of the implementation of the Third Directive across the EEA, reference should be made to the Europa website[5] or the website of the International Bar Association Anti-Money Laundering Forum.[6]

All institutions subject to the requirements of the Third Directive must be supervised for compliance by a supervisory authority or regulator in accordance with Article 37 of that Directive. In the UK this is the FCA.[7] A list of regulators in other EEA countries can be found on the JMLSG website.[8]

Credit or financial institutions outside the EEA
In order to benefit from simplified due diligence, credit or financial institutions situated outside the EEA must be located in a jurisdiction that has anti-money laundering provisions equivalent to the Third Directive and must be supervised for compliance with such provisions. Details of those jurisdictions which are considered to have equivalent AML provisions have been set out in Chapter 7. Institutions that are situated in such countries must also be subject to supervision for compliance and a list of regulators in FATF counties can be found on the JMLSG website.

Application of simplified due diligence to credit and financial institutions
It must be remembered that simplified due diligence only applies in respect of client identification and so does not therefore exempt the firm from carrying out ongoing monitoring of the business relationship with the client, or from the need for such other procedures as may be necessary to enable a firm to fulfil its responsibilities under POCA or TA.

Other regulated bodies
Other bodies which are regulated by the MLR 2007 are not covered by r.13 with the result that simplified due diligence does not apply. As such, their identity needs to be verified in accordance with their legal status, for example as private companies, but if it is a professional practice its identity can be checked by reference to the membership directory of its professional society, for example the Law Society's Find a Solicitor search.

Statutory licensing

Certain companies may not have their securities listed on a relevant market and yet be subject to statutory licensing and regulation due to the nature of their industry, for example, water, gas, electricity or telecommunications. Although the MLR 2007 do not state that these companies can be subject to simplified due diligence, the JMLSG guidelines indicate that they may be treated in this way if it is considered that there exists "an equivalent level of confidence in the company's public accountability" (part 1 para 5.3.149). As such they state that evidence that a company is subject to the licensing and prudential regulatory regime of a statutory regulator in the EU will satisfy the firm's obligation to verify its identity. Such regulatory companies in the UK include Ofgem, Ofwat and Ofcom.

Subsidiaries of existing clients

The LSPN states at para 4.6.3 that if the firm starts to act for a subsidiary of an existing client, it may refer to the CDD checks carried out on the parent company client for verification details of the subsidiary. This is subject to the proviso that the existing client has been identified to the level required by the MLR 2007. However, such checks may not be up to date and reliance on these checks does not obviate the need for ongoing monitoring.

Companies well-known in sector/household names

Companies that are household names or well-known and long-established within their particular sector may be considered to be low risk. It may be appropriate to rely on details from their website and the fact that written correspondence is sent to the recognised business address and replies are received from that address on official headed notepaper. It is, however, always appropriate to ensure that the firm is dealing with an authorised representative of the company who has the authority to give instructions, and for the firm to know who has the relevant authority to sign any legal documentation.

Private and unlisted companies

Private unlisted companies may present a standard or higher risk depending on their structure, ownership, purpose and nature of activities. The smaller private companies are generally owned by a small number of individuals and are subject to some, but not extensive, public disclosure and controls. Nonetheless, the structure, ownership and commercial activities of such companies are usually clear and relatively comprehensible. As such, they generally only require standard due diligence, with verification of identity relating not only to the company but also the directors and, in certain circumstances, their shareholders as beneficial owners.

Private companies may be considered to be higher risk if the structure, ownership or purpose is complex or unclear or their activities fall into areas which increase the likelihood of money laundering or terrorist financing occurring. They may also be situated in a high risk jurisdiction (see Chapter 7).

The JMLSG guidelines state that corporate clients may be higher risk if they are "smaller and more opaque entities, with little or no industry profile and those in less transparent jurisdictions..." (part 1 para 5.3.151). Where such a client is linked to a PEP or a jurisdiction assessed as carrying a higher money laundering/terrorist financing risk, this will put the entity into a higher risk category in which case reference should be made to the list of higher risk jurisdictions issued by FATF (see Chapter 7). Money laundering risks are likely to be lower where the company is incorporated or operating in an EEA state or a country which is a member of FATF.

Identification and verification

To identify a private limited company, the firm needs to obtain the following information:

- Full name;
- Registered number;
- Registered office; and
- Details of directors and beneficial owners.

The extent of verification of identity depends on the level of risk presented in any particular case. Verification of identity needs to be undertaken in relation to the company, its directors and beneficial owners. For standard verification in the UK, the firm needs to undertake a Companies House, or similar electronic, search to verify the registered name, number and office of the company. This can be done by undertaking a free WebCheck search, which is available on the Companies House website.[9] For non-UK companies, it is possible to carry out the equivalent of Companies House searches in many jurisdictions – the list of world-wide registries can be viewed on the Companies House website.[10]

Verification for higher-risk companies could include further questions being asked of the instructing directors, relating not just to the identity of the firm but also its business activities, financial position and source of funding. Further evidence could also be obtained from Companies House, such as a copy of the last financial accounts.

Directors

The identity of directors does not necessarily have to be verified in accordance with the provisions for individuals. The spectrum of checks available depends on the nature of the risk presented and will range from gaining the names and addresses of the directors to full identity checks as for individuals. Suggested checks (ascending in accordance with the level of risk) are:

- Obtaining a copy of the current appointments register which details past and current directors and their home addresses, available from a Companies House search;
- Undertaking an online check for individuals using a reputable electronic verification database provider; or
- Carrying out a full identity check in accordance with the provisions for individuals depending on whether or not they are seen in person.

A director may also be required to be identified as a beneficial owner if they own or control more than 25% of the company's shares or voting rights. In the early days of the AML regime it was necessary to conduct full personal checks against at least two directors, but this requirement was relaxed some time ago so that, as now stated:

"The key identification particulars are the company's name and its business address, although the registration number and names of directors may also be relevant identification particulars." (LSPN para 4.6.3)

The effect of this is to relax the requirements in relation to directors to the lower level of those holding beneficial interests, but many firms continue to adopt the 'belt and braces' approach on this issue and conduct full personal checks on the individuals concerned, particularly when dealing with new instructions. The LSPN states at para 4.6.3 that identity checks need only be taken in respect of two directors, but the number of directors checked will again depend on the level of risk. If only two are subject to verification, then preferably this should be the director who is authorised to give instructions and the director who is responsible for the financial dealings of the company, usually the finance director.

Similar steps should be taken in respect of directors of overseas companies.

Beneficial owners

The firm needs to identify and verify the identity of those shareholders or other persons who fall within the definition of beneficial owners. In the case of a body corporate r.6(1) provides that a beneficial owner means "any individual who [...] ultimately owns or controls (whether through direct or indirect ownership or control, including through bearer share holdings) more than 25% of the shares or voting rights in the body; or [...] otherwise exercises control over the management of the body."

The MLR 2007 do not provide a definition of shares and voting rights and, in any event, such terms are increasingly too general and simplistic to take into account the different classes of share ownership and voting rights often found in modern company structures. The LSPN states at para 4.7.4, "Voting rights are only those which are currently exercisable and attributed to the company's issued equity share capital." The best approach is probably to take into account only ordinary and preferred ordinary shares which have full voting rights when looking at beneficial ownership, whilst preference shares which do not have voting rights should be disregarded.

Beneficial ownership is easy to ascertain where there is one corporate body but is not so straightforward where there are several layers in a corporate body. The ESAs' 2012 report[11] indicates that there are two ways to assess the percentage shareholding to see if the 25% threshold has been met. Under a "top down approach" the ultimate beneficial owner is one who owns or controls more than 25% of the shares or voting rights of the client company, but under a "bottom up approach" the ultimate beneficial owner is the person who owns or controls more than 25% of any entity that owns more than 25% of the client company. This is best explained in diagrammatic form (see Figure 1).

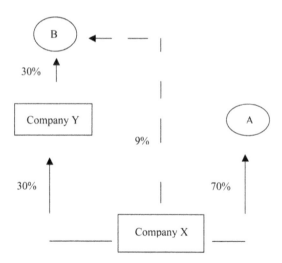

Figure 1: 'Top down' and 'bottom up' assessments of percentage shareholdings

In the example given, Company X is the client. The question is whether B is the ultimate beneficial owner. B owns more than 25% of an entity which owns more than 25% of Company X and would therefore be a beneficial owner on a bottom up approach.

However, on a top down approach B ultimately owns (indirectly) only 9% of Company X and so does not qualify as an ultimate beneficial owner.

According to the ESAs' 13 member states follow a "top down" approach and 11 take "the bottom up" approach, with the UK appearing to take a top down approach. The Law Society, at para 4.7.4 of the practice note, recognises that it may be disproportionate to search through multiple layers to find an individual in ultimate control, and therefore provides that the firm should apply a proportionate approach to the identification of beneficial owners. The most important thing is for the firm to have an overall understanding of the ownership and control of the client structure.

The verification requirements under the MLR 2007 are different as between a client and a beneficial owner. Regulation 5 states that the identity of clients must be verified on the basis of documents obtained from a reliable and independent source, whereas the obligation to verify the identity of a beneficial owner is for the firm to take "adequate measures on a risk-sensitive basis" so that it is satisfied it knows who the beneficial owner is, which includes the ownership and control structure of the company (r.5(b)).

As a pre-requisite to any CDD, the firm needs to identify if there are any beneficial owners and obtain their names. This information may be available from the client but, if not, a list of shareholders could be obtained from a copy of the latest filed annual return, together with any amendments made since that date. This information can be obtained from Companies House (or similar overseas registry). It may also be necessary to obtain a copy of the articles of association, to determine the voting rights which attach to the various classes of shares. The identity of the person who is in ultimate control through its shareholdings at the highest level may be disclosed in the latest copy of the audited accounts at Companies House.

Verification of the identity of beneficial owners needs to be carried out on a risk-sensitive basis. Examples of the type of checks that could be carried out, in ascending order of risk, are:

- Written assurance from the client as to the existence of beneficial owners;
- Written assurance from regulated bodies, such as banks, independent legal professionals or external accountants who have been acting for the client and who have the relevant information;
- Online search at Companies House or similar overseas online registry;
- Electronic search from a reputable service provider; or
- Full identity checking as for individuals who are not physically present for the purposes of verification.

Companies with capital in the form of bearer shares are considered to be higher risk as they are often incorporated in countries without equivalent AML or CTF provisions and it is also difficult to ascertain the beneficial owners. The firm needs to obtain an undertaking in writing from the beneficial owner stating that immediate notification will be given to the firm if the shares are transferred. It may also be advisable to have this undertaking certified by an independent legal professional or external accountant. As an alternative the shares may be held by a regulated person who will notify the firm of any changes of ownership.

The firm also needs to be aware if there is any individual who "otherwise exercises control over the management of the body" as required by r.6(1)(b). Such an individual may have the power to manage funds or enter into transactions without requiring specific authority from the directors or shareholders to do so. In ascertaining the ownership and control structure of the company, the firm should check whether there is anyone who might be in such a position and verify their identity as for other beneficial owners, depending on the level of risk posed.

Notes

1   'Prevention of money laundering / combating terrorist financing: Guidance for the UK financial sector', JMLSG, 2014 Revised Version, part I, para 5.3.137.
2   Markets in Financial Instruments Directive 2004/39/EC, as amended 2008/10/EC.
3   See http://ec.europa.eu/internal_market/securities/isd/mifid_en.htm.
4   https://www.gov.uk/government/publications/overseas-registries.
5   http://ec.europa.eu/internal_market/company/docs/official/080522web_en.pdf.
6   http://www.anti-moneylaundering.org/globalchart.aspx.
7   See http://www.fca.org.uk/.
8   See http://www.jmlsg.org.uk/other-helpful-material/useful-information-resources.
9   See http://wck2.companieshouse.gov.uk//wcframe?name=accessCompanyInfo.
10 *Ibid (4)*.
11 EBA, ESMA and EIOPA's "Report on the legal, regulatory and supervisory implementation across EU Member States in relation to the Beneficial Owners Customer Due Diligence requirements under the Third Money Laundering Directive [2005/60/EC], April 2012.

CHAPTER 11

Identification procedures for other bodies

Some of the most troublesome of CDD issues for compliance partners or personnel can involve not-for-profit and non-commercial organisations, the difficulties arising because they tend to be outside the normal range of clients for most firms. This chapter deals with the most obvious of all such legal entities and other bodies, including public authorities, schools, trusts, charities, churches and clubs. Many such organisations comprise the so-called "third sector" and the various factors that make up their identity and the verification differ according to the constitutional make-up of the body. Sometimes it is necessary merely to verify the body itself but on other occasions it will also be necessary to verify the identity of those in control of the body, including its beneficial owners. Many of the clients covered by this chapter can be considered to be low risk and therefore qualify for simplified due diligence – public authorities most obviously – whilst others might require standard or even enhanced due diligence depending on the complexity of their structure and the nature of their objects. Charities and trusts, in particular, have become a favoured device for those pursuing illegal objectives, especially those relating to terrorist activities. We cover also partnerships, estates of deceased persons, foundations and pension funds. Each category in this area must therefore be judged on its particular merits and the factors that are special to it.

Trusts

There is a wide variety of trusts, from small testamentary or local trusts to large national or international ones, for a wide range of objectives. The firm needs to consider the size, area of activity and nature of business conducted in deciding the level of risk presented. When dealing with non-UK trusts, the geographical location should be considered and whether this presents a higher risk of money laundering activity. Trusts are not separate legal entities and so it is the trustees who enter into the business relationship with the firm, in their capacity as trustees.

Trusts which present a standard risk are generally for a limited purpose, such as inheritance planning, or have a limited range of activities. Factors which may indicate that a trust presents a higher risk include situations where:

- There is no apparent reason for the trust;
- The trust is established in or has financial links with a jurisdiction that does not have equivalent AML/CTF legislation; and
- The trust has a lack of transparency of ownership or has a complex structure with numerous layers.

In identifying a trust, the firm needs to obtain the following information:

- "Full name of the trust
- Nature, purpose and objects of the trust (e.g., discretionary, testamentary, bare)
- Country of establishment
- Names of all trustees
- Names of any beneficial owners
- Name and address of any protector or controller".[1]

For trusts that are considered to be standard risk, the identity of the trust must be verified from relevant extracts of the trust deed or through reference to an appropriate register in the country of establishment. The firm needs to understand the ownership and control structure of the trust.

The firm must also verify the individual identity of the trustee or, if there is more than one trustee, of at least two trustees (see the Law Society practice note at para 4.6.4) and in accordance with the status of the trustee, for example, individual or corporate. If the trustees are individuals, the form of verification will depend on whether or not the trustee is seen in person. Where the trustee is another regulated person it is acceptable to rely on their listing with their supervisory body, for example, the Law Society or the FCA. It is also advisable for the firm to take appropriate steps to be reasonably satisfied that the trustees it is dealing with are properly authorised to give instructions on behalf of the trust.

In a higher risk situation, it is necessary to conduct enhanced due diligence which would include extra verification of identity of trustees and possibly the settlor, and greater monitoring of the nature of the trust. This could include:

- The conduct of CDD on all the trustees, or perhaps the settlor even after the creation of the trust;
- Making enquiries about the purpose of the trust and the source of the funds used; or
- Checking the trust deed or making searches in the appropriate register in the country of establishment (LSPN para 4.6.4.).

Beneficial ownership

Securing agreement on who precisely would be regarded as being a beneficial owner of a trust proved to be one of the greatest difficulties in finalising the MLR 2007, with the Law Society in particular regarding the first drafts on this issue as unworkable. Agreement was finally reached and the issue is now as set out at r.6(3) to the effect that, in the case of a trust, beneficial owner means:

"(a) any individual who is entitled to a specified interest in at least 25% of the capital of the trust property;

(b) as respects any trust other than one which is set up or operates entirely for the benefit of individuals falling within sub-paragraph (a), the class of persons in whose main interest the trust is set up or operates;

(c) any individual who has control over the trust."

Trustees will always fall within r.6(3) as they have control over the trust and will therefore need to have their identities verified as beneficial owners at least, assuming they are not clients of the firm. For further details relating to the identification of beneficiaries and trusts, refer to Chapter 16.

For standard due diligence, verification of identity can be obtained by gaining assurances from trustees on the existence and identity of beneficial owners but, in the case of higher risk, further enquiries and verification may be undertaken by:

- Obtaining assurances from other regulated persons;
- Reviewing the trust deed;
- Undertaking an electronic search of names and addresses; and/or
- Undertaking a full ID check according to whether the beneficiary is present or not.

In relation to beneficiaries falling within parts (a) or (c) of r.6(3), verification of identity will relate to a named individual. In relation to part (b) beneficiaries, the identity of the class is all that is required; for example, the children of X.

Where a company is the beneficial owner of a trust under part (a) (specified interest in the capital of the trust property) or part (c) (having control over the trust), any individual who is a beneficial owner of the company is also treated as falling under the provisions of parts (a) or (c). Individuals who hold more than 25% of the shares or capital, or otherwise exercise control over the management of the company, will therefore be beneficial owners of both the company and the trust.

Foundations

A foundation is the civil law equivalent of a common law trust and operates in many EEA countries and other civil law jurisdictions. It will be regarded as a legal entity and managed by a board of directors. In most countries a foundation's purpose must be public but there are countries in which foundations may be created for private purposes. Normally, foundations are highly regulated and transparent.

Foundations should be well understood by law firms in their country of operation. However, if a UK law firm receives instructions from a foreign foundation, it should consider why it is seeking advice outside of its home jurisdiction.

The information required to identify a foundation is the same as for a trust. Verification of the identity of the founder and beneficiaries should be undertaken on a risk-based approach, in accordance with the principles used for individuals and beneficiaries. In some jurisdictions the identity of the founder remains anonymous and in these circumstances it is necessary to see if assurances on the identity of relevant persons can be obtained from any intermediaries who are also regulated bodies for AML/CTF purposes.

The word 'foundation' can also be a loose term for a charitable institution in the UK and the USA, in which case they must be verified in accordance with the procedures for verifying charities.

Partnerships and other unincorporated bodies

Partnerships and other unincorporated businesses are not legal entities but a collection of individuals with an underlying business purpose. Identification needs to be based not only on the individual partners but on the business as a whole. To identify a partnership a firm needs to obtain the:

- Full name of the partnership;
- Business address;
- Names of all partners who exercise control over the management of the partnership; and

- The names of individuals who are classed as beneficial owners.[2]

Verification of the identity of a partnership or other unincorporated business depends on its size, public profile and the professional status of its members. Where a partnership is a well-known, reputable organisation, which is long established within its industry and has substantial public information about it, confirmation of the client's membership of a relevant professional or trade association is likely to provide the necessary reliable and independent evidence required for CDD. In addition there needs to be verification of the identity of any beneficial owners.

Where a partnership is made up of members of a recognised professional body, it will be sufficient to confirm the firm's existence and the business address from a reputable professional directory or search facility with the relevant professional body, such as the SRA's Find a Solicitor database, but bearing in mind the warnings now being issued by the regulator as to the prevalence of bogus law firm activity. Any beneficial owners will also need to be identified.

For other partnerships with a lower profile, it will be necessary to see the partnership deed or gain assurance from a regulated body that such a deed exists. This will prove that the partnership actually exists and verification of the identity of the partnership will then depend on the size of the partnership. Where there are relatively few partners, they should be treated as a collection of private individuals and ID checks carried out in accordance with the provisions relating to individuals. It is necessary to obtain evidence on the identity of at least the partner instructing the firm and one other partner (preferably the one in control of the finances), and evidence of the firm's business address. Where the numbers are larger, the checks should be in accordance with guidelines for private companies. For a UK LLP, and Scottish partnerships, verification should be undertaken in accordance with the requirements for corporate bodies.

It is always advisable to ensure that the partner giving the instructions is authorised by the other members of the partnership to do so. For all types of partnerships, it is also necessary to make reasonable and proportionate enquiries to establish whether beneficial owners exist and, where relevant, verify their identity in a risk-based manner. This may involve investigating the voting rights within the partnership.

Beneficial owners

In the case of a partnership (but not a limited liability partnership), r.6(2) provides that a beneficial owner is an individual who:

> "(a) ultimately is entitled to or controls (whether the entitlement or control is direct or indirect) more than a 25% share of the capital or profits of the partnership or more than

25% of the voting rights in the partnership; or

(b) otherwise exercises control over the management of the partnership."

It is necessary to make reasonable and proportionate enquiries to establish whether beneficial owners exist and, where relevant, verify their identity in a risk-based manner. According to the Law Society, "enquiries and verification may be undertaken by:

- receiving assurances from the client on the existence and identity of relevant beneficial owners
- receiving assurance from other regulated persons more closely involved with the client, particularly in other jurisdictions, on the existence and identity of relevant beneficial owners
- reviewing the documentation setting up the partnership such as the partnership agreement or any other profit-sharing agreements" (Law Society practice note, para 4.7.5).

Public sector bodies, governments, state-owned companies and supra-nationals

Public authorities in the UK

Simplified due diligence is permitted for public authorities situated in the UK under r.13(5) MLR 2007. This includes both local government and central government departments and also NHS trusts with the only requirement for simplified due diligence being to check that the client falls within the relevant category (r.13(1)). This can be undertaken by checking the home website of the authority in question, and a dated copy should be made for the firm's records.

Although not required by the MLR 2007, it is advisable to ensure that the official instructing the firm has authority to give instructions and to sign any necessary documents. Written confirmation from the head of the relevant department is one way in which to do this.

Community institutions

Simplified due diligence also applies to community institutions, provided they meet the following criteria laid down in r.13(6) and Schedule 2, para 2 MLR 2007:

"(a) the authority has been entrusted with public functions pursuant to the Treaty on the European Union, the Treaties on the European Communities or Community secondary legislation;
(b) the authority's identity is publicly available, transparent and certain;

(c) the activities of the authority and its accounting practices are transparent;

(d) either the authority is accountable to a Community institution or to the authorities of an EEA state, or otherwise appropriate check and balance procedures exist ensuring control of the authority's activity."

In order to qualify for simplified due diligence, the law firm must have reasonable grounds for believing that the community institution qualifies for such treatment and should make a dated copy of the relevant website or other material which confirms its status as such an institution.

Non-UK public authorities

In identifying non-UK public sector bodies – including governments, state-owned organisations and supra-nationals – which are standard risk, the firm needs to obtain the following information about the client:

- "Full name of the entity
- Nature and status of the entity (e.g., overseas government, treaty organisation)
- Address of the entity
- Name of the home state authority
- Names of directors (or equivalent)".[3]

Their identity can be verified by a web-based search of official government websites, as well as using a search engine to find confirmatory evidence of the information supplied. A dated copy should be retained for the firm's records. In addition the firm should be reasonably satisfied that the officials do actually have the authority to give instructions and to sign any documentation.

Those public sector bodies, governments, state-owned organisations or supra-nationals which are situated in higher risk jurisdictions should be subjected to enhanced CDD. It should also be borne in mind that some governmental or supra-national bodies may be managed or controlled by PEPs. Firms should be aware of this risk and the fact that funds of such bodies may be used for improper purposes and in such cases the names of any officials should be checked against an electronic global database of PEPs.

State schools, colleges and universities

State schools, colleges and universities should be treated in the same way as public authorities, meaning that in the UK they qualify for simplified due diligence. The Department for Education maintains on its website a list of approved educational establishments and firms should therefore use this list to ascertain the existence of these institutions.[4] A dated copy of the relevant entry should be taken from the website and retained as part of the firm's record-keeping obligations.

Independent schools and colleges
The identity of independent schools and colleges should be verified in accordance with their legal status, be this a registered charity, private company or unincorporated association. The Department of Education website will again prove to be useful with this type of institution.

Estate of a deceased person
The identities of executors or administrators of an estate need to be verified in accordance with their status – for example, as an individual or a company – and if more than one individual is acting it is necessary to verify the identity of at least two of them. It is also advisable to verify their authority to act on behalf of the estate by obtaining copies of the grant of probate or letters of administration.

During the course of the administration, the executors or administrators are also the beneficial owners (r.6(8)). The effect of this regulation is such that the only CDD checks required are those relating to the executor or administrator. The firm does not have to identify the beneficiaries under the will or on intestacy until the administration of the estate has been completed and any will trust has come into effect. At that stage the firm will need to undertake ID checks of the trustees (if they differ from the executors) and will also need to verify the identity of any beneficial owners. For more detail on verification of beneficial owners under a trust, see Chapter 16.

Pension funds
Simplified due diligence is permissible in respect of an occupational pension scheme under r.13(7)(c) MLR 2007 if it complies with the following definition:

> "a pension, superannuation or similar scheme which provides retirement benefits to employees, where contributions are made by an employer or by way of deduction from an employee's wages and the scheme rules do not permit the assignment of a member's interest under the scheme (other than an assignment permitted by section 44 of the Welfare Reform and Pensions Act 1999 (disapplication of restrictions on alienation) or section 91(5)(a) of the Pensions Act 1995 (inalienability of occupational pension))."

It is necessary only to have evidence that the product is such a scheme to show that it qualifies for simplified due diligence. This can be done by obtaining:

- A copy of the page showing the name of the scheme from the most recent definitive deed; or
- A consolidating deed which shows the name of the scheme, plus any amending deed subsequent to that date.

The person taking the copy must sign and date it so as to satisfy the firm's record-keeping procedures.

Pension schemes which fall outside the above definition will be subject to standard CDD according to their specific business structure. A UK pension fund may be one of several legal entities: a trust, a company limited by guarantee or an unincorporated association. If, however, it has HMRC or Pensions Regulator registration then confirmation of the scheme's registration will be sufficient evidence.

If a scheme takes the form of a trust, an individual does not qualify as a beneficial owner through having control solely as a result of any discretion delegated to him or her under s.34 Pensions Act 1995 (r.6(5)(b)(ii) MLR 2007). As always, it is advisable for a law firm to ensure it is dealing with persons who have authority to give instructions and/or approve the movement of funds.

Charities

A charity may take a number of forms: incorporated by Royal Charter or Act of Parliament, a company limited by guarantee, a trust or an unincorporated association. For charities it is necessary to obtain the following information:

- "Full name and address
- Nature of body's activities and objects
- Names of all trustees (or equivalent)
- Names or classes of beneficiaries".[5]

Verification of identity will depend on whether the charity is registered, unregistered or excepted (churches).

Registered charities

Details of registered charities (including the charitable number) can be obtained from:

- The Charity Commission of England and Wales at www.charity-commission.gov.uk; or
- The Office of the Scottish Charity Regulator at www.oscr.org.uk.

Other countries may also have charity regulators that maintain a list of registered charities.

The Charity Commission of England and Wales holds a central register of charities and allocates a registered number to each charity; the Scottish Regulator carries out a similar procedure for Scottish charities. A search of the register of the Commission or Regulator will confirm whether the charity is registered and will also give details of its registered number and the name and address of the charity's correspondent, together with details of the governing document and the objects of the charity.

In Northern Ireland there is currently no regulator for charities and so the identity of such charities needs to be verified in accordance with unregistered charities set out below.

Unregistered charities

The firm should undertake the relevant CDD checks for all unregistered charities in accordance with their legal structure. The charitable status of such organisations can be checked with HMRC. In cases of higher risk, the firm should see the constitutional documents of the charity. Owing to increased interest in the vehicles of charities and not-for-profit organisations from terrorist organisations, it may be prudent in certain cases to consult the HM Treasury sanctions list to ensure that the charity is not a listed organisation. This can be achieved by using one of the many online search providers which include the sanctions list as part of the search undertaken.

Churches and places of worship

Places of worship may either register as a charity or apply for registration as a certified building of worship from the General Register Office (GRO), which will issue a certificate. Further, their charitable tax status may be registered with HMRC. Identification details may be verified by one of the following:

- GRO certificate/register;
- As a charity;
- Through an enquiry to HMRC; or
- Through the headquarters or regional organisation of the denomination or religion.

Clubs and associations

The following information is required to identify the club or association:

- Full name;

- Legal status; and the
- Purpose of the club or society.[6]

Many clubs and associations will be low risk, particularly where they exist for a limited social or regional purpose. On the other hand, risk may be higher if they are more sophisticated or have geographical or financial links to countries that are considered to be higher risk.

For lower or standard risk, the firm should verify the identity of those officers who have authority to give instructions or deal with the funds. It is also advisable that the firm checks that the person it is dealing with is authorised to give instructions or enter into transactions on behalf of the club or association. Where the risk may be higher, further checks may include examining the constitution of the club and obtaining a copy of its bank statement or any recent audited accounts (see the LSPN at para 4.6.4).

Notes

1   'Prevention of money laundering / combating terrorist financing: Guidance for the UK financial sector', JMLSG, 2014 Revised Version, part I, para 5.3.246.
2   *Ibid*, part I, para 5.3.156.
3   *Ibid*, part I, para 5.3.174.
4   http://www.education.gov.uk/edubase/home.xhtml;jsessionid=F39E54FE6E8E85A200A1233D21E7C7C3.
5   *Ibid (1)*, part I, para 5.3.226.
6   *Ibid (1)*, part I, para 5.3.266.

PART C

Related Financial Crime Reporting Obligations

Introduction

In this part of the book we examine some of the other areas of potential liability for law firms, be it criminal or regulatory, with particular emphasis on the reporting obligations that may arise in certain circumstances. Away from AML and CTF concerns the duty to report is more likely to fall – for the time being, at least – to the COLP, or in the case of Accounts Rules breaches showing dishonesty, the COFA. Determining who is responsible for which areas of non-compliance or illegal client conduct is one of the issues that will need to be addressed in the office manual or the "compliance plan", which is referred to in the guidance notes to the SRA Authorisation Rules and which all firms are, in effect, required to adopt.

We consider first the more general risks of fraud, along with the Bribery Act 2010. The obligations in relation to market abuse and insider dealing will be of concern to commercial firms and those in relation to data protection and information security to many more. The troublesome issue, as most would see it, of the Foreign Account Tax Compliance Act 2010 is then worthy of a brief mention. The most significant reporting obligation – in terms of the risks to law firms at least – is mortgage fraud, which therefore merits a chapter in its own right.

The areas we cover in this part of the book are not without controversy. As of October 2014 there had still not been a corporate conviction under the Bribery Act 2010, which apparently led the Serious Fraud Office to suggest that the provisions of the Bribery Act should be extended to other areas of financial crime. In response the head of fraud and investigations at one leading firm dismissed this as an "empty threat" on the basis of actions taken to date under the Act.

If the future of the Bribery Act is uncertain then a much safer tip is that data protection breaches will attract increasing attention and levels of retribution. In the November 2014 update to its "Risk Outlook" publication the SRA elevated "breach of confidentiality: information security and cybercrime" to be one of its "other priority risks". All of the areas covered in this part of the book pose risks to law firms, and future developments should be monitored with care.

CHAPTER 12

Fraud, bribery and market abuse

The Fraud Act 2006

Fraud is a common ingredient of many of the other areas of financial crime that a firm should safeguard against, but not necessarily so. Since the risk of fraudulent activity underpins many of the risks faced by law firms, however, a summary of the main provisions of fraud is a useful starting point.

Prior to the Fraud Act 2006 there was no comprehensive definition of fraud in English law, the law instead being a compendium of case law and various statutory offences. Even now there are numerous offences that are not contained in the Act, but there is at least a clear statement of the general principles that underpin this area of the criminal law. The most significant change to the previous law was that, whereas previously it was generally necessary to prove that someone had been deceived for fraud to have arisen, it is now sufficient for the prosecution merely to show that somebody lied with dishonest intent. Fraudulent intent is therefore now more clearly culpable in its own right, regardless of whether that intent is accomplished in practice.

Section 1 of the Act creates a general offence of fraud and defines three ways in which it might be committed:

- False representation;
- Failure to disclose information; and
- Abuse of position.

In addition, the Act introduced certain new offences of obtaining services (such as loans or other financial products) dishonestly and of possessing, or making and supplying articles for, use in fraud. The Act replaced certain of the offences in the Theft Act 1968, most notably the deception offences at ss.15 and 16. The maximum penalty for the main offence of fraud is ten years' imprisonment.

Section 2 makes it an offence to commit fraud by false representation, which will be relevant in relation to so-called "application frauds" where conveyancing clients are dishonest in mortgage applications, or legal aid clients in relation to applications for funding from the Legal Aid Agency. On the basis of *R v Ghosh* 1982[1] an applicant would be dishonest for these purposes if their conduct would be regarded as dishonest by the ordinary standards of reasonable and honest people. If so, it would also be necessary for the defendant to have been aware that their conduct was dishonest and that it would be regarded as such by reasonable and honest people. Since subsection 2(1)(b) requires only an intention of causing a loss to the lender or a gain to themselves as being necessary, there is no need for that loss or gain actually to have materialised, meaning that a dishonest application for funding which is rejected could nonetheless amount to an offence. Further definitions of "false" and "representation" are also provided.

Fraud by failure to disclose information is covered in s.3, which makes it clear that the duty to disclose can be contractual as well as statutory. Interestingly, the example provided in the accompanying guidance note at the time of the Act being passed concerned a solicitor who failed to share vital information with a client in order to perpetrate a fraud on them.

The other major offences under the Act include fraud through an abuse of position under s.4, which might be relevant where a participator in a mortgage fraud scheme obtains a position in a lending institution or a firm, and the possession and supply of materials to be used in a fraud under ss.6 and 7. These offences could be used against those concerned with the websites that offer "novelty item" false documents such as passports and utility bills that enable identity frauds to be perpetrated.

Finally, it should be noted that the general common law offence of conspiracy to defraud remains and is still used in cases involving the most complex of fraud rings, especially those with an international element to them.

The Bribery Act 2010

The Bribery Act had been intended to take immediate effect when passed in 2010, but its implementation was postponed until July 2011 while further consultation continued in relation to its key provisions. The Act was in part a consolidation measure, replacing such enactments as the Prevention of Corruption Acts of 1906 and 1916 and the Public Bodies Corrupt Practices Act 1889. The new law was based on the Law Commission's 2008 report 'Reforming Bribery' and was passed with cross-party support, but doubts as to the possible impact on the business community have continued to this day, the

---

Confederation of Business Industry having maintained its concerns that the new law would unduly hamper the competitiveness of British business.

Sections 1 to 5 set out the "general bribery offences". The main offence of giving or offering a bribe (s.1) is described in rather confusing terms as having two "cases", the first being where a person:

"offers, promises or gives a financial or other advantage to another person, and [...] intends the advantage–

(i)   to induce a person to perform improperly a relevant function or activity, or

(ii)   to reward a person for the improper performance of such a function or activity."

The second case arises where a person:

"offers, promises or gives a financial or other advantage to another person, [knowing or believing] that the acceptance of the advantage would itself constitute the improper performance of a relevant function or activity."

Further explanation is provided to the effect that in the first case, "it does not matter whether the person to whom the advantage is offered, promised or given is the same person as the person who is to perform, or has performed, the function or activity concerned", and that in both cases it does not matter whether the advantage is offered, promised or given directly or through a third party.

Section 2 deals with the other side of the bribery transaction by prohibiting the request or receipt of a bribe, again confusingly set out in a number of illustrative cases. Under this offence it is necessary only to agree to receive or accept a financial or other advantage in circumstances where the person concerned should not do so, meaning that the crime will have been committed even if the payment or other benefit is not forthcoming.

Section 3 deals with the range of functions and activities that might be involved for possible liability under the Act, while s.4 sets out the provisions on when such an activity might be said to have been "improperly" performed. Section 5 then completes this part of the Act by introducing a reasonableness test in relation to ss.3 and 4, reflecting the core problem of the legislation in attempting to differentiate between normally accepted business practice – especially in relation to marketing events – and what should be regarded as criminal behaviour. The offence of bribing a foreign official is dealt with separately within the Act in order to meet the specific requirements of the OECD Anti-Bribery Convention.

Notwithstanding the rather confusing definitions of the key offences by illustrative cases, the core offences are easily summarised: it is an offence to offer or request a bribe, regardless of whether that bribe, be it money, goods or other advantage, is paid or received. The relatively low threshold for criminality might therefore mean that illegal acts of bribery are encountered much more frequently than might be thought, as where a client offers a payment for their adviser to misrepresent the position in a matter or to lie in court. Fortunately such behaviour falls short of the requirements to make a report to the NCA under the relevant provisions of POCA, since although the offer of a bribe will amount to "criminal conduct" under the definition of money laundering at s.340 of that Act there will at that point be no "criminal property" in anyone's possession. The adviser would simply be required to dismiss the offer and point out the inappropriateness of the offer in whatever terms were considered appropriate.

There might, however, be a need to involve the MLRO where it becomes apparent that a client has been party to some act of bribery. Suppose, for example, that a company director attributes the success of the organisation to having well developed contacts elsewhere and to keeping them on board by providing them with "regular sweeteners". The adviser would now have knowledge or suspicions that bribery offences had been committed, with the criminal conduct of the bribe having been accompanied by criminal property in the payments made, thus satisfying the POCA test for money laundering.[2] As such, a duty to report would seem to arise under s.330 POCA, assuming that the work falls within the parameters of the regulated sector. The consultation would, however, be likely to be covered by privilege if the comments could be regarded as being germane to the matter in question, meaning that it should not be reported to the NCA under the provisions on privilege at s.330(6). In this situation the firm should feel constrained, however, in acting for that client further in any transactional work in particular for fear of entering an arrangement whereby money laundering would be facilitated under s.328 of the Act. If the client were instructing the firm to act in litigation they might be free to continue to act without fear of entering an arrangement under the authority of *Bowman v Fels,* but the appropriateness of so doing might be questionable taking into account the fundamental duty of all solicitors to "uphold the rule of law and act in the interests of justice" at Principle 1 of the SRA Handbook.

Compliance concerns

The publicity that has accompanied the Bribery Act might suggest that those responsible for law firm management might fairly leave the issue of compliance with the law to common sense and personal judgement, but it would be unwise to do so. Section 7 of the Act introduces the concept of corporate responsibility by providing that the firm itself will be liable for any transgressions under the preceding offences if it has failed to put in place "adequate procedures" to prevent representatives of the organisation from committing any such offence. In the absence of a suitable policy, preferably accompanied by appropriate training, the firm itself therefore stands to be liable for the acts of any of its workforce as a "relevant commercial organisation", whether incorporated or a partnership (though not, it would seem, an unincorporated sole practitioner).

This provision has led many larger firms in particular to adopt lengthy, complex policies, sometimes based on those in place at larger client concerns that have instructed them to advise on this issue. A policy is indeed required, but a sense of proportion is required. The advice booklet from the Ministry of Justice stresses that the requirement on organisations is for "proportionate" measures to be in place, and so account might be taken of the essentially compliant nature of most lawyers and law firms and the additional prohibition imposed by the SRA on illegal activity.[3] Most law firms should be capable of being viewed as low risk organisations for these purposes, therefore, in which case a concise policy should suffice. However long and detailed the drafting, the policy should:

- Explain and prohibit any form of bribery involvement by anyone within or acting for the firm;
- Assert the obligation of all personnel to "uphold the law and the proper administration of justice" under Principle 1; and
- Appoint a management representative to be responsible for this policy (usually the COLP or the MLRO), also establishing a reporting line to them.

For a template policy along these lines see *The Solicitors Office Procedures Manual*. To ensure compliance some form of training should be provided, as the guidance booklet produced by the Ministry of Justice provides:

"Like all procedures training should be proportionate to risk but some training is likely to be effective in firmly establishing an anti-bribery culture whatever the level of risk. Training may take the form of education and awareness raising about the threats posed by bribery in general and in the sector or areas in which the organisation operates in particular, and the various ways it is being addressed."[4]

One potentially troublesome element in relation to the Bribery Act for law firms could be in relation to the marketing programme, and client entertaining events in particular. The sort of benefits that can arise at such events are clearly covered by the heading of "financial or other advantage" under s.2 of the Act and all such events are arranged with the hope of encouraging new or continued instructions or referrals of work from those attending. Unfortunately the line between established business practices in relation to entertaining and the provision of illegal inducements is poorly defined, with seemingly little middle ground between the two. This confusion might have been avoided had there been a need for the prosecution to show an "intention to corrupt",[5] but the standards of fault are instead limited to tests based on "reasonableness" and what amounts to acting "improperly", with the "expectation test" in s.5 merely stating that:

> "For the purposes of sections 3 and 4, the test of what is expected is a test of what a reasonable person in the United Kingdom would expect in relation to the performance of the type of function or activity concerned."

Quite how the average juror might view an invitation to a major sporting event if not themself familiar with this sort of activity remains to be seen, but a lack of familiarity with the world of big business could cause complications with the proportionate enforcement of the law. To date there have been few proceedings under the Act, with the case of a foreign student who sought to influence their university tutor to review his marking as reported in March 2013 being only the third conviction under the Act. Furthermore, all of these early convictions were of individuals rather than organisations, leading to the headline story in the *Law Society Gazette* of the 22nd July 2013, "Bribery Act lying dormant, SFO admits". It was further reported in the *Daily Telegraph* of the 3rd February 2014 that the Head of the Serious Fraud Office wanted to see more corporate bribery prosecutions, with a threat of "vast fines" and the prospect of being excluded from EU tender processes where convictions were recorded. For those with an interest in jurisprudence it remains a "glass half full or empty" debate to judge the effectiveness of the Act from the dearth of proceedings. The Act might be deemed to have been a great success by having changed opinions throughout the commercial world on what might fairly be done to win business without the need for prosecutions, or it might equally be judged to have been an utter failure through a lack of resolve or resources to make a success of the new law by achieving convictions.

How, therefore, should a law firm approach a client entertaining event to ensure that it does not become a test case on quite where the boundaries should be drawn between lawful marketing and illegal conduct? It is worth consulting the Law Society practice note on the Bribery Act and section 3.5 (7th June 2011 version) in particular, but this seems merely to repeat the Government advice – issued as required by s.9 of the Act – that entertaining must not be lavish. Given that the main objective of any marketing campaign is likely to be to influence the recommendations or buying of those involved, the comment by Chris Walker – head of policy at the SFO in 2010 – may not be quite as reassuring as was probably intended:

"Sensible and proportionate promotional entertainment expenditure is not an offence under the Act. However, when hospitality is done so that people will be induced to act in a certain way – when the expenditure is beyond what is sensible and proportionate, the relevant provisions of the Act will be triggered."[6]

For the time being doubts are likely to continue as to what might be judged "improper" behaviour under ss.1 or 5 of the Act, but it may well prove to be the case that the more generous marketing budgets of large multinationals will be more likely to prompt any test case on the point rather than the more parsimonious entertainment budgets of most professional advisers.

Market abuse and insider dealing

Depending on the profile of the firm the COLP and MLRO may well need to be aware of their responsibilities under the linked areas of market abuse and insider dealing. The term "market abuse" is sufficiently wide to embrace all action intended to distort the market so as to result in some form of improper gain, and so would extend to the practice of insider dealing. This is the illegal trading in shares or securities by someone with inside knowledge of unpublished business information that might affect the price of those investments and is now dealt with under s.52 of the Criminal Justice Act 1993. The offence involves either "dealing" on the basis of such data or information or "tipping" others about it through improper communication. The other main heading of market abuse is the more general process of market manipulation.

The formal definition can be found at s.118 of the Financial Services and Markets Act 2000, which provides that:

"For the purposes of this Act, market abuse is behaviour (whether by one person alone or by two or more persons jointly or in concert) which—

(a) occurs in relation to—

(i) qualifying investments admitted to trading on a prescribed market,

(ii) qualifying investments in respect of which a request for admission to trading on such a market has been made, or

(iii) in the case of subsection (2) or (3) behaviour, investments which are related investments in relation to such qualifying investments, and

(b) falls within any one or more of the types of behaviour set out in subsections (2) to (8)."

There then follows a series of outlines of various types of behaviours which will amount to breaches of this provision. These can be summarised as:

- Dealing or attempting to deal with a qualifying investment or related investment in reliance of insider information;
- Disclosing inside information to someone other than in the course of the proper exercise of their "employment, profession or duties";
- Falling below the standard of behaviour reasonably expected by the market in relation to information that is not generally available to regular users of the market;
- Being responsible for transactions or orders to trade where the price is distorted in some way;
- Being responsible for transactions or orders using fictitious devices or other types of "deception or contrivance";
- The dissemination of information by any means which gives a false or misleading impression; and
- Behaving in a manner that would be likely to be regarded by a regular user of the market as being likely to distort the market in relation to this investment.

As is made clear by the wording of this provision, along with the various leaflets available from the Financial Conduct Authority website, professional advisers who become involved in any behaviour which might be termed market abuse are just as culpable as any other party. Any such behaviour would have to be regarded by the firm's COLP as a "material breach" of the firm's obligations to ensure compliance with all material obligations and would also be likely – as a financial crime – to be reportable under O(10.4) of the SRA Code of Conduct as "serious misconduct" in any event. It might also be necessary to report the conduct to the FCA under the terms of the Markets Abuse Directive under a process that is analogous to the reporting regime applying to money laundering and terrorist financing, on which see FCA, "Obligation to report suspicious transactions", 12th February 2014.

Data Protection Act 1998

The Information Commissioner is appointed under the terms of the Data Protection Act 1998 with responsibilities to uphold information rights in the public interest. The Commissioner has extensive powers to punish breaches of the data protection principles to which all relevant organisations are subject through their obligation to be registered with the Commissioner's office – the ICO. The whole issue of data usage looked very different in 1998, when relatively few people had their own email address or internet access. It can be argued that the burgeoning use of electronic data since that time has left the Act out of date with modern practice and a major overhaul is now being planned through a proposed EU Regulation to be implemented in the next few years. Although still under review, this major change to the law is proposed to be by way of Regulation rather than Directive and so will take direct effect in all Member States without the involvement of the various domestic parliaments, on grounds that the objectives envisaged are not capable of being satisfactorily achieved by Member States.

As yet there is no general legal obligation to disclose data breaches to the ICO but this will change if the current draft Regulation is approved. The likely timetable is also unclear, but 2017 has been suggested by some observers. At that stage a duty to report data breaches "without undue delay" will take effect, though the actual extent of the obligation is as yet unclear. For the time being the professional reporting responsibility for breaches of the duty of confidentiality imposed by O(4.1) of the Code of Conduct will remain with the COLP, this being an area where the prospects of any breach being "material" (and so requiring to be reported to the SRA "as soon as reasonably practicable") are quite high.

The Information Commissioner issued some useful advice on what would be regarded as bad practice in the legal sector by way of a news release of the 5th August 2014. Along with a reminder that the ICO has a power to impose penalties of up to £500,000 for serious breaches it went on to warn that "the regulator has recently included solicitors and barristers in their sights". Particular risks that were highlighted included:

- Carrying information in folders when taking them to court;
- Thefts of mobile phones, laptops or computers;
- The use of such facilities as Dropbox or memory sticks, which were regarded as more suited for private individuals rather than professionals holding sensitive data; and
- Hosting arrangements for the firm's website and email being offshore and not meeting regulatory requirements.

Also, and worryingly, the ICO suggested that it was a "common misconception" that requiring a login would provide adequate protection because of the growing ease of circumventing them with modern software, or moving hard drives from computer to computer. The greater levels of safeguards that are likely to be expected are the ability to wipe data remotely on the loss of the device and the greater use of secure encryption. The text of the full release, along with further tips for lawyers, can be found on the ICO website under the listing of 'News Releases 2014'.

UK trusts: The UK/US Intergovernmental Agreement

Finally, all firms undertaking trust administration work need to be aware of the Foreign Account Tax Compliance Act (FATCA), which is a piece of American legislation aimed at reducing tax evasion by its citizens. In certain circumstances financial institutions outside the US are required to pass information about their American clients to the Internal Revenue Service (IRS) – the tax authority in the USA. This legislation became binding within the UK on the signing of a treaty by the UK Government in September 2012 (the UK-US Agreement to Improve International Tax Compliance and to Implement FATCA). These provisions have triggered considerable adverse comment in the UK financial press by requiring extensive checks to be made of savers in relation to certain investments even where no American citizens are involved.

The checking has been required because financial institutions within the UK (including law firms, depending on their work profile) must meet their obligations in order to avoid the penalties that can arise under the legislation. The provisions mean that it might be necessary to register with the IRS, on which there is a long and highly complex HMRC document (which can be found at www.hmrc.gov.uk/fatca/130814-guidance.pdf) and a joint notice from the Law Society, the ICAEW and STEP of the 2nd May (which can be found at http://www.lawsociety.org.uk/advice/articles/fatca-important-guidance-for-trustees).

Notes

1   *R v Ghosh* [1982] 1 QB 1053.
2   See s.340 POCA 2002.
3   See Principle 1 and O(7.5).
4   The MOJ guidance booklet can be downloaded from https://www.gov.uk/downloads/legislation/bribery-act-2010-guidance.pdf
5   See Mansell, J. "Gold-plating of anti-bribery legislation threatens competitiveness of UK business Perils of the Gold Standard", *Law Society Gazette*, 6th May 2010.
6   Quoted by Harrison, K. and Ryder, N. in *The Law Relating to Financial Crime in the United Kingdom*, Ashgate, 2013. Page 173.

CHAPTER 13

Mortgage fraud

Mortgage – or property – fraud has come to represent one of the most significant operational risks for law firms in recent years, and for smaller property-reliant practices in particular. The number and value of claims arising from this type of fraud has led to sharp increases in the cost of indemnity insurance for many firms, thereby reducing profits or, in more extreme cases, leading to practice failures. Little wonder, therefore, that money laundering and the misuse of money and assets remain "current priority risks" in the latest version of the SRA Risk Outlook document, with "inadequate systems and control over the transfer of money" being highlighted in particular.[1]

Mortgage fraud has been defined as "a generic label for dishonest conduct involving deception as to the existence, value or ownership of property in order to obtain a mortgage advance".[2] Since mortgage fraud is one form of "criminal conduct" that will lead to "criminal property" it can also be seen as being – potentially at least – one form of money laundering. There may also be overlaps with terrorist fundraising, the Land Registry having reported in 2011 that it was seeing increasing numbers of suspected mortgage irregularities that were thought to be terrorist inspired.

As to the value of mortgage fraud activity, estimates of £1bn annually have been suggested with Steve Wilmott, Head of Fraud Intelligence at the SRA, having described mortgage fraud some time ago as "the biggest growth industry" then facing the profession. At one end of the scale the lender might be persuaded through dishonesty to make an offer, or to lend a higher sum of money to the borrower than it might otherwise have done. In the more extreme cases, persons relying on fictitious identities might abscond with substantial sums of money that will never be recovered. Although the lenders are themselves responsible for identifying the borrower, checking the valuation report and carrying out their own checks on the affordability of the loan, they are nonetheless always likely to look to their lawyers to recoup their losses as a result of the client-friendly indemnity insurance arrangements that are imposed by the SRA.

It is, furthermore, not just lenders and their advisers that might find themselves out of pocket – other innocent buyers can also become victims. In the widely reported Thamesmead fraud of 2007, a property company sold a number of flats to a development company that then set about creating false identities to borrow from lenders at inflated prices. Not only were the main lenders involved left with losses reckoned to be in the region of £40m, but other lawful purchasers of other units in the development were fooled into paying inflated prices on the basis of the recorded sale prices, with losses per unit of over £100,000 having been reported at the time. One of the lenders most heavily involved – Alliance & Leicester – reviewed its entire exposure to the buy-to-let market as a result of its losses in this single case.

A further complication is that potentially all or any of the players in the property market could stand to make improper gains at someone else's expense in the more sophisticated scams: the developer who commissions false valuation advice to fix the price of units in their development; the mortgage brokers who have a vested interest in exaggerating the borrower's circumstances to meet targets and bonus incentives; the valuer providing misleading advice; and, sadly, any legal advisers who are paid to knowingly facilitate the illegal transaction. From the fraudster's point of view the involvement of a solicitors' firm will be quite an achievement as law firms are involved in every transaction and are in the best position to hide the proceeds of crime. They also occupy an unrivalled position of trust, not least in their ability to deal directly with the Land Registry. Not surprisingly, therefore, the SRA has continued to issue warnings that property firms of all types and sizes might be targeted by skilled fraudsters seeking to purchase or infiltrate the firm and have reported growing numbers of investigations against members of the profession.

Risks to law firms

There are various risks to the firm in even unwitting involvement in mortgage fraud:

- Criminal liability under s.330 POCA or the Fraud Act 2006;
- Lenders' claims for their losses in negligence or breach of trust;
- Removal from lenders' panels (usually in an arbitrary manner);
- Land Registry compensation claim under the Land Registration Act 2002;
- Civil claims for any losses by other third parties; and in all cases,
- Increased PII premium as a consequence of any of the above.

Those solicitors who deliberately turn to fraud remain a tiny, but newsworthy, minority.

One notable example from 2014 concerned the imprisonment of the former solicitor Jonathan Martin Gilbert who was sentenced to 12 years' imprisonment and who had been struck off the roll of solicitors in 2010 for having assisted a fraudulent client to make multiple bogus mortgage applications. It was reported in the Law Society Gazette of the 20th October that the two had been part of a conspiracy which had also involved mortgage brokers and an accountant and which had netted over £30m over a four year period. The Solicitors Disciplinary Tribunal described the case as "without a doubt one of the worst cases" to come before them.

For most, however, the dangers are of unwitting involvement through a combination of carelessness, naivety and poor management controls. Every firm, regardless of profile, size, location or client base is at risk from fraudsters. The smaller firm, lacking in bespoke compliance officers and often more trusting in its dealings with a largely local clientele, will often be a more attractive target for the more sophisticated fraudsters. For firms of all types and sizes there is also the risk of infiltration by an accomplice seeking employment in the conveyancing department. For those who consider such risks to be exaggerated, the case of *Pulvers v Chan and Others* 2007[3] provides a chilling illustration of this form of risk.

In the initial case of *Halifax plc and Bank of Scotland v Curry Popeck and Pulvers* 2008[4] two owners of a property and a corrupt conveyancer employed by a small firm were able to defraud the Bank into believing that they had taken a charge over a bungalow, whereas the title had in fact been split into several small strips of land, garages and the main property itself. The charges referred to the strips of land or the garages, and not the bungalow which the fraudsters had transferred to themselves through an alias. This case examined which of the lenders had priority in relation to the various transactions. In the linked case of *Pulvers v Chan and Others*, the court ruled that the firm concerned was entitled to recover its losses from the those concerned in the perpetration of over 20 frauds.

Key to this case was the lack of supervisory control exerted by the two-partner firm on the new employee who turned out to be a fraudster. Using a pseudonym she had signed her own certificates of title. This, and other similar cases, may explain why the "compliance plan", which firms are encouraged to adopt in the guidance notes for COLPs and COFAs at s.8 of the SRA Authorisation Rules, includes "appropriate checks on contractors and new members of staff". The risks of fraudsters using false or stolen identities also featured in an advisory paper put out by the SRA in November 2014 – "Cleaning up: Law firms and the risk of money laundering" – with the comment that "we have seen cases over the last few years where criminals have targeted law firms to launder money by placing someone at the firm". Other SRA requirements that are intended to counter the risks of complicity in property fraud by solicitors and their staff can be found in chapter 10 of the SRA Code of Conduct to the effect that firms must notify the SRA of:

> "a significant change to your firm, for example:
>
> (a) key personnel, such as a manager, COLP or COFA, joining or leaving the firm;
>
> (b) a merger with, or an acquisition by or of, another firm" (IB(10.8)).

This provision reflects concerns at instances where fraudsters have acquired failing practices as a front to conduct short term frauds under the cover of an established firm.

The other regulatory requirement of note is to be found at O(8.5) of the Code, which requires that in addition to the words "authorised and regulated by the Solicitors Regulation Authority" being shown on letterheads, websites and emails the "firm's registered name and number if it is an LLP or registered company, or, if the firm is a partnership or sole practitioner, the name under which it is licensed/authorised by the SRA and the number allocated to it by the SRA" must be shown. This provision is intended in part to counter the increasing involvement of bogus firms in conveyancing transactions, the SRA having reported in its Risk Outlook 2015/2016 that whereas they had had 548 reports of suspected bogus firms in 2013 there were 701 in 2014, showing that the risks of this form of fraud are clearly on the increase. The required details should enable other parties to transactions to check on the credentials of the firms they are dealing with, but bearing in mind the increasing risks of bogus firms impersonating valid firms in relation to these and all other pertinent details with sham notepaper and websites.

Categories of mortgage fraud

In order to develop a strategy for countering the risks of involvement in mortgage fraud it is necessary first to understand the different formats it can take, the simplest classification being that all such frauds are either "application" or "identity". Application frauds arise from any misrepresentation to the lender as to the borrower's circumstances, whereas identity frauds involve deception as to the parties involved or the property details. The more complex category of identity fraud has a number of sub-types such as valuation and registration frauds.

Application frauds are committed in the main by otherwise honest people who have every intention of maintaining their payments and being good customers of the lender, but identity frauds will inevitably involve dishonest intent to steal funds at some future stage.

Whereas application frauds might be very much more commonplace, identity frauds pose the most significant risks to law firms. Application frauds are termed as being "opportunistic" in the Law Society practice note on the topic and occur when the borrower seeks to obtain an offer, or a higher mortgage than they would otherwise be entitled to, by providing untrue or misleading information. Many perpetrators of such offences might be surprised to know that their conduct would amount to an offence under s.2 of the Fraud Act where a false representation is made, or under s.3 through failing to provide relevant information as required by the lender for its decision making process, and it should be part of the adviser's role to make these risks clear to them. Identity frauds, by contrast, are termed "large scale mortgage fraud".

The sort of information involved in application frauds will classically concern income, employment status or other financial particulars including the existence of other borrowing, but can also embrace failure to disclose private loans or arrangements for discounts from the vendor or developer. Other points to look out for are previous names and addresses: borrowers might often fail to disclose time at an address where the details might reveal CCJs or other adverse credit information. A recent change of name might be entirely explicable, as through recently having married, but can also represent an attempt to avoid the borrower's full credit history coming to light.

Advisers should always be wary of any information that contradicts anything that has been disclosed to date. Discrepancies, or significantly changed circumstances, should be challenged and a careful file note should be made of any response provided. Where the borrower reveals plans to mislead the lender they should be warned of the risks they face of criminal liability if they do so. In so doing it would be worthwhile to explain the shared systems within the industry to cross-check data provided to different lenders, such as the National Hunter programme as operated by the Credit Industry Fraud Avoidance System (CIFAS) with the involvement of the Council of Mortgage Lenders (CML). This, of course, will not amount to the offence of tipping off under s.333 POCA as no disclosure would have been made at that stage. Warning the client of the risks they face could instead be seen to be offering advice in furtherance of Principle 4 of the SRA Handbook by acting in the best interests of the client through advising them of the risks they face in taking actions that they might not think of as criminal conduct.

Identity fraud

Whereas many cases of application fraud will be unplanned and often not thought through, cases of identity fraud are almost bound to be premeditated and quite possibly part of a larger conspiracy. Cases of identity theft have become more commonplace in recent years, with the Fraud Prevention Service CIFAS reporting that there were 77,500 reported cases in 2007 but 123,600 cases by 2012.[5] One of the benefits of conducting online data checks as part of the firm's identity checking processes is that they should alert the firm to more frauds of this kind by, for example, checking if the number appearing on a passport copied in the office is recognised by the Passport Office. One of the more distressing aspects of identity fraud is the use of the details of deceased people, especially children – a practice also reported recently in relation to under-cover police operations.

Given the prevalence of identity fraud in the property market any failure to establish the client's true identity will probably give rise to a *prima facie* case that the firm has failed in its duties to the lender and/or the Land Registry. The requirements of the CML Lenders' Handbook to check on the vendor's advisers if they are not known, on the client, and also on their signature are to be found in section A3. The Land Registry requirements are contained in their Practice Guide 67 which deals with the confirmation that must be given to the Land Registry rather than the methodology of identity checks, with sections 12 to 14 of form AP1 requiring the applicant to confirm that sufficient steps have been taken to identify the client and also the conveyancers to the other parties.

Registration fraud

Most identity frauds will involve the falsification of the Land Registry details, but the cases that involve deception as to the true ownership of properties deserve special mention. Various elements of Land Registry practice could be seen to have contributed to the problem, none more so than the much-criticised abolition of land and charge certificates through the Land Registration Act in 2002. Further concerns have also been expressed as to the ease with which fraudsters might change the address for service in relation to the proprietorship register. Add to this the ease with which any individual might change their name and it does seem to have become worryingly easy to perpetrate this particular form of crime. Once the registration details have been fraudulently changed the criminal is then likely to find it fairly simple to take out a mortgage on that property or even sell it outright and pocket the proceeds.

In one case reported on Radio 4 in March 2009, an elderly couple from Birmingham who wished to trade down to a smaller property discovered that, according to the Land Registry, they no longer owned their property. They later discovered that two people had impersonated them and instructed a solicitor to change the ownership of the house to someone claiming to be their son-in-law. Subsequently the fraudsters obtained a substantial mortgage against the property and promptly vanished. It was reported in the 'You and Yours' programme that £36m had at that time been paid out to landowners caught up in such situations as the Land Registry guarantees the title to all registered properties.

In another case a London property was subject to a fraudulent sale where the owner had willed her property to her adult children and they then put it up for sale through probate. A fraudulent buyer instructed a firm on a purchase and provided the details of the sellers' solicitors, who were not in fact instructed by the rightful owners, thereby excluding the owners and the estate agents. When the buyer's solicitors could no longer contact their supposed counterparts they made contact with the owners direct and a race to prevent the fraudulent registration ensued. Disciplinary action was subsequently taken on two of the partners of the firm that had been represented as acting for the sellers.

Registration fraud might involve a bogus solicitors' firm or licensed conveyancers acting for the vendor, or an elaborate scam whereby an entirely respectable firm might be cloned or impersonated. So-called cases of "application hijack" also feature in the Law Society advice on the topic, where outsiders step in at a late stage claiming to be the new representatives of the other party, often with the complicity of a dishonest estate agent who is able to provide information on the intended completion date. All such risks should be capable of being countered by checking on the SRA website the identity of any firm that is not well known to the adviser, and using only the phone number shown by the SRA – the number shown on what might be cloned notepaper being that of the fraudsters and not the firm being impersonated. Unfortunately several of the reported cases in this field involve bogus firms that actually appeared on the Law Society's database of members (as in *Nationwide v Davisons* 2012 at page 184). Either way, a change of advisers at the point of completion should always be regarded as suspect and it would be wise to make contact with the advisers to date to see if they are aware of the development.

Certain properties are more susceptible to this form of fraud, especially unoccupied properties where the mail is unlikely to be opened, and buy-to-let properties. Fraudsters might also claim to be someone who has recently deceased or the rightful heir, especially where there is a delay in probate. It should therefore be seen as good practice to warn certain clients, such as buy-to-let investors or those that are working or retiring elsewhere, of the risk of this form of fraud and of the benefits of registering address or other contact details at the Land Registry for notification in the event of any attempted dealings with the property. Common indicators of registration fraud include instructions to transfer the property for nil value or the obtaining of loans soon after such transactions. It is probably only a matter of time until failure to advise such clients to notify the Land Registry of addresses for service (to alert the owners of any attempted dealings on the property) is seen as a cause of action in negligence. On the advisability of this see also Land Registry Practice Guide 55 – "Address for Service".

Mortgage fraud practices

There are clever minds involved in frauds and the practices continue to develop. One of the best sources of advice on the "tricks of the trade" is the Law Society practice note on the topic.[6] Common practices include the development of false identities – cloned or fictitious – by the use of birth certificates or change of name deeds. Also:

- The use of false identities to purchase a property and obtain a mortgage, sometimes compounded by then obtaining false valuation advice so as to obtain subsequent mortgages for inflated amounts. This may enable the first mortgage to be paid off, but eventually the fraudster will abscond with the greatest amount possible;
- The use of equity release schemes to assist owners in known financial difficulties, with the fraudsters perhaps paying off the known current debts but then taking out much greater loans, leaving the original owners – now mere tenants – to respond to the later demands for repayment;
- Flipping and back-to-back purchases are often indicators of this form of activity and have led to new restrictions on successive transactions with many lenders. Variations include not registering the first charge and not redeeming it on the second purchase;
- Use of non-bank lenders, such as property clubs, which have less stringent checking procedures;
- Use of deceased estates, sometimes claiming to be the deceased where there are notices trying to locate heirs; and
- Seller/buyer collusion, in which related parties agree on a transaction at an artificially inflated price so as to support a larger mortgage than would otherwise be available.

It is important to see this form of fraud as applying to commercial transactions and not being confined to residential conveyancing, as illustrated by the case of *Cheshire Building Society v Dunlop Haywards and Others* 2008.[7] An application had been made to Cheshire Building Society (CBS) for a loan of £10.5m to a company called Goldgrade Properties to fund the purchase of a property in Birmingham at a price of £14.5m. It was informed that, following the purchase, the property would be occupied by three business tenants taking leases at favourable rates.

CBS instructed Dunlop Hayward, a local firm of surveyors, to value the property. A director of the company provided what transpired to be a dishonest valuation of £16m with the leases and £10.5m if vacant possession. Later a further loan was applied for and the same director confirmed the valuation. The advance was duly made; it soon became apparent that the true vacant possession value was only £1.5m. The claimant building society sued the surveyors and the advisers that they had instructed on the loan – Cobbetts – for their losses.

An award of £10m was made for the building society's losses for deceit, with Cobbetts' insurers paying out roughly half of this in a settlement (the law firm having limited its liability), as disclosed in a separate claim brought by Nationwide BS who by that stage had taken over CBS. In that later case it was held that Cobbetts had been at fault in not alerting CBS to the "indicia of fraud, which they should have spotted. But, had they done so, CBS would be likely to have carried out, albeit somewhat earlier, exactly the same sort of investigations into the extent of the fraud that they carried out later".[8]

It might be worth adding, in passing, that this decision also shows that property lawyers should no longer regard the valuation reports as being none of their concern, a gross over-valuation suggesting mortgage fraud, as in this case, whilst an extreme under-valuation might suggest money laundering activity, as in *R v Griffiths and Pattison* 2006[9]. The need to monitor the value of the property as a warning sign of fraud is also referred to in the Law Society practice note on mortgage fraud at para 4.2.

Vendor frauds and breach of trust cases

Although mortgage fraud is most obviously associated with those acting for borrowers and purchasers, there has been an increasing trend for the vendor's representatives to fall victim to the crime. This occurs where the firm is duped into acting for bogus vendors. The steps in this growing form of property fraud are to:

* Gain information from the Land Registry as to properties that are not mortgaged;
* Change the address for service;
* Depending on the age of the rightful owners, transfer the property to one of the conspirators; and
* Obtain a mortgage.

A variation to this form of fraud is for the criminals to change the address for service for an empty property and then pose as builders who are entitled to payments for work done. If the court does not receive a reply from the person at the address it can order the house to be sold to meet the claimed sum, with the balance of the sale proceeds then being paid to the fraudsters.

In order to recoup their growing losses a number of lenders have started to take proceedings against the firms that fall prey to this practice based on breach of trust, rather than contract. This is made possible as the CML Handbook provides that the law firm holds its monies on trust until completion is achieved, and does offer various advantages to the lender if it chooses to go down this route. These include:

- A lesser evidential burden;
- The prospect of higher damages; and
- Reduced risks of contributory negligence affecting the award.

The first major report on this line of cases was *Lloyds TSB v Markandan & Uddin* 2012.[10] Here the Bank was successor to a building society that had offered a loan to buyers with the defendant representing the buyers and the lenders under the CML Handbook. The sale was a sham and the vendors' solicitors did not exist. There was no suggestion that the defendants were a knowing party to the fraud but it was held that the payment of completion monies by them was in breach of trust since they would only have had authority to release the funds if in receipt of the documents necessary to register title, or on receipt of a solicitors' undertaking to provide such documents. As to the nature of the trustees' duties it was held that completion:

> "must mean the completion of a genuine contract by way of an exchange of real money in payment of the balance of the purchase price for real documents that will give the purchaser the means of registering the transfer of title to the property that he had agreed to buy and to charge".

This decision was followed in the later case of *Nationwide Building Society v Davisons* 2012.[11] Here the law firm again acted in good faith for a bona fide purchaser. The vendors were represented by a newly opened branch office of a local sole practitioner, which transpired to be a sham operation. Not knowing of this office Davisons checked the SRA directory and found that the office did indeed appear on the Law Society listing of firms. Critically, this was the case throughout the transaction and remained the case until a month after completion in March 2009.

The claimant building society contended that its instructions were on the basis of the then current version of the CML Handbook. It was an express term of those instructions that the loan was to be secured by a first legal charge over the property and that all existing charges had to be redeemed on or before completion. There was a prior charge on the property to another lender – GE Money. The claimant duly released money to the defendant and the fake branch wrote to the defendant to provide a TR1 Transfer Deed purportedly signed by the vendor and requisitions on title. The transaction therefore duly completed but the property was, of course, still subject to the GE charge.

Nationwide issued proceedings against the defendant seeking damages for breach of contract or an order for the restoration of a trust fund and for equitable compensation. The defendant claimed that it had shown reasonable care and skill in its handling of the transaction and was therefore not in breach of either contract or trust.

The other issue in this case was whether the firm should be entitled to equitable relief under s.61 of the Trustee Act 1925, but this failed through Davisons having failed to notice "suspicious" features in the correspondence (para 47 of the judgment) to the effect that neither the requisitions, nor any other document, contained anything capable of being construed as a solicitor's undertaking to discharge the first charge on completion.

It was held that the careful, conscientious and thorough solicitor, who conducted the transaction by the book and acted honestly and reasonably in relation to it in all respects but still did not discover the fraud, might still be held to have been in breach of trust for innocently parting with the loan money to a fraudster. As such it would usually be subject to equitable relief, but in this case no suitable undertaking was received that the fraudster had GE's authority to receive the sum intended to pay it or an undertaking from a solicitor to redeem or obtain a discharge for the charge. Relief was not therefore granted and judgment was given in favour of the building society.

On appeal, however, it was held that although the firm had acted in breach of trust by handing over the mortgage monies when completion had not, in fact, taken place it was entitled to relief from liability since it had acted honestly and reasonably and the loss had been caused by the fraud of an unconnected third party rather than lack of care by the solicitors' firm. It was also reported in the appeal decision that the sole practitioner who had been impersonated by the fraudsters had informed the SRA and the Law Society of the false entry, but they had failed to remove the entry from their website. The Court of Appeal took the view that the judge had placed too much emphasis on the fact that the fraudsters had responded on an Oyez form rather than a TA13 given that the wording used amounted to an undertaking to redeem or obtain discharges for the existing charges, even though not in fact from a solicitor.[12]

If matters seemed to have taken a turn for the better in this latter decision, there was a reminder of how real the risks can be in *Santander UK Plc v R.A. Legal Solicitors* 2014.[13] It was held that the conveyancer's poor performance of their duties contributed to the loss suffered by Santander when completion monies were misappropriated by the vendor's solicitor ('Sovereign') who were in fact fraudsters. The court refused to grant the purchaser's solicitors, RA Legal ('RA'), relief under s.61 of the Trustee Act 1925 and found the firm liable to the lender for the loss of the mortgage funds.

In this case the law firm RA acted for the lender and for the purchaser in the acquisition of a residential property. The real owner was unaware of the sale and RA was also unaware that the transaction was not genuine. RA was due to exchange contracts and complete the transaction simultaneously, but it released funds to Sovereign the day before and prior to the actual exchange of contracts. There was no letter notifying

Sovereign that the money had been released nor any requirement that the funds were to be held to the order of RA. RA did however check with the Law Society that Sovereign was registered as a law firm.

The court emphasised the fundamental principle that solicitors who hold a loan advance on trust until completion necessarily commit a breach of trust if they part with the advance otherwise than upon completion. In assessing the degree of fault of the purchaser firm Lord Justice Briggs undertook an examination of each stage of the process, covering completion by post and the purpose of Requisitions on Title. He held that the following departures from best practice were connected with the lender's loss:

1. **Making and receiving inadequate requisitions on title**

   Sovereign answered "confirmed" to the whole of paragraph 4(B) of the requisitions which raises a series of questions about the discharge of the mortgage including details of the terms of the undertaking to be provided.

   Under paragraph 5(A) regarding the arrangements for completion, Sovereign answered "formula B". This was a meaningless answer in relation to completion as it is a reference to a standard method for exchange of contracts. RA did not question any of these inadequate replies nor raise any supplemental Requisitions.

2. **Failure to obtain the vendor's solicitors written commitment to follow the Completion Code before transferring the completion money to them**

   Sovereign did not answer paragraph 7(D) of the Requisitions where it was asked to confirm that it would comply with the Law Society Completion Code. This meant that the completion money was transferred to Sovereign the day before completion without RA imposing any written obligation upon Sovereign to hold it to its order.

3. **Failure to appreciate that completion had gone seriously wrong when no confirmation that the mortgage had been discharged was received in the post**

   The fact that its client had not received the keys by 4th August 2009 and it had not received the mortgage discharge form did not alert RA to the possibility that there was a problem with the transaction. RA's post completion correspondence with Sovereign was confused, on the one hand stating that the sale had been completed and on the other it served a notice to complete on 10th August. The completion monies remained in client account from the date of purported completion until the misappropriation took place on 13th August.

The court was also critical of the practice of submitting an unqualified Certificate of Title before investigation of title had been completed. RA had yet to inspect a 1986 transfer when it sent it off. This was on the basis that it could halt the transaction if a defect in title was subsequently discovered. RA submitted that this practice was common amongst conveyancers to minimise delays by lenders in releasing mortgage monies, but this explanation was frowned upon by his Lordship who regarded the practice as a deliberate misrepresentation to the lender, even if not one which in this case had contributed to the loss. The view was also expressed that even if RA had followed best practice the fraud would probably have succeeded, but that was not in his view the legal basis for granting relief under s.61 which was therefore denied under the general equitable discretion of the court.

The clear inference from this decision is that whatever the pressures imposed by clients or others in the chain, conveyancers should adhere meticulously to the correct procedure – a counsel of perfection, perhaps, for those involved in the more competitive end of the residential market. Close attention should be paid to the requisitions and to the arrangements for completion. The fact that duties are owed to two clients, namely the purchaser and the lender, can often be overlooked in the strain of complying with unrealistic timescales. The judgment also provides a stark reminder that residential conveyancing is not a purely administrative process – it is a legal transaction upon which legal advice and expertise is required.

Preventing mortgage fraud

Any law firm undertaking conveyancing work should adopt a mortgage fraud prevention policy as an important component of its overall risk management policy, and those that seek to be certified to the Law Society's Lexcel standard will need to do so in any event even though in the revised standard (v6) such a policy is stated to be a "should" item rather than a "must".[14] The two essential components of any such strategy should be based on the level of supervision required by Principle 8 of the SRA Handbook and chapter 7 of the Code of Conduct and a thorough approach to the issue of identity checking as required by the MLR 2007.

A good starting point for most practices will be to check their obligations under the Council of Mortgage Lenders' Handbook, along with the similar provisions to be found in the Building Societies Association Mortgage Instructions. Both sets of guidelines provide that the primary obligation is to ensure compliance with the standards expected by the Law Society as contained in its practice note on Money Laundering.[15] Much the same duty will be found in relation to the firm's obligations to the Land Registry in relation to compensation claims under the Land Registration Act 2002, though the joint practice note of the Law Society and the Land Registry – which can be consulted most easily under the title 'Property and Registration Fraud' in the library of practice notes on the Law Society website – recognises that the exercise of reasonable care when checking identity will not be foolproof.

To date it has been accepted that the losses which arise for the lender or the Land Registry will be borne by them where it is clear that they have arisen despite the application of due diligence of the law firm rather than its failure to meet the required standard. The Law Society practice note on Money Laundering, for example, provides that:

> "You should not ignore obvious forgeries, but you are not required to be an expert in forged documents." (para 4.3.3)

It was easier to assert that the standard expected by the Land Registry was one of reasonableness before a practice note 'Identity evidence for the Land Registry' was withdrawn. This included the helpful statement that:

> "You are not legally obliged to guarantee that information provided by you is genuine. The Land Registry state that they regard you as being satisfied with the validity of any identity detail included in an application, whether or not you have personally verified the information given" (para 2.4).

Even in this now obsolete guidance, however, it did go on to say that "the extent of the obligation may be a matter for the courts" and para 3(1) of the Property and Registration Fraud note (11th October 2010) now rather worryingly states that:

> "Even where you have followed usual professional practice the court may hold that the steps taken exposed someone to a foreseeable and avoidable risk and amounted to a breach of duty of care. See Edward Wong Finance Co Ltd v Johnson Stokes & Master [1984] 1 AC 296."

Regardless of the enthusiasm that might be shown by the lenders or Land Registry to pursue firms for their losses, all firms exposed to the risk of mortgage fraud need to adopt anti-money laundering policies that are at least compliant with the Law Society guidelines, imposing additional checks where a risk assessment might suggest that these would be merited. Many firms, for example, conduct electronic identity checks in addition to the usual practice of checking the usual identity and address evidence documents in all conveyancing matters, or where the client is not already well known to the firm.

The decision in the Santander case provides a timely reminder of the need for effective supervision in all conveyancing matters – an issue also addressed by the relevant provisions in the Law Society's Conveyancing Quality Scheme requirements, especially at section G.

Finally, the SRA has suggested that all firms should establish occasional monitoring of their identity on the web to see if they are being cloned. Likewise, any miscellaneous post in the property department that cannot be traced to any known matter should be checked out carefully as it might be evidence that the firm is being impersonated with this item getting through to your actual address rather than the one established by the fraudsters.

Notes

1 SRA Risk Outlook 2015-2016.
2 'Mortgage fraud: pitfalls for the professional', webinar presented by David McCluskey and Neil Swift, Peters & Peters: Central Law Training September 2009.
3 *Pulvers v Chan and Others* [2007] EWHC 2406 (Ch).
4 *Halifax plc and Bank of Scotland v Curry Popeck and Pulvers* [2008] EWHC 1692 (Ch).
5 See http://www.cifas.org.uk/identity_fraud.
6 'Mortgage Fraud', Law Society practice note, 31st July 2014.
7 *Cheshire Building Society v Dunlop Haywards and Others* [2008] EWHC 51 (Comm).
8 *Nationwide Building Society v Dunlop Haywards and others* [2009] EWHC 254.
9 *R v Griffiths and Pattison* [2006] EWCA Crim 2155.
10 *Lloyds TSB v Markandan & Uddin* [2012] EWCA Civ 65.
11 *Nationwide v Davisons* [2012] All ER (D) 141 (Apr).
12 *Davisons v Nationwide Building Society* [2012] EWCA Civ 1626.
13 *Santander UK Plc v R.A. Legal Solicitors* [2014] EWCA Civ 183.
14 Lexcel v6 – 5.14.
15 "You must follow the (Law Society's guidance) relating to money laundering and comply with the current money laundering regulations and the Proceeds of Crime Act 2002 to the extent that they apply" (CML Handbook, part 1, para 3.1.2).

PART D

Practice Areas

Introduction

In this part of the book we switch the focus from the requirements of the AML and CTF regimes to an overview of the compliance obligations within the main departments that exist in most firms. What are the main risks of possible liability under the main Acts and when might a disclosure to the NCA be required? Likewise, what are the main challenges in attempting to comply with the regulatory requirements of the Money Laundering Regulations 2007, especially in relation to identity checking?

We have arranged this part around what we see as the four critical areas of general and commercial practice:

- Chapter 14: Company and commercial
- Chapter 15: Litigation and family law
- Chapter 16: Private client
- Chapter 17: Property and Conveyancing

Other more specialist areas of practice are likely to be seen as sub-sets of the above.

A template AML and CTF policy then follows.

CHAPTER 14

Company and commercial work

Risk profile

The application of AML and CTF principles to corporate work produces some of the most challenging issues that those nominated officers concerned are likely to face. So far as money laundering activity is concerned, the complexity of corporate structures and the amount of money that can be involved have obvious attractions for those wishing to launder funds. On the regulatory side, difficult issues often arise in relation to understanding the structure and ownership of the more complex corporate entities, especially when there is an international element to the transaction. There may be further complications in relation to identifying the beneficial ownership of any client entities, often deliberately so on the part of the client. It follows that many firms will take the view that this category of work is likely to be unusually taxing in relation to complying with the regulatory requirements and amongst the highest risk work for these purposes that the firm undertakes.

Money Laundering Regulations 2007

Corporate work is specifically addressed by the MLR 2007, and will be quite clearly within the sphere of the firm's regulated activities, but this will not necessarily be the case in relation to any commercial drafting work which could be interpreted as being the "provision of legal advice" under the exemptions set out at s.1.4.5 of the LSPN. Few practices seem to make this distinction, however, with the result that all of the work of company commercial departments is likely to be subject to the regulatory requirements. For the record, the key provisions that bring corporate work within the regulated sector are:

* The buying and selling of business entities;

- The organisation of contributions necessary for the creation, operation or management of companies; and
- The creation, operation or management of companies or similar structures.[1]

These headings cover the staple diet of most corporate departments: share and asset sales; company formations; and corporate financing operations such as MBOs and the raising of private equity.

If a client is setting up a company, it is important that the firm establishes the intended purpose of the company and the source of any funding. Companies owned by nominee shareholders or multiple owners can be used to disguise ownership and any such issues will need to be investigated. Often companies are created at one firm to be then used elsewhere, in which case it would be advisable to question why the firm is merely being asked to create a company or subsidiary with no further work to follow, especially if the client has no obvious local connection.

If the firm is going to hold funds as part of a transaction and these are to be held as stakeholder or escrow agent, then it is advisable for it to carry out CDD against all those on whose behalf it is holding the funds.

Private equity work is generally considered to be low risk because private equity firms are FCA regulated and the investors are generally large institutions which are often themselves regulated. In addition, any investment is generally illiquid and the return of capital unpredictable.

The Law Society has issued warnings about lawyers being approached to act as company directors in client companies as this could be a means to misuse their professional status to gain respectability. Such an appointment should only be accepted once suitable financial and CDD checks have been carried out and the aims and the purpose of the venture have been clearly shown to be beyond reproach.

The firm should also be wary of being asked to bank large amounts of money in client account pending further instructions, not least as this could easily fall foul of s.14(5) of the SRA Accounts Rules which prohibits the use of client account as a banking facility – an issue which is now being strictly enforced by the SRA. The general principle is that there must be current underlying instructions to explain why the funds in question are being held by the firm, and as soon as this is no longer the case they must be returned to the client under s.14(3). In *Fuglers LLP v Solicitors Regulation Authority* 2014 the original decision of the Solicitors Disciplinary Tribunal that there must be a reasonable nexus between the nature and scope of activity and the original retainer was upheld where funds had been held on behalf of Portsmouth Football Club whilst it was suffering from its widely reported financial difficulties at the time.[2]

A further complication arises where potentially large sums of money have been deposited into client account only for the client to instruct that the matter is abortive and for them then to request their return. Since this might be little more than a ruse to get money into and out of a law firm's client account the consent of the NCA might be required before repayment is made, even if it is to be returned to the same account from whence it came. It follows that caution is required when the client is anxious to make a substantial payment into client account at an early stage to "get things moving".

Proceeds of Crime Act 2002

Given the relatively high risk profile of corporate work for AML purposes it follows that the issue as to whether or not to make disclosures to the NCA may well present itself quite frequently, but in practice many commercial firms will admit to having made very few reports indeed, or fewer in this area of the practice than in others. More than any other area of legal work, corporate transactions seem to highlight the widespread confusion as to the requirements of the disclosure regime and how they should be interpreted in practice. There are some specific guidelines on this area of work in the LSPN at chapter 12 – which have, therefore, been Treasury approved – but they do contain some of the most confusing elements of the entire practice note. The guidance distinguishes the different processes of the asset sale or purchase as opposed to share transactions, seemingly to attempt to introduce some degree of proportionality into the regime. There is no getting away, however, from the fact that the wide definitions at s.340 POCA for criminal property and criminal conduct, with no *de minimis* considerations to take into account, cause problems of interpretation – at the very least – for the corporate lawyer.

Criminal offences

The principal offences at ss.327-329 POCA apply to all parties of the corporate transactions: the vendor may be liable for transferring criminal property, the purchaser for acquiring criminal property and both for entering into an arrangement. It follows that their advisers may also be liable under s.328 for becoming involved in an arrangement, the "*Bowman v Fels* exemption" (whereby a lawyer is not to be seen to be entering an arrangement with their client simply through acting for them) being quite specifically limited by that judgment to litigation work and not therefore applying to corporate work. As to the risks of the non-contentious lawyer entering an arrangement, the judgment in *Bowman v Fels* suggested that:

- To enter into an arrangement involves a single act at a point of time;

- An offence cannot be committed until an arrangement has been made; and
- An arrangement could not be made by any intermediate step which does not itself involve the acquisition, retention or use of criminal property.[3]

It could therefore be argued that the lawyer and their client can safely undertake all of the preparatory steps towards an assets or share sale as long as they do not become involved in the transfer of any property or funds until the position relating to the criminal property has been resolved. In practice more care might be required since the lawyer would be under an obligation to report any offences already committed by the target company pursuant to s.330 unless privilege applies and, as the case of *Fitzpatrick v MPC* 2012[4] shows, the authorities seem to be increasingly likely to launch enquiries at an earlier stage than the judgment in *Bowman v Fels* suggested.

Criminal property

Problems also arise from the definition of criminal property which covers benefits arising "directly or indirectly" from criminal conduct, along with obtaining a pecuniary advantage in connection with any such conduct. The more serious financial or tax related offences which may only come to light as part of a due diligence exercise are obviously covered by this definition, but it also encompasses an extensive range of other predicate offences in the corporate arena, including those that are simply regulatory in their nature. Examples include health and safety and environmental issues, and registration requirements under the Companies Act 2006. Such provisions are often minor and of strict liability and have little to do with acquisitive crime. They generate "saved costs" in that the target company does not incur expenditure which it would have done had it complied with the relevant statute or regulations. These may take many forms, and could arise from saved expenditure arising from a breach of legislation due to a failure to:

- Purchase safe equipment, plant or machinery;
- Engage consultants to prepare necessary reports; or
- Pay a registration or other type of fee, such as the annual payment required of all data handlers to the Information Commissioner under the Data Protection Act 1998.

This extra money could be seen to taint the assets of the company, which would then be considered to be criminal property, meaning that any dealing with the assets of the company could give rise to potential liability under one or other of the principal offences under ss.327-329 POCA. In practice most advisers seem to take the more pragmatic view that all such irregularities are capable of being remedied and can therefore be dealt with quite adequately by warranties or monies which are withheld. Under this approach the view is taken that there will be no illegality still to report and therefore the issue is resolved from all parties' points of view.

Taking this line of approach further, the key question in share and asset sales is whether the assets have been tainted by criminal proceeds. On an asset sale, if the business is sold in its entirety, it is immaterial whether all or just some of the assets constitute criminal property and there would appear to be no *de minimis* provision. The difficulty arises where only part of the assets or business is sold. The question arises as to which of the assets have been tainted and whether they are the ones which are the subject of the transaction.

In share sales, the issue is more complex. It has to be decided whether the criminal property in the underlying assets of the target has affected the share price of the company so that the shares themselves have become criminal property because they have conferred a benefit or pecuniary advantage on the vendor.[5] Again, this will not usually be the case, especially in relation to regulatory breaches, in which case there would be no need for a disclosure.

The key question might therefore be seen to be the degree of variation to the share price for there to be a material effect. The LSPN suggests at chapter 12 that an arrangement offence under s.328 might be committed in such circumstances "particularly if the criminal property represents a large percentage of the value of the target company", which seems to indicate that the effect needs to be material; an example of 10% of profits is given. Later in the same chapter the guidance states, "if the value of the criminal property is not sufficient to affect the purchase/sale price, the transaction is unlikely to be considered a prohibited arrangement", with the example here being a situation of £25 saved costs when a company is purchased for £100m, in which case the purchase price would not be affected.

What is clear is that the share price needs to be affected before the shares can be considered as tainted and thus amount to being criminal property in their own right. The degree to which the share price is affected is unclear – whether there should be a material effect or just greater than *de minimis*. It should also be noted that in practice the affect on share price will be determined by the method adopted for valuation of the share price in the share sale and purchase agreement. If there are detailed completion accounts on a share sale then it can be argued that the criminal property will have affected the share price, even if this is of an extremely low amount.

Disclose, remedy or abort
The discovery of tainted assets means that the legal adviser has to give serious

consideration to the course of action open to his client. The adviser might advise their client to waive any privilege and make a joint disclosure to the NCA and seek consent. This causes at the very least a risk of unwanted delay which might put the deal itself at risk, and much may also depend on whether the NCA needs to liaise with external authorities, such as HMRC. The unit that deals with requests for consent to continue to act at the NCA will discuss cases on the telephone and endeavour to deal with urgent cases quickly. However, this can only be done once a formal disclosure has been made and– since October 2014 – accepted by them as a valid SAR.

An alternative course of action is for the vendor's lawyer to recommend to their client that they voluntarily resolve any outstanding problems, for example by paying the tax or other saved costs before proceeding with the sale. The advice should almost certainly spell out the risks of not doing so, including the likelihood of a disclosure to the NCA by the purchaser or the funder's advisers, without fear of 'tipping off' since at that stage no disclosure would have been made. Even then the adviser could probably claim that they did not believe that any investigation would be prejudiced and that they were simply acting to prevent the commission of an offence by their client.[6]

If the vendor agrees to pay the saved costs, his lawyer and the other side can – according to *Bowman v Fels* – continue with any preparatory steps but not the actual completion before the payment has been made. Although in theory a disclosure should be made in advance of repayment being made, warranties against future complications seem to be acceptable to most firms or there may be a decision to put aside the money, representing the saved costs, to be held in the firm's client account. The completion would take place and the payment made post completion. The disadvantage with this is that the offence has not been discharged and the firm arguably is holding criminal proceeds, but the longer that time goes on and complications do not arise the safer the corporate lawyer and their MLRO are likely to feel with this widespread practice.

In a share sale, the saved costs may not be sufficient to have an effect on the share price, so unless the predicate offence is rectified the target company will still contain tainted assets and therefore further offences under ss.327-329 are likely to be committed post completion. If the vendor were to refuse to remedy the irregularity and did not agree to a disclosure to the NCA, the firm would have to seriously consider refusing to act for fear of liability itself or out of professional considerations such as Principle 1 of the SRA Handbook and the need to uphold the rule of law. The firm would also need to consider whether it is required to make a disclosure to the NCA under s.330 unless privilege were to apply. The crime/fraud exception might apply depending on the level of the assets which are tainted and the intentions of the parties, in which case if the level of tainted assets were significant there would be a need to disclose as privilege would not apply.

Disclosure and privilege

In relation to the duty to disclose offence at s.330 the vendor's advisers will usually be exempt from the duty to make a disclosure through the operation of the statutory privileged circumstances defence at s.330(6). The lawyer will be taking instructions in order to provide their services to the client and there should seldom be any circumstances to displace the normal operation of the defence, but there could be further complications arising from future communications to lawyers on the other side arising from information posted in a data room. This depends in part on the distinction between common law advice privilege and the statutory format of the defence found in POCA and the TA.

The LSPN suggests that a request for further information from the purchaser or another party will amount to a "second communication" meaning that the original information would no longer be subject to privilege, this interpretation flowing from the problem highlighted in Chapter 3 of analysing privilege not, as is usually the case in the legal process, in relation to documents but the state of the lawyer's mind.

> "That second receipt from the purchaser, or their solicitor, would not be protected by privileged circumstances. It will lose its exemption from disclosure unless the information was also subject to LPP which had not been waived when it was placed in the data room (e.g. a letter of advice from a solicitor to the vendor)."[7]

The situation under the principal offences and the need to make a disclosure is more clear-cut. Where the information that leads to the knowledge or suspicion of money laundering emanates from privileged information – usually the client's instructions – it will be necessary under the Law Society guidance following *Bowman v Fels* to obtain the client's waiver of privilege before a disclosure can be made. Where the client does not agree to this course of action, the lawyer would have to cease to act rather than risk entering an arrangement without having first gained permission to do so, but would usually still be protected by privilege in relation to their duty to make a disclosure under s.330 POCA.

It is more likely that the advisers working for all parties other than the vendor will be more prone to the need to make a disclosure on grounds of the duty to do so at s.330 POCA. This is because they are less likely to come by their knowledge or suspicion of money laundering in privileged circumstances – most obviously because they are in receipt of the information from the vendor, as a result of the due diligence exercise, rather than through their client's instructions. It should be remembered that the scope of communications that are covered by the privileged circumstances defence is more limited for non-contentious lawyers as opposed to their litigator colleagues, being confined to communications with their client only in non-contentious work but extending to "any person" if acting "for the purpose of or in connection with contemplated legal proceedings".

It should also be borne in mind that a confidentiality undertaking will not in itself be effective in overcoming the statutory obligation to make a disclosure, since it is only privileged information that is immune from disclosure under the relevant POCA offences.[8] Much the same considerations apply to the need to disclose to gain a defence to the principal offences.

Tipping off

Legal advisers might sometimes wish to disclose to the other side that they will be making a disclosure or have done so. Revealing this information in advance of triggering the disclosure process by making a formal report to the nominated officer will not amount to tipping off since at that stage no disclosure will have been made, though care will be needed as to the dangers of the separate and ill-defined offence of "disclosing an investigation". Even where the disclosure has already been made there is now also the defence at s.333C POCA and 21F TA of disclosures being permitted between professional legal advisers in relation to "a transaction involving them both", but only where "the disclosure is for the purpose only of preventing an offence under this part of the Act". Quite how this rather odd form of statutory wording will be interpreted remains to be seen, notwithstanding that it has been in place since 2007.

Other defences

The LSPN also discusses the significance of the defence of adequate consideration in transactional work. This is unlikely to be of great significance in practice since if a charge were to be brought it would, on past experience, be likely to be that of entering an arrangement under s.328 POCA as above. It is possible, however, that the offence of acquisition, use or possession under s.329 POCA could be brought instead on the basis that the firm is handling criminal proceeds when they are paid into the client account. In such circumstances the defence of adequate consideration might apply, to the effect that the firm would have simply been party to paying a fair market price for the undertaking. It should be borne in mind, however, that this defence only applies to the acquisition, use and possession offence and not the other "principal" offences of concealing and arrangements. The LSPN suggests at 12.3.2 that perhaps a s.328 arrangement and the acquisition, use and possession offences should be "read together" but this concept is untried, and it therefore suggests that the point should be "considered" and may need "legal advice as appropriate".

Post completion

Until such time as any predicate offence is remedied by payment of the "saved costs", the tainted assets will remain within the target company post completion. This remains the case whether the sale was by way of asset or share sale and could in theory mean that further use, possession or other dealing with those assets by the directors will continue to be an offence under ss.327-328 POCA.

The concept of fungibility, which means that the entire assets are considered tainted, featured heavily in the Home Office review of the reporting system in 2008 and is a concept which has caused considerable problems in the banking sector. If criminal proceeds are paid into a bank account, then this is taken to taint all the money in that account, with the result that any subsequent dealings with the account could give rise to an offence under POCA. The banking industry has argued that this concept means that it needs to ask for the consent of the NCA every time a transaction is carried out via that bank account, although the Home Office disagreed with this interpretation.[9] The Law Society in its response to the consultation stated that the concept of fungibility means that there is "frequently the necessity for multiple consent reports relating to a single, non-serious technical offence."[10] Notwithstanding the stated intention at the time for the Home Office to find ways of reducing the burden of seeking consent little has since been achieved in this regard, so until reforms are implemented the best course of action continues to be to remedy the offence that has occurred. This is the case even if the tainted assets did not have an effect on the share price and so no consent was obtained for the original share sale.

Summary

The main considerations to arise through a transaction can be summarised as follows:

Vendor/Vendor's legal advisers

The instructions provided to the vendor's legal advisers will generally be covered by privilege and thus they will be immune from having to make a "required disclosure" under the "failure to disclose" offences at s.330 POCA and s.21A TA. The adviser should inform the vendor client of the need to address irregularities that amount to offences out of their duty to do their best for the client (Principle 4 of the SRA Handbook). They should also advise the vendor of the purchaser's adviser's duty to disclose under s.330 POCA and should also explain that the vendors will be obliged to disclose pre-completion if the problems are still unresolved and if they have a bearing on the consideration being paid. This will not be tipping off since no disclosure will have been made at this stage.

If any irregularities affecting the share price remain and cannot be dealt with adequately by elements of the agreement, the vendor's advisers would only be able to continue to act if they make an "authorised disclosure" in advance of completion to protect themselves from liability under the principal offences. Since their information is likely to be privileged information that has been received from the client they are likely to have to gain their client's waiver of privilege, under the Law Society's *Bowman v Fels* guidance. If the consent to disclosure is not forthcoming, and if the client also declines the alternative of correcting the underlying problems, they would have to withdraw from acting further or accept the risk of liability under the principal offences. Although not quite so clear-cut as under the former 2007 Code of Conduct, which had a direct rule prohibiting the involvement of solicitors in any illegal action[11], to do so could be seen to be in breach of the firm's professional obligations under Principle 1 (the duty to observe the rule of law and to uphold the administration of justice) and O(7.5) (the need to comply with legislation).

Purchaser/Purchaser's legal advisers

The purchaser's adviser, seeing disclosure details that reveal criminality, will not be covered by privilege and would appear to be under a duty to disclose their knowledge or suspicion of money laundering by "another person" – i.e. the vendor – under s.330 POCA. In practice they are unlikely to do so if they can be satisfied that the problem will be resolved at some stage. A confidentiality agreement will not override the duty to disclose offence: only privilege excuses non-disclosure where there is an obligation to do so. Much the same would apply to any funders and their representatives.

The purchaser's adviser would also seem to need to make an authorised disclosure in advance of completion where problems are still outstanding to protect themselves from liability under the principal offences, and might well advise their client to join in on this disclosure so that they also can gain immunity. A particular consideration for the purchaser is the offence of acquisition, use and possession at s.329 POCA post completion.

Case study

The firm is instructed in a management buyout deal worth £15m. Environmental and health and safety due diligence reveals that the target has failed to obtain certain reports required by health and safety law. The reports required include a machinery risk assessment, legionella survey and electrical survey. There are insufficient internal resources to compile the reports as nobody in the company has the requisite skills or expertise. The reports therefore would have to be commissioned externally at a cost to the firm.

The question arises as to whether any money laundering offences have already been committed or will be committed as a result of the buyout.

Before completion

- It would appear that the target is already in possession of criminal property, in the form of saved costs. These have arisen from the money saved by not commissioning the writing of the reports by an external body. If the reports had been capable of being produced internally by existing resources no costs would have been saved and so no criminal property would be in existence.
- The legal advisers (both vendor and purchaser) arguably have a duty to disclose under s.330 unless the defence of privileged circumstances applies. This defence would appear not to be available if the information relating to health and safety has been put into the data room and viewed by the purchaser and is then subject to questioning.

Share sale

- The question is whether the cost of the reports, which constitute the saved costs, is sufficient to have an effect on the share price. Arguably there is no effect on share price because the cost of reports is immaterial in relation to value of the target as a whole, so no criminal offence is committed by the share transfer.
- If there is an effect then the offences and defences set out in ss.327-329 POCA apply and the parties to the buyout and their legal advisers need to decide whether to make a disclosure, remedy the offence or abort the deal.
- Any possible effect on the share price could be remedied before completion by commissioning the report and making payment in advance. Any required adjustment to the share price should be made before completion.
- The lack of time before completion might make the commissioning of a report and payment not possible. It might therefore be decided that one of the legal advisers holds the funds in their client account pending the commissioning/production of the reports. Arguably this money is still criminal property and the law firm is committing the offence of possessing criminal property (s.329 POCA) but this is very unlikely to have legal ramifications. Such risk as does exist might be avoided if the law firm holds the money to the order of the external consultant to be paid on completion of the work and if the work is not completed within three months then the money is to be donated money to a charity. This will ensure that the money does not revert to the target in the event that the work is not carried out.

Post completion

- Unless the reports were commissioned, or money was held on account pending their completion, the target will still be in possession of criminal property after the buyout has taken place. This will result in post completion offences being committed by the new directors. To avoid this, the tainted assets need to be cleansed before completion by the

> commissioning and advance payment for the report. Although this will not remedy existing breaches, the assets of the target will cease to be tainted and therefore the directors will be able to deal with those assets including money in the bank account without committing a criminal offence.

Notes

1   MLR 2007 r.3(9)(a), (d) and (e).
2   *Fuglers LLP v Solicitors Regulation Authority* [2014] EWHC 179 (Admin).
3   *Bowman v Fels* [2005] EWCA Civ 226, para 67.
4   *Fitzpatrick v Metropolitan Police Commissioner* [2012] EWHC 12 (QB).
5   POCA s.340(3) and (6).
6   POCA s.333A(1)(b) and 333(D)(2).
7   LSPN para 12.3.2.
8   Section 330 and the principal offences at ss.327-329.
9   'Obligations to report Money Laundering: Consultation document 2007', The Home Office.
10 'Obligations to report Money Laundering: The consent regime. The Law Society's response to the Home Office Consultation', The Law Society, March 2008.
11 The Solicitors' Code of Conduct 2007, rule 2.01(a).

CHAPTER 15

Litigation and family law

Risk profile

Of all the main legal disciplines, litigation and family law are likely to be the lowest risk in terms of their AML and CTF profile in most firms, meaning that the problem for those with compliance responsibility in these areas of work can instead be one of complacency. Since litigators are less likely to have to make disclosures to the NCA, and with many areas of litigation being exempt from the MLR 2007, the temptation is to think that the regime does not apply to the litigious parts of the practice. This is not the case, however, particularly in areas of civil litigation. Here, at least, there are compliance risks to be recognised and avoided, though criminal law as a practice area may in practice bring fewer such concerns.

Money Laundering Regulations 2007

The conduct of disputes is not specifically included in the definition of regulated activities within the MLR 2007. Furthermore, the exemptions from the regulations to be found at para 1.4.5 of the Law Society's practice note include:

- Provision of legal advice;
- Participation in litigation or a form of alternative dispute resolution; and
- Publicly-funded work.

Notwithstanding the reference to litigation, the LSPN at para 1.4.5 counsels caution on exempting areas of the practice and suggests that in determining their position firms should "take the broadest of the possible approaches to compliance with the regulations." The reasoning seems to be that it does not follow from the regulations and the practice note that anything of a litigious nature will necessarily be exempt from the regime. The boundaries between transactional work and disputes can easily become blurred, especially where the parties are still in negotiations, and what might have started out as a debt action can soon become more transactional in its nature. For much the same reasoning family law is usually included within the regulated sector, most obviously because of the ancillary issues surrounding the joint assets, tax issues and any property that is owned or occupied by the parties. Likewise, a commercial dispute might well be transferred to a non-contentious colleague who will continue the work done by the firm by way of negotiation, in which case it will not be clear if the matter remains litigious in its nature or has become transactional in its outcome.

It follows that one of the first steps for the firm to carry out is to take a view on which parts of the practice are covered by the regulations. Much will depend on this as CDD checking processes and the duty to make disclosures under s.330 are limited to the regulated sector. If, as is highly probable, the firm takes the view that certain of its litigation work, for example its personal injury work, is outside the scope of the regulations, it would also exclude this area of work from the obligation to disclose suspicions of money laundering under s.330 POCA. It is not clear if the firm's own decision on whether its constituent parts are regulated or not is conclusive, or whether this might be subject to review in a subsequent money laundering or terrorist financing prosecution.

The approach most adopted in practice can be summarised as:

- Firms that practise exclusively, or almost exclusively, in areas of legal aid or publicly-funded services, such as crime-only practices, are likely to see themselves as being exempt from the regulations;
- Where there are distinct parts of the practice and little overlap between clients, as with a largely self-contained personal injury department that obtains its work from referral sources, that part of the practice will generally be exempted by the firm from the need to comply with the MLR 2007. The advantage of this approach is not having to obtain CDD evidence from individuals who are not met in person, at least in the early stages of the dispute; and
- In most other mixed practices, whether high street or commercial, the safest and most practical approach is to apply the same degree of compliance under the regulations to all departments or groups, and all clients.

Proceeds of Crime Act 2002

As always, it is important to consider the need for disclosures under the separate headings of the *duty* to disclose under s.330 POCA and the *need* to disclose to gain a defence to the principal offences under ss.327-329 POCA.

The duty to disclose

As far as the duty to disclose is concerned, there should seldom be any cause to make a disclosure because of the operation of the privilege defence found at s.330(6) POCA or s.21A(5) TA for those lawyers who are inside the regulated sector, and at s.19(5) TA for those who are not. The process of taking instructions from the client is one of the clearest examples of discussions that are covered by common law litigation privilege, and is also subject to the statutory format of the "privileged circumstances" defence. There might be a need, however, to consider the need for a disclosure where the crime/fraud exception applies, and this might arise in certain categories of litigation such as personal injury, where there is sham litigation. Since privilege will not arise where the lawyer is, in effect, the means by which the fraud will be committed, there would then be a duty to make a disclosure, but only where the work is regulated in its nature. All therefore again depends on whether the instructions in hand and the work of the department or group in question are subject to the MLR 2007.

Examples: Obligation to disclose

There is a personal injury department in a large mixed practice. The view taken, and recorded in the firm's policy manuals, is that the work of this department is exempt from the MLR 2007 and is not regulated.

Client A consults the firm about a possible claim for compensation arising from a road collision. On closer inspection it seems that the incident that gave rise to the injuries that are alleged to have been sustained is a scam and that the injuries are either fabricated or severely exaggerated.

The lawyer, as required by Principle 1 of the SRA Handbook, declines to act since to do so would be unprofessional and/or illegal. She concludes that the crime/fraud exception would apply since there was an attempt to commit a crime of fraud through her, with the result that the instructions are not therefore covered by privilege.

There would be no need to make a disclosure under s.330 POCA since the department in question is outside the regulated sector – thus no duty to do so arises. In these circumstances it might be argued that making a voluntary disclosure might be contrary to Rule 4 of the Code of Conduct but the fraudulent nature of the client's instructions might also waive confidentiality. The usual rule, however, is that client information should only be disclosed when there is a requirement to do so and it would therefore be unlikely that a disclosure is made on a voluntary basis for fear of professional liability.

The final consideration is that although money laundering is defined at s.340(11) POCA to include an attempt to commit an offence, the LSPN at para 6.4.3 suggests that as long as no offence is committed there is no fraud to be reported to the NCA under s.330 POCA.

Much the same considerations would apply to client B who asks to be paid his or her compensation to the bank account of a friend or relative where this is suspected to be to

---

avoid any changes to the client's entitlement to benefits. Most firms would decline to make the payment as requested on grounds that it would be improper to do so and for fear of entering an arrangement under s.328 POCA. Having refused to make the payment to the third party, most firms will not then make a disclosure to the NCA in relation to the incitement, attempt or other inchoate offence on grounds that criminal conduct has been prevented.

It should be noted that where terrorist financing is present or suspected, different considerations apply as a result of the duty to disclose extending beyond the regulated sector through s.19 TA and the specific reference to attempts in s.21A TA.

The principal offences

The main effect of the *Bowman v Fels* decision[1] is to take contentious work outside the scope of the principal offences, particularly s.328 POCA, and so remove the need for an authorised disclosure to be made and consent to be obtained where there is a suspicion of illegal activity. The justification for this approach is to be found at paras 83-84 of the judgment. Describing legal proceedings as a "state-provided mechanism for the resolution of issues according to law", their lordships went on, crucially, to rule that:

> "Parliament cannot have intended that proceedings or steps taken by lawyers in order to determine or secure legal rights and remedies for their clients should involve them in 'becoming concerned in an arrangement which ... facilitates the acquisition, retention, use or control of criminal property', even if they suspected that the outcome of such proceedings might have such an effect." (para 84)

The effect of this "central issue" of the case, as it was referred to, was an immediate reduction in the frequency of disclosures by solicitors' firms, especially in the field of family law. No longer would the divorce lawyer told of the nanny being paid in cash to avoid national insurance, or learning of some other taxation irregularity in a family business, risk entering an arrangement themself. It follows that they would not therefore have to make a disclosure since there was no need to acquire a defence to such charge.

Since *Bowman v Fels* limited itself to s.328 arrangements, concerns have since been expressed about possible liability for the other principal offences. The same family lawyer might be at risk of "concealing" relevant information contrary to s.327 POCA, or to be in use or possession of the funds while they are in the client account contrary to s.329 POCA. Such concerns, although they have been acknowledged by the Law Society in the past, do not seem as yet to have materialised in practice, and it is to be hoped that this remains the case so far as the prosecuting authorities are concerned.

The LSPN at para 5.4.3 on the impact of the *Bowman v Fels* decision remains that all

---

forms of disputes, including ADR, mediation and tribunal proceedings, will be covered by the judgment and that its scope includes the distribution of damages or other funds through the client account. The more practical concern is where the client then goes on to instruct a non-contentious department in the same firm. The share of the matrimonial proceeds were not disclosable while they featured in the ancillary dispute, but if the client then instructs a conveyancer in the same firm, the conveyancer would not be subject to the *Bowman v Fels* exemption and might need to make a disclosure before completing any transaction, for fear of committing one of the principal offences. This wholly unwelcome complication has caused various firms to create a "warned list" where concerns that arise in litigation matters can be recorded (whatever the data protection considerations) as a warning to their non-contentious colleagues.

The risk of a conveyancer entering an arrangement contrary to s.328 by acting in any transaction where they know or suspect that criminal property is involved is recognised in updated Law Society advice on the application of the statutory disclosure requirements to family law – "Matrimonial property challenges" (2nd December 2014). Anyone with an interest in the application of the statutory disclosure principles to family law, and perhaps litigation more generally, should take heed of this advice which for the most part restates the Society's position that litigators do not enter an arrangement with their clients through acting and may also therefore handle any assets without the risk of criminal liability. On the other hand greater caution is now recommended in relation to tax evasion in particular. The advice note also confirms that where the adviser receives allegations of criminal conduct by their client from an opponent or a third party that they should put these to their client so as to give them an opportunity to respond. Even if any such allegations do transpire to be valid the information is still likely to be privileged, with the result that the adviser might sometimes wish to withdraw from acting further, but would not be obliged to do so or to make a criminal report on their client in most cases.

Finally, it should be noted that the *Bowman v Fels* litigation exemption does depend on there being a genuine dispute between the parties. 'Sham' litigation would not be covered and where there is a fraudulent claim – in personal injury cases, for example – the crime/fraud exception would apply so that the instructions would not be protected by privilege. Litigators should also not regard themselves as being immune from liability for an "arrangement" under s.328 POCA if, for example, they make payments to unrelated third parties whereby benefit fraud or tax evasion might knowingly be facilitated.

Note

1   *Bowman v Fels* [2005] EWCA Civ 226.

CHAPTER 16

Private client

Risk profile

Private client solicitors operate in law firms of all different shapes and sizes, from high street practices and local law firms through to large regional, niche and City law firms. The work covers most obviously the core areas of will drafting, probate and trusts but can also include instructions in relation to personal tax planning, charities, agricultural and residential conveyancing. This chapter concentrates on the core areas of wills, probate and trusts, and also personal tax planning. The risk profile of this core area is varied in nature: wills, probate and the administration of testamentary trusts will almost invariably be low profile under the risk assessment required by the MLR 2007, whereas more complex investment trusts are probably amongst the higher risk transactions that firms are likely to encounter.

As ever, the application by a practice of a lower risk banding to its wills and probate work does not mean that there is no risk of having to make disclosures to the NCA under POCA or TA in these areas. For example, where there has been dishonesty by the deceased in an administration, a disclosure is a distinct possibility even if the need to do so is circumvented by the practical steps taken. Non-payment of tax is another area where disclosure may be required.

Trusts, charities and other such vehicles are increasingly being used to disguise ownership by criminals and terrorists. Trusts might also be created at one firm to be used elsewhere, in which case it would be wise to question why the firm is being asked to create any such scheme if no further instructions follow.

Any request to a legal adviser to act as a trustee could be a means to misuse their professional status to gain respectability and so acceptance should be made only after careful financial and other checks are made. As ever, the firm must also be wary of being asked to bank large amounts of money in client account pending further instructions. This is a common means of laundering funds and could also be a breach of the SRA Accounts Rules.[1]

Money Laundering Regulations 2007

The core work of a private client department should generally be viewed as being caught by the provisions of the MLR 2007; the provision of taxation advice is specifically mentioned at r.3(8) as an area that is embraced within these provisions. There is a possible exemption for will-writing, according to the Law Society practice note at para 1.4.5, but even here care would be needed because of the possibility of incorporating taxation advice as part of the service provided – a point which is now acknowledged in the LSPN at para 1.4.5.

There are certain warning signs which indicate higher risk and should also be taken into account whether taking initial instructions or conducting ongoing monitoring. They include:

- Obscure source of funds, especially those which emanate from a foreign jurisdiction;
- The deceased was accused or convicted of acquisitive crime during his or her lifetime;
- The deceased had business interests in a high risk jurisdiction;
- Discretionary and complex offshore trusts;
- Trusts which have unusual structures or jurisdiction, especially those with strict bank secrecy and confidentiality rules or without equivalent money laundering procedures; and
- Non-payment of tax or wrongful receipt of benefits giving rise to 'saved costs'.

Beneficial ownership

Amongst the most difficult concepts in the MLR 2007 in relation to private client work are the rules relating to beneficial interests involving trusts. They require a good understanding of trust law to decide if an interest is vested, contingent, in possession, in residue, or defeasible or indefeasible.

Regulation 6(3) sets out three types of beneficial owners of a trust:

- Part (a): "any individual who is entitled to a specified interest in at least 25% of the capital of the trust property";
- Part (b): "[…] the class of persons in whose main interest the trust is set up or operates"; and
- Part (c): "any individual who has control over the trust."

Individual with specified interest (part (a))

Individuals have to have a specified interest in at least 25% of the capital. This means that those with life interests are not considered beneficiaries under this heading, as their interest is in income and not capital.

A specified interest means a "vested interest" which is "in possession or in remainder or in reversion" and is "defeasible or indefeasible" (r.6(4)(a)-(b)). A vested interest is one that is not subject to any future condition, so "to my children in equal shares" is a vested interest whereas "to my children as shall survive me and attain the age of 25" is subject to a future event and is thus a contingent interest, and in this case is subject to both an age and a survival condition. If an interest is given to a child, but is not subject to a condition precedent, it is still vested. This is so notwithstanding the fact that until the beneficiary reaches the age of 18 he or she cannot receive the capital because they cannot give a valid receipt to the trustees or executors.

The interest can be:

- In possession, which means the beneficiary has the immediate right to use the trust fund:
- In remainder, which means there are prior interests; or
- In reversion, which means the trust fund reverts to the settlor.

By way of example, if a testator provides a life interest for his wife, with remainder to his children in equal shares, his children have a vested interest in remainder, as their interest is subject to the prior life interest of their mother.

Defeasible and indefeasible interests are included. This means that a beneficiary who has a specified interest in at least 25% of the capital at the time the instructions are taken has to be verified under part (a), even though the will or trust gives the trustees overriding power to vary the trust and thus reduce the share of a beneficiary below 25%. With defeasible interests it is necessary to consider the shares of the beneficiaries at the time instructions are taken.

If a trust has one or more persons who are individuals with a 25% specified interest, but has other beneficiaries who fall below the 25%, the former will fall under part (a) but the rest have to be considered as beneficiaries under part (b).

The LSPN contains at para 4.7.6 detailed definitions of the various trust terminology set out in part (a).

Class of persons to benefit (part (b))
Beneficiaries falling under this heading are generally identified as a class – for example, 'the children of A'. All discretionary trusts are covered, as are those with beneficiaries who have contingent interests, and as such might be specifically named but cannot fall under part (a).

If there are several classes of beneficiaries it is necessary to decide which class is more likely to receive the trust property. The LSPN at para 4.7.6 gives the example of a trust for the children of X, but if they all die, for the grandchildren of X, but if they all die, for charity Y. The suggestion is that the class is likely to be the children of X as it is unlikely that they will all die before the funds are disbursed. If there is doubt about which class has the main interest, it is necessary to identify all the classes.

Control of the trust (part (c))
Control is defined in r.6(4) MLR 2007 as "a power (whether exercisable alone, jointly with another person or with the consent of another person) under the trust instrument or by law to:

(a) dispose of, advance, lend, invest, pay or apply trust property;
(b) vary the trust;
(c) add or remove a person as a beneficiary or to or from a class of beneficiaries;
(d) appoint or remove trustees;
(e) direct, withhold consent to or veto the exercise of a power such as is mentioned in sub-paragraph (a), (b), (c) or (d)."

The definition of control applies equally to trustees and beneficiaries, and to situations where their powers have to be exercised collectively. A protector, in respect of offshore trusts, may also fall under this category.

According to r.6(5)(b), "an individual does not have control solely as a result of:

(i) his consent being required in accordance with section 32(1)(c) of the Trustee Act 1925 (power of advancement);

(ii) any discretion delegated to him under section 34 of the Pensions Act 1995 (power of investment and delegation);

(iii) the power to give a direction conferred on him by section 19(2) of the Trusts of Land and Appointment of Trustees Act 1996 (appointment and retirement of trustee at instance of beneficiaries); or

(iv) the power exercisable collectively at common law to vary or extinguish a trust where the beneficiaries under the trust are of full age and capacity and (taken together) absolutely entitled to the property subject to the trust".

Examples of the application of parts (a), (b) and (c) to certain trusts:

Mrs A sets up an *inter vivos* trust 'to such of my grandchildren who attain the age of 25'. The trustees have power to vary the shares of the beneficiaries. None of the grandchildren are yet 25.

- The grandchildren have contingent interests and so are identified as a class under part (b);
- The trustees need to be identified under part (c);
- When a grandchild reaches 25, its interest will vest. If its interest is 25 per cent or more it will need to be identified under part (a) at that time, otherwise it will remain under part (b).

Mr B's will trust provides for a life interest in income for his wife C, with a remainder to their children who shall survive C and attain the age of 25. In the event of no children surviving C, then everything is to go to charity D. Mr B has died.

- During the administration of B's estate, his personal representatives are the beneficial owners and there is no need to verify the identity of any other beneficiaries;
- C has a life interest and so does not have an interest in capital and therefore does not fall under part (a);
- The children have a contingent interest in remainder. Even if they are 25 at the date of B's death, they still have to survive their mother. As such they fall under part (b);
- The charity D has an interest in remainder but it does not have the main interest and so will not fall under part (b); and
- The powers given to the trustees are likely to mean that they fall to be identified under part (c).

Proceeds of Crime Act 2002

The client's assets may be tainted by criminal conduct giving rise to criminal proceeds as, for example, where a deceased testator has failed to pay tax, and has therefore involved him or herself in criminal conduct leading to criminal property. The effect of the tax evasion is to taint the client's assets since the estate has been increased by the funds which should have been paid by way of tax.

If assets are tainted in this way, the firm should advise the executor client to rectify any tax issues before the estate is distributed. The alternative is for the client to waive privilege and make a joint report with the firm to the NCA, but if the client refuses both options the firm will be unable to act further. The instructions to that point of time would be privileged, meaning that no duty to disclose would arise under s.330 on grounds of the privileged circumstances defence at s.330(6). Furthermore, in the unlikely event of a disclosure being made to the NCA for the adviser to gain a defence to an arrangement offence under s.328, the executor's waiver of privilege would usually be necessary since the lawyer would almost certainly form their knowledge of the illegal activity through taking instructions that were subject to advice privilege. The client should be advised that a disclosure will mean that the matter will be reported to the HMRC and so the outstanding tax would need to be paid in any event. Such advice would not amount to tipping off as no disclosure would have been made at that point, but care would have to be taken in relation to the linked offence in s.333 of disclosing an investigation.

Note

1   SRA Accounts Rules 2011, Rule 14(5).

CHAPTER 17

Property and conveyancing

Introduction

Property work is likely to be the highest risk area of work for AML purposes in most law firms. Not only are property purchases the most common high value transactions undertaken by law firms, but the conveyancing transaction also represents the most obvious way for criminals to launder large amounts of funds. A further complication is the pace of the modern property transaction, leaving the conveyancer little time to investigate anomalies as to client identities or the source of funds, especially if they arise shortly before completion. It is therefore no coincidence that most of the AML prosecutions against lawyers to date have involved conveyancing purchases, with the convictions of David McCartan and Phillip Griffiths being prime examples.[1] Add to this the increasing incidence of mortgage fraud and it follows that property lawyers need to be on their guard, both for illegal funds being invested by clients and for transactions that are themselves an attempt to perpetrate a fraud against their lenders. These risks have brought with them an increased weighting in professional indemnity insurance premiums, making effective risk management in this area of work all the more important.

Money Laundering Regulations 2007

Property transactions are directly addressed by the MLR 2007. Regulation 3 provides that "independent legal professionals" are covered by the regulations "when participating in financial or real property transactions concerning [...] the buying and selling of real property or business entities". The one exception of note for conveyancers is that preparing a Home Information Pack or any of its contents is specifically exempted from the scope of the Regulations (r.4(1)(f)).

There are some specific warning signs in relation to property transactions, set out in chapter 11 of the Law Society's practice note, which should be taken into account when undertaking risk assessments at matter level and as part of ongoing monitoring. These are summarised and explained below but should be consulted in full by those with responsibility for AML and CTF compliance in property work.

Ownership

Ownership by multiple parties or nominee companies may be an attempt to obscure the true ownership of the property or to make it difficult to ascertain the audit trail. There may also be sudden and unexpected changes in ownership. 'Flipping' is one such example of this, where fraudsters seek to re-sell a property very quickly for a substantially increased price; though given the prevalence of this practice in recent years in numerous mortgage fraud scams the lenders are unlikely to be involved in any such transactions, with the result that they are therefore now much less likely to be encountered.

Funding

The firm should be wary if the source of funding for a property purchase is obscure or unusual for the type of transaction involved. If large payments are made from the client's own funds then the origins of those funds should be ascertained; in other words, it becomes just as important to know the source of wealth of the client as the source of funds, such as the bank account that will be used to remit the completion monies. In this regard it should be remembered that the fact that a payment is made via a well-known clearing bank does not necessarily mean that the funds are clean – a point that many lawyers continue to overlook. It is possible that criminal funds might have been successfully "placed" in an account, in which case its subsequent "layering" is as easily culpable as the introduction of the funds to the bank in the first place. Property lawyers in particular need to remember that from their point of view it is layering that carries the greater risk of their becoming involved in AML or CTF activity, rather than the receipt of cash.

A good example of the importance of this form of checking was provided by the SRA by way of a case study in its advice note "Cleaning up: Law firms and the risk of money laundering" which was issued in conjunction with the November update of its Risk Outlook document for 2014-15. A client was purchasing a flat using his own funds and the conveyancer therefore requested the last six months' bank statements. These showed no regular payments-in but several large receipts were shown from a named company within a short period of time. Given that no information could be obtained on this company through an internet search a disclosure was made. The firm's file was requested and a successful prosecution was subsequently brought against the client, who turned out to be a drug dealer who was acquiring premises for cannabis production.

Where funding is contributed, whether in whole or in part, from a third party the source of those funds also needs to be ascertained. There are two levels of checking that might apply here: first, any contribution above the €15,000 level in the MLR 2007 will count as an occasional transaction and so trigger the obligation to conduct CDD at r.7(1)(b); but more generally there is always the need to understand the transaction being handled, not least so as to be able to counter any charge under the failure to disclose and the principal offences in part 7 of POCA. The LSPN states at para 11.4.1 that in such circumstances the firm needs to consider the relationship between the client and the third party and the proportion of funding being provided by the third party. Many firms apply a lower level of checking when the funds are received initially by the client rather than being received directly into client account, but this is questionable since the lawyer is responsible for the transaction whether they receive the funds directly or indirectly. It is also advisable to have a clear understanding of the source of all intended completion monies from the outset of the matter so as to avoid the panic that might ensue from an unexpected receipt immediately before completion; see the "source of funds" form at Chapter 18, which has been designed to assist in this process.

Direct payments between the buyer and seller should also be closely monitored, not least as they may amount (unwittingly, perhaps) to an application fraud against the lender through misrepresenting the actual sale and purchase price, thus distorting the loan to value percentage which will often be an important part of the lender's risk calculations. Direct payments between the parties, whether for payments for carpets or other fixtures and fittings or not, can also often be a device to commit stamp duty fraud by artificially reducing the price below a threshold, a practice which the lawyer must, of course, be wary to avoid at all costs.

Cash payments

Property transactions are usually funded in part by mortgage borrowing so, depending on the factors of the transaction, if the whole or a large part is funded by private funding this is likely to add to the checks that need to be made. Here the original source of wealth becomes all the more important, but taking into account all relevant circumstances; for example, a well established private client who is well known to the firm from his successful business activities locally over many years, purchasing a holiday home as he or she nears retirement, can fairly attract less questioning than someone 40 years their junior who is making a purchase with little or no borrowing, especially if they are not working.

A particular problem relating to cash payments can arise at auction sales where the vendor requests that the cash is put into the solicitor's client account as soon as the sale is agreed, in that the source of the funds will lie with the purchaser and it is likely to be difficult for the firm to carry out the necessary CDD checks in advance of receiving the funds. In relation to this issue the Law Society guidance on property work suggested that the firm may be able to use the checks carried out by the auctioneers as part of its CDD even though they would not count as one of the groups that might offer formal reliance under r.17 of the MLR 2007.[2] This would not, however, prevent them from being regarded as a "reliable and independent source" within the meaning of r.5 as one of the approved methods of "customer due diligence measures". The guidance does nonetheless suggest that "ultimately the solicitor may feel more comfortable not banking the cash into their account and would prefer their client to do so." This might assist the vendor's lawyer in the situation, but does rather leave open the question of the client's potential liability for the principal offences and the advice that should therefore be offered to them, most obviously for acquisition, use and possession under s.329 POCA. In practice the risks here should not be too pronounced since the principal offences all require normal *mens rea*, so liability should not arise unless some illicit activity by the purchaser was known about or suspected. The client would also probably be able to claim the defence of adequate consideration if questioned on any such transaction.

The firm needs to have a policy on not accepting large cash payments into its client account. Most firms seem to have introduced a cash receipts limit for partners and staff – £500 to £1000 are figures commonly encountered. It should also be noted that banks have been known to permit large cash payments direct into client account without asking for the permission of the firm, especially where the payment is offered in another location. The Law Society advises not giving out client bank account details until CDD has been completed to try to lessen the risk of this happening, but client account details do, of course, appear on all client account cheques.[3] It follows that accounts departments need to monitor receipts into client account and question those that are by cash.

The firm should not allow its client account to be used where there is no underlying transaction, and must ensure that it is holding and disbursing money on behalf of a client for a proper purpose. The SRA Accounts Rules make it clear that it is not a proper part of a lawyer's role to operate a banking facility for third parties, whether they are clients or not.

Valuation

Law firms are not required to offer valuations of property, but this does not mean that they can ignore the issue, especially where the amounts being paid are questionable or it is known that the issue is being discussed between the parties. Sales at an over-value might suggest mortgage fraud activity, as in the commercial property case of *Cheshire Building Society v Dunlop Haywards & Others* 2008, but sales at an under-value might be an indicator of money laundering, as in *R v Griffiths & Pattison* 2006. The issue was particularly relevant in the Cheshire Building Society case, where one of the main grounds in the finding against the Society's legal advisers – notwithstanding that the client had appointed its own surveyors to advise it on the valuation – was that they had overlooked emails that questioned the apparent discrepancies in the valuation advice being provided, and so had overlooked "the indicia of fraud". Reported separately as *Nationwide Building Society v Dunlop Haywards and others* 2009[4] (the Nationwide Building Society having taken over the Cheshire Building Society largely as a result of its losses in this single case), a payment to the lender was ordered to the level set by way of limitation of liability in the retainer agreement.

Unless the firm specialises in bulk conveyancing from referred sources, the receipt of standard residential instructions from elsewhere in the country where there is no obvious local connection might trigger suspicions as to the client's intentions. It is possible that the parties hope that distant lawyers might not question what would be regarded as suspect pricing for the property in question closer to home. In such circumstances various websites might assist, or it might be necessary to make contact with independent local estate agents. The conveyancer must also take into account if the value of the property has increased significantly in a short period of time so as to take it out of line with the market in the area or the data available to them from the Land Registry. Another obvious concern is to establish if the valuer who has provided the valuation report actually exists or was actually involved in the evidence provided. Although those who are members of the Royal Institution of Chartered Surveyors can be checked on its website there is no equivalent for those who are unregulated.[5]

Mortgage fraud

Mortgage fraud activity has become increasingly common in recent years and is dealt with in more detail at Chapter 13. Fraud is defined in the Fraud Act 2006 to include fraud by false representation and by failure to disclose information where there is a legal duty to disclose. Mortgage fraud occurs when a mortgage is arranged by misleading the lender as to the borrower's circumstances ("application fraud") or the identity of one or more of the parties ("identity fraud"). Common fraud practices include:

- The true purchase price is not disclosed to the lender;
- The borrowers mislead the lender about their financial position;
- The lender is not told about allowances for additional items such as carpets and fittings, or incentives by builders selling new properties, such as free holidays;
- The price paid is actually less than reported;

- The buyers are not providing the balance of the price from their own resources.

The facilitation of mortgage fraud by solicitors is usually attributable to incompetence rather than dishonesty, but the latter has featured in various findings by the Solicitors Disciplinary Tribunal in recent years. Where there are reasonable suspicions that the other side's advisers are acting dishonestly the firm should consider the obligation to report their suspicions to the SRA under O.10(4) of the Code of Conduct, which talks about the need to report "serious misconduct". If doing so after a disclosure to the NCA has been made there is a specific defence in relation to the offence of tipping off at s.333D(1)(a) POCA and s.21G(1)(a) TA.

A conveyancing solicitor's obligations to a lender client are clearly set out in the Lenders' Handbook[6] and in chapters 3-4 of the Code of Conduct. Where the lawyer is acting for the lender as well as the purchaser they have a potential conflict of interests, but since there is no intrinsic conflict in acting for lender and borrower this is more an issue under chapter 4 of the Code of Conduct, dealing with confidentiality and disclosure, than chapter 3 and professional conflicts as such. The firm's primary obligation is the duty of confidentiality to the client that the firm already represents, or has represented in the past. This duty will need to be reconciled with the duty of disclosure to other clients, however, and the general rule is that where the adviser is unable to be fully open with another client (as the lender will be seen to be for these purposes) unless it compromises the duty of confidentiality to the original client (the purchaser), then it may not act or continue to act for the new lender client. Where the solicitor is informed of or discovers information that might be relevant to the lender it is likely to be confidential to the purchaser, so it follows that this may only be passed on to the lender if the purchaser consents to the lender being informed. If the purchaser refuses to give such consent then the adviser is placed in a position of conflict and will not be able to continue to act for the lender through its duty of disclosure at O(4.2).

If the lawyer ceases to act he or she may still wish to report an attempted fraud to the lender. The position here is complex in that there is still a continuing duty of confidentiality to former clients, but it is nonetheless suggested by the Law Society's practice note that the crime/fraud exception might arise in which case the duty of confidentiality might be waived. This is far from clear-cut, however; the same advice talks about the need for a "strong prima facie case that the client, or third party, was using you to further a fraud or criminal purpose" for the normal duty of confidentiality to be waived, and suggests that the advice of an AML specialist might be needed in such cases. It is more likely that the lender could be informed where the purchaser has made a deliberate misrepresentation. If this is not the case, the Law Society practice note on mortgage fraud states that "you should simply return the mortgage documents to the lender and advise that you are ceasing to act due to professional reasons, without providing any further information."[7] If privilege has been lost, then the lawyer must also consider making a disclosure to the NCA.

By way of a footnote to this issue, the Law Society has taken the view that the solicitor might obtain the purchaser's consent to relay any such information to the lender in its retainer process as long as it specifically draws the client's attention to this term (in other words, it must be more than just a clause in the terms of business document) and obtains the client's signature by way of acceptance of the point. This suggestion can now be found at para 6.1 of the LSPN on mortgage fraud of the 31st July 2014, but might nonetheless be open to challenge by the SRA through the principles of the SRA Handbook, especially Principles 3 (to act with independence) and 4 (to act in the best interests of each client). Careful consideration would be required as to whether it was consistent with the duties to the client to report damaging information to the lender without first consulting the purchaser client on the issue in each individual case.

Proceeds of Crime Act 2002

There is a duty to disclose a knowledge or reasonable suspicion of money laundering or terrorist financing under s.330 POCA and the relevant provisions of the TA where the information or suspicions are not covered by legal professional privilege. Commercial and domestic property have become some of the prime investments for terrorist and criminal funds and it follows that property transactions can quite easily give rise to offences under ss.327-329 POCA, especially an "arrangement" under s.328 POCA for any adviser who proceeds with a transaction without first reporting their suspicions and obtaining consent to continue from the NCA and their reporting officer.

Property that is bought with criminal proceeds becomes criminal property itself as s.340(3)(a) POCA provides that the property is criminal property if "it represents such a benefit ...whether directly or indirectly". In addition, information about tax evasion or welfare benefit fraud may come to light during the course of a conveyancing transaction, which may indicate that the property is criminal proceeds due to the principle of "saved costs". Mortgage fraud might also give rise to criminal proceeds in the form of the mortgage money received, though the defence of "adequate consideration" has been held to apply to dishonest borrowers who maintain their repayments.

Any disclosure to the lender is unlikely to be tipping off as there is little likelihood of prejudicing an investigation provided the lender is reputable. Discussing the disclosure with the client is permitted if this is for the purpose of dissuading him or her from engaging in a money laundering offence.

Notes

1   See page 21.
2   'Anti-money laundering guidance for solicitors undertaking property work', The Law Society, 22 December 2005.
3   LSPN para 11.2.3.
4   *Nationwide Building Society v Dunlop Haywards and others* [2009] EWHC 254.
5   www.rics.org.
6   See www.cml.org.uk/cml/handbook/frontpage.aspx.
7   LSPN Mortgage Fraud, 31st July 2014, para 5.2.

PART E

Source Materials

Anti-money laundering and terrorist financing sample policy

CHAPTER 18

Anti-money laundering and terrorist financing sample policy

This is a generic sample policy which will need to be edited in the light of the particular circumstances of each firm. It will be too complex for some and insufficiently detailed for others. The policy, along with the four appendix forms, is taken from the 'Solicitors Office Procedures Manual' (v2) which is also published by Professional Compliance Publishing (www.solicitors-opm.co.uk).

This policy, along with its accompanying forms and all of the other materials forming part of this template manual publication, is available for download exclusively by subscribers to the Infolegal compliance service: see www.infolegal.co.uk. Advice and training on this topic can also be obtained from Infolegal.

Within this sample policy all financial limits marked * are by way of example only and are not based on available guidance.

1 Introduction

1.1 The firm must safeguard against becoming involved in the processing of illegal or improper gains for clients. As a professional practice the firm is particularly attractive to criminals wishing to convert gains to a respectable status. It is the policy of the firm not to assist them to do so. Breach of this policy could in any event be an unlawful act on the part of anyone concerned and could place the firm and/or its representatives at risk of criminal and/or civil proceedings.

1.2 We are also obliged to establish the identity of our clients as a result of the Money Laundering Regulations 2007 ("MLR 2007") and also to screen all work to ensure that:

- We know the identities of other related parties who might be involved (those with a beneficial interest);

- We extend these searches to anyone paying us more than £10,000; and
- We are satisfied that we are aware of the nature and purpose of the instructions and that the work will not put us at risk of involvement in illegal or unprofessional conduct.

1.3 The partners have determined that all work conducted by the firm should be regarded as being covered by the MLR 2007 with the consequential need to conduct identity checks in all areas of our practice. [*Or justify the non-application of the regulations to all or parts of your practice. see page 68.*]

2   Client checking ('CDD')

2.1 Fee earners must ensure that we obtain evidence of identity for all clients as soon as possible after contact is first established between the firm and the potential client, often with the assistance of receptionists and secretaries. The Law Society guidelines make the distinction between 'identification' (being told or coming to know a client's identifying details) and 'verification' (obtaining some evidence which supports this claim of identity). In general 'customer due diligence' (as it is referred to in the MLR 2007) requires both elements to be addressed. The evidence of identity check must be undertaken by completion of forms ML1 and ML2 (Appendices 1 and 2) which must appear on the matter file in question.

2.2 The main requirements for client checking are:
- *Individual client met in person*
  You should ask the client to bring the normal documentation as listed on form ML1 into the office for inspection and copying. The top half of form ML1 must be signed and dated by the person checking the documents along with the Passport/Driving licence checking form (form ML2). When undertaking this process please refer any concerns to a partner (e.g. you do not think that the photo is a likeness of the client presenting it). Where we are acting for co-clients we must certify each of them – it is not permissible for one to bring in the documents of the other where the person checking has not met that other client.
- *Individual client not met in person*
  Please note that every attempt should be made to meet the client in person to verify the evidence provided, but where this is not possible the client should be asked to obtain certification through local solicitors or other professionals. Certification is permissible if received from:
    - Other solicitors in private practice;
    - Accountants in private practice;

- Mortgage brokers or other agents if regulated by the FCA and well known to us; or
- The Post Office's documentation checking service.

Wherever distant certification is obtained from another professional the adviser must make a check of the validity of the referring firm or organisation in a current directory such as the SRA website and print off the relevant entry if possible and place this on the matter file. Where the referrer is not well known to us you must also phone the person who has provided the certification to check if they did indeed do so: be sure to use the number in the professional directory rather than the number on the notepaper in front of you as that notepaper might be false and therefore part of a 'bogus firm' scam. Where repeat usage is made of a particular referrer (e.g. a mortgage broker who introduces multiple matters to the firm) there is no need to have this copy on every matter file.

Finally, we should also commission, with the client's agreement, an electronic search on the basis of copy documents and details provided.

- *Companies*

   In the case of commercial clients a companies search must be obtained at the outset of the first matter for that client, along with a companies search or evidence of the identity of at least two directors or officers, if possible, unless the representatives are known to the firm and have had personal ID checks undertaken already. Further checks may be needed in the case of non-domiciled companies. It is, in any case, important to check that those who purport to represent an organisation are actually entitled to do so.

- *Other types of client*

   For other types of client consult [*name or title*].

2.3 *PEPs and Sanctions*

An electronic search should also be conducted wherever there is a risk that the client or someone else involved in the matter is or could be a 'politically exposed person' ('PEP') or might be on the UN/UK Sanctions list. You should question any client with a foreign connection (including UK passport holders who have recently been based abroad) if they have held a high ranking position in a foreign government or international organisation and/or conduct an electronic search.

Much the same considerations apply to anyone that might, from their activities or profile, appear on one of the sanctions lists. To check this for yourself go to https://www.gov.uk/government/publications/financial-sanctions-consolidated-list-of-targets.

2.4 *Third parties*

2.4.1 It is becoming increasingly common for third parties to make payments to us, especially as more purchasers in conveyancing transactions obtain assistance from parents or other relatives. The approach of the firm is that the source of funds must always be known about in advance and where the sum is for a significant amount (again, a matter of judgement depending on the circumstances, but always where more than £1000* – see introduction – is to be received) questions must be made as to how that money was acquired. If 'savings' then you do need to profile how this person might have acquired this sum, such as detailing their occupation. Where possible check the information with a Google search and file any useful information that you find and/or request six months of bank statements to look for regular salary payments or unusual and large receipts.

2.4.2 Where more than £10,000* is to be received by us (whether directly from the third party or through the client's account) you must conduct an identity check as if the party was a client, save that it is permissible to undertake an electronic search only if the client or third party prefers. Be sure to maintain any evidence collected on the matter file together with an attendance note detailing what checks you have made and why.

2.4.3 If the client or third party resists your questions you may be apologetic but should point out that the firm has no option but to comply with the duties that are placed upon it by law. If the required information is not forthcoming please consult [*a partner/director/supervisor*] and it may well be that we will have to cease to act.

2.5 *Form ML1*

In line with Law Society advice it is permissible for a partner to 'sign in' a client they know well in all cases other than where the CML Handbook applies. In all cases the 'lawyer certification' part of the form must be ticked by a fee earner (not a secretary) and signed. Where you feel unable to do so please refer to a partner.

3   Ongoing monitoring

3.1 In relation to regular, established clients the firm will compile a directory of standing checks of identities. Even then the current address should always be checked in relation to any future instructions.

3.2 For those more occasional clients that have instructed the firm before, the usual CDD process should be conducted if there is a gap of three years since the end of the client's last matter with us, save that it is open to a partner to verify that the client is well known to him/her in accordance with 2.5 above. Where possible we should be sure to be relying on up to date documents – i.e. passports should be current if possible. The full CDD process should therefore be repeated if possible where a passport has expired

---

and must also be conducted whenever there is any doubt as to the identity of the client or the matter itself.

4   Records

4.1 The firm is obliged to maintain records for at least five years of:

- What has been done for the client; and
- Any disclosures made (completed form reference or name).

Please bear this in mind when deciding a destroy date when archiving files. In addition the firm must maintain ID evidence for at least five years from the end of the 'business relationship' or the close of the 'occasional transaction'.

5   Cash receipts

5.1 The mere fact that a client pays in cash or wishes to do so is not in itself a cause for suspicion. Nonetheless, the larger the intended cash payment, the more likely it is that the client actions are suspect. Substantial amounts of cash might be criminal in origin or are often the result of failure to declare income to HM Revenue and Customs and, as tax evasion, would amount to criminal conduct under the anti-money laundering regime.

5.2 The approach to cash receipts is therefore as follows:

- In the absence of any complicating factors the firm will accept sums of up to £500/ £1000* in cash (complicating factors could include, doubts as to the source of funds.
- Sums of over [*£500 or £1000 are common levels*] should not be accepted and can only be accepted with the permission (to be noted on file) of the MLRO or, if (s)he is unavailable, another partner, save that you are authorised to accept cash of up to [*a higher figure might be justified for payment of the firm's fees in the light of the adequate consideration defence to s.329 POCA*].

[*On the reasoning of accepting higher sums of cash for the firm's fees see the defence of adequate consideration at page 32. Some firms have now increased their general cash limits to £1000, and sometimes more than this, on grounds that the banks do not ask questions where these sorts of sums of money are withdrawn in person by the customer.*]

5.3 Where a significantly larger payment than you can accept is offered you must speak to [*name of MLRO*] and may have to complete a report form (ML4) in order that (s)he can consider if a disclosure should be made. Some judgement is needed here as the circumstances will vary from case to case, but it is envisaged that an offer of [*consider a suitable figure for your firm – usually £2000* at least*] or more of cash should always be reported by you to the MLRO.

6 Reporting to the National Crime Agency ('NCA')

6.1 A disclosure could be necessary for one of two reasons. First, the Proceeds of Crime Act 2002 (POCA 2002) s.330 imposes a duty to make a disclosure if, in the course of practice in the regulated sector, a person forms a suspicion (or should reasonably have done so) that money laundering is or could be occurring. The position is complicated by the fact that this is stated to be subject to legal professional privilege. The defence of privilege will mean that in most circumstances there is no need for the practice to make a report to the NCA on the basis of instructions received. This is not always the case, however, especially where third parties are involved, so please refer any concerns to [*name of MLRO*] in case a disclosure is required.

6.2 You are encouraged to have a discussion with [*name of MLRO*] at any time and you might then need to make a formal report by use of form ML4. Even if (s)he does not share your concerns it is your entitlement to send him/her a completed ML4 as in most cases this will be your defence to a charge that you have committed an offence under POCA.

6.3 Secondly, it should be noted that a disclosure might also be necessary to gain a defence to a charge under the principal offences under POCA 2002, ss.327–329, most probably that of 'entering into an arrangement' whereby money laundering is facilitated under s.328. There are similar offences in relation to terrorist fundraising in the Terrorism Act 2000, ss.15–18. Where a suspicion arises the firm may, subject to the complex provisions relating to legal professional privilege, need to make a disclosure and gain permission to continue to act. The rules on this requirement differ according to work type, so again please contact [*name of MLRO*] if any concerns arise.

6.4 Do not store a completed ML4 report form on the matter file to which it relates. This would create a risk that the client might see the disclosure report, especially if the file is sent out of the office. Please make sure that any of your colleagues who might become involved in the work being done on the file are informed that the issue of a possible disclosure to NCA has arisen so that they may also proceed with caution.

7 Responsibilities

7.1 As Money Laundering Reporting Officer (MLRO) [*name of MLRO*]'s duties are to:

- Ensure that satisfactory internal procedures are maintained;
- Arrange for periodic training for all relevant personnel within the firm;
- Provide advice when consulted on possible reports and receive reports of suspicious circumstances;
- Report such circumstances, if appropriate, to the NCA on behalf of the firm;
- Direct colleagues as to what action to take and not take when suspicion arises and a disclosure is made; and
- Report annually to the partners on the operation of the anti-money laundering policy and procedures.

7.2 It is the duty of all personnel within the practice to:

- Attend training arranged within the firm if required to do so;
- Conduct identity checks and other due diligence enquiries unless the MLRO signifies that this is not necessary in the particular case in hand;
- Report without delay all circumstances which could give rise to suspicion that the firm is being involved in some element of the money laundering process for a client;
- Be wary of payment arrangements different from those anticipated or deposits of cash into client account;
- Follow the directions of the MLRO when a disclosure has been made, bearing in mind the personal risk to the adviser of 'tipping off' the client in question either expressly or by implication; and
- Maintain the utmost caution in maintaining confidentiality for the client and the firm when suspicious circumstances arise.

7.3 In certain circumstances fee earners/advisers may or must report to the client that a disclosure will be made. They might also sometimes have the option in exceptional circumstances of informing a client that a disclosure has been made concerning another party or even the client themself, notwithstanding the offences of 'tipping off' and 'disclosing an investigation' (POCA 2002, s.333) or, in relation to work outside the regulated sector, 'prejudicing an investigation' (POCA 2002, s.342). There are, of course, significant risks in doing so and in all such cases the advice of the MLRO must be sought and his/her instructions must be closely followed.

7.4 Property lawyers should note the source of funds form (ML3) and use it as part of our duty to obtain information on the funds to be used in any purchase.

8   Other resources

8.1 Helpful details on the obligations on all firms in relation to money laundering and terrorist financing can be found on the Law Society website in the practice note of October 2013, which has been approved by HM Treasury.

8.3 There are also practice notes of interest to conveyancers in relation to 'Mortgage fraud' (31st July 2014) and 'Property and registration fraud' (11th October 2010); the latter guide was compiled in conjunction with the Land Registry.

FORM ML1: PROOF OF IDENTITY: CLIENT SEEN IN PERSON

(Keep a photocopy of all documentation on file)

Exemption?

Client is another regulated business under the MLR 2007

(If so print off directory listing and place on file)

Private individuals

Identity: One of	–	Full Passport
	–	Full driving licence
	–	Other evidence of identity *(specify)*
Verification: One of	–	Utility bill
	–	Recent bank statement
	–	Other evidence of address *(specify)*

Trustees and executors: perform as individuals, preferably on two persons

Non-professional partnerships (other than LLPs) and other unincorporated associations: deal with as individuals; professional partnerships and LLPs deal with as companies

Private companies

- Names and addresses of two officers/directors
- Company search, copy certificate of incorporation, or directory entry on professional firm
- Evidence of authority of representatives

If none of the above, client accepted because: (e.g. partner sign-in: see s.2(5) of AML policy)

Identity check completed by (sign) .... date ....

Lawyer Certification

From the instructions received and the checks undertaken in this matter I believe that:

1) this matter does not involve a politically exposed person, including an associate or any family member of such a person
2) this client is not acting as an agent of another person, other than as set out above, and there are no significant (over 25%) beneficial interests by others
3) the nature and purpose of the instructions is clear and causes no concerns
4) there is no undue risk to the firm in this matter in relation to client identity or the instructions received

If you are unable to tick any of these four statements, or if you are dealing with a high risk matter, please consult [*name of MLRO*] or another partner.

Signed .... date ....

FORM ML2: IDENTITY DOCUMENT CHECKING FORM

The client and matter

Full name of client	
Former name(s) if any	
Address	
Description of matter	

Passport check

		Expiry date
Does the photograph match the appearance of the holder?		
Does the colour and quality of the passport look as if it is a genuine document?		
Does the passport number at the front match the number on the identification page?		
Is there a watermark on the identification page that also includes the photograph?		

Photo driving licence check

Does the photograph match the appearance of the holder?	
Does this appear to be a valid driving licence?	
What is the expiry date of the licence?	

Check completed by ………………………………… (signature) ………………………… (date)

Please sign or initial a photocopy of the passport identification page or licence.

Conveyancing matters

Does the signature on the above document match the signature that you hold on file? (Note answer at or before exchange of contracts if not when initial passport check is undertaken)

Check completed by ………………………………… (signature) ………………………… (date)

This form is to be retained on file or placed in central records. This form must not be returned to the client if they request return of their papers on completion of any matter.

FORM ML3: SOURCE OF FUNDS

CLIENT	Mr	Mrs	Ms	Surname	
Forenames			Previous name (or alias)		
Address					
Postcode					
Capacity [when acting on behalf of a business]: Director / Secretary / Partner / Other					

Source	Details required	tick	£ approximately and comment
1 Sale of existing property	Address Approximate amount		Net proceeds after agents' fees
2 Building Society or Bank mortgage	Copy mortgage offer or loan to be applied for		Name of institution and amount
3 Inheritance	Copy Estate Accounts or Copy solicitors letter with cheque or Other evidence		
4 Savings	Building Society passbook or Bank statement Consider need for 6 months statements Provide explanation of how acquired		Evidence of source of wealth needed and on file?
5 Gift	Donor(s) name Donor(s) address Over £5,000 source of wealth? ID check on donor also required?		Relationship to client?
6 Private loan	Lender(s) name Lender(s) address Over £5,000 source of wealth? ID check on lender also required?		Relationship to client?
7 Proceeds of sale of investments or securities	Broker's/adviser's letter with cheque or Contract notes or other evidence		
8 Other source(s):			Give details

The importance of advising my solicitors of any changes to the above has been explained to me. I understand that completion of the purchase might be delayed if there are late changes to the above that have not been explained by me/us to my/our adviser in advance.

Signed (client 1) .... Date: ....

Signed (client 2) .... Date: ....

FORM ML4: REPORT FORM: STRICTLY CONFIDENTIAL

Before completing this form speak first to [name of MLRO] or, if (s)he is unavailable, another partner. Great care must be taken to ensure that this form is not seen by the client at any time.

Client

(Mr) (Mrs) (Miss) (Ms) ( ) Forenames _____

Surname _____ Any alias? _____

Phone (day)_____ Evening _____Mobile_____

Address _____

_____

e-mail (if any) _____

Date and place of birth, if known _____NI no if known_____

Source of client

Nature of Instructions

Reason for Report (attach confidential memo if necessary)

Signed _____ **(adviser)**

MLRO Date Received _____ Date of report to NCA _____

Or, reasons for not reporting and/or any further action taken

INDEX